Teachers and Teacher Unions in a Globalised World

Teachers and Teacher Unions in a Globalised World asks a series of pressing questions of teacher educators, teachers and teacher unions worldwide in this era of global capitalism. As governments around the world support austerity politics in the face of financial meltdowns, social inequalities, terrorist threats, climate catastrophe, wars and mass migrations, the book questions whether practitioners in teaching and teacher education are succumbing to pressures to dismantle their nation-state systems of education.

The authors present a clearly argued case in Ireland for teachers and teacher educators organising to realise their moral and social responsibilities of free and fair schooling for all when it is most needed, as well as insisting on policy debates about a free publicly funded school system. At a time when teachers are feeling overwhelmed with workload and frustrated by the visible turning of events away from the historical record, the book emphasises the importance of practitioner research in informing decisions about a strategic and democratic way forward for education around the globe.

Teachers and Teacher Unions in a Globalised World will be of great interest to academics and researchers in the field of education, as well as teacher educators, practitioners and policymakers.

John Carr, MA (Ed) is the immediate past General Secretary of the Irish National Teachers Organisation (INTO), now retired, and chairs the Vere Foster Trust.

Lori Beckett, PhD was the inaugural Winifred Mercier Professor of Teacher Education at Leeds Metropolitan University, now retired, and works with the Vere Foster Trust. She is also an adjunct Professor at the Griffith Institute of Educational Research, Griffith University.

Routledge Research in Education

This series aims to present the latest research from right across the field of education. It is not confined to any particular area or school of thought and seeks to provide coverage of a broad range of topics, theories and issues from around the world.

Recent titles in the series include:

Manufacturing the Mathematical Child
A Deconstruction of Dominant Spaces of Production and Governance
Anna Llewellyn

The Arts as Learning
Cultivating Landscapes of Democracy
Edited by Jay Hanes and Eleanor Weisman

The Changing World of Outdoor Learning in Europe
Edited by Peter Becker, Chris Loynes, Barbara Humberstone and Jochem Schirp

Democratic Education and the Teacher-As-Prophet
Exploring the Religious Work of Schools
Jeffery W. Dunn

Teachers and Teacher Unions in a Globalised World
History, Theory and Policy in Ireland
John Carr and Lori Beckett

Learning Beyond the School
International Perspectives on the Schooled Society
Edited by Julian Sefton-Green and Ola Erstad

For a complete list of titles in this series, please visit www.routledge.com/Routledge-Research-in-Education/book-series/SE0393

Teachers and Teacher Unions in a Globalised World

History, theory and policy in Ireland

John Carr and Lori Beckett

LONDON AND NEW YORK

First published 2018
by Routledge
2 Park Square, Milton Park, Abingdon, Oxon OX14 4RN

and by Routledge
711 Third Avenue, New York, NY 10017

Routledge is an imprint of the Taylor & Francis Group, an informa business

© 2018 John Carr and Lori Beckett

The right of John Carr and Lori Beckett to be identified as author of this work has been asserted by him/her in accordance with sections 77 and 78 of the Copyright, Designs and Patents Act 1988.

All rights reserved. No part of this book may be reprinted or reproduced or utilised in any form or by any electronic, mechanical, or other means, now known or hereafter invented, including photocopying and recording, or in any information storage or retrieval system, without permission in writing from the publishers.

Trademark notice: Product or corporate names may be trademarks or registered trademarks, and are used only for identification and explanation without intent to infringe.

British Library Cataloguing-in-Publication Data
A catalogue record for this book is available from the British Library

Library of Congress Cataloging-in-Publication Data
A catalog record for this book has been requested

ISBN: 978-1-138-29011-2 (hbk)
ISBN: 978-1-315-26654-1 (ebk)

Typeset in Galliard
by Apex CoVantage, LLC

Contents

Acknowledgements	xi
Endorsements	xvi
Foreword by Gary McCulloch (UCL Institute of Education)	xviii
Co-authors' introduction: Ireland as a prima facie case	1

PART 1
The history of teachers' organising — 23

1 Historical revisions — 27
2 Introducing Vere Foster (a key figure in Ireland's struggle) — 50

PART 2
Theories of teachers organising: the options in edu-politics — 71

3 The INTO and activist teachers — 75
4 Irish national schools — 95

PART 3
The practical politics of teachers' organising — 115

5 Ireland in the global neoliberal policy regime — 119
6 Teachers' case for the defence — 142

Co-authors' closing: the rebuttal — 165

Afterword The politics of teacher unions and archives:
Bob Lingard School of Education, the University
of Queensland   186

Bibliography   195
Index   212

A nation's greatness depends on the education of its people.
Vere Foster (1819–1900)

THE TILLERS OF THE MIND.

A SONG FOR THE NATIONAL TEACHERS.

Respectfully dedicated to Vere Foster, Esq., the philanthropic advocate of education and progress.

Air—"The Cruiskeen Lawn."

"Let us, then, be up and doing
With a heart for any fate;
Still achieving, still pursuing,
Learn to labour, and to wait."
—*Longfellow.*

I.

The farmer's honest toil
Can draw riches from the soil,
The artisan spreads luxury around,
The soldier may be brave,
And the sailor plough the wave,
While the miner delves for wealth far under ground;
But there's still a nobler field—
A rich harvest may it yield—
May the nation trusty labourers e'er find
Who will sow the precious seed,
And destroy each noxious weed
That may spring up in that glorious soil—the mind!

II.

Neglected and despised,
Unrewarded and unprized,
Long suffering these labourers have been,
Yet they still preserved the light
That shone steadily and bright
Through the mists that floated o'er our island green:
And when the brighter day
Now dispels these mists away,
Say will a grateful nation be inclined
Approval to accord,
And to yield a just reward
To the men who toil to cultivate the mind?

III.

What though their lot be cast
Amid penury's chill blast,
And their path of life be strewn with many a thorn,
Yet knowledge ever bright
Yields a calm and pure delight,
That's proof against adversity and scorn:
And the blessings that must flow
From the gifts which they bestow
In the hallow'd bonds of brotherhood shall bind,
Till the tongues of future days
Shall carol forth the praise
Of the men who toiled to cultivate the mind.

IV.

No monument they claim,
For they yearn not for fame,
But the silent work of progress to be done
In majesty shall rise,
Mounting upwards to the skies,
Till science shall beam forth another sun!
Then why should we regard
Vain endeavours to retard
A destiny that Heaven hath design'd?
For *all* shall happy be,
Educated and made free
By the men who toil to cultivate the mind.

V.

Let us, then, join hand in hand,
North and south, throughout the land,
Unanimous for once to act as men;
In the warfare that we wage
There is no sectarian rage,
And the weapon that we fight with is the pen:
And standing side by side,
Let us point with honest pride
To the services we render to our kind,
And wish success to those
Who to ignorance are foes,
And who advocate the culture of the mind!

Source: "Tillers of the Mind" by Patrick Reilly, The Rural Harp, Publisher J. Hughes, 1861, pp 111–113. From the collection of Agnes Halpenny. Photographs courtesy of Gavin Byrne.

Acknowledgements

We first came together a decade ago, the direct result of a chance meeting, so a very special mention needs to be made of Aggie Halpenny and the late Sean Halpenny, who provided early answers to two burning family history questions about the Irish diaspora from nineteenth-century rural Ireland: how did the children of poor tenant farmers listed in the ship's register come to emigrate, and how did they learn to read and write English? Agnes and Sean not only shared their knowledge of Vere Foster (1819–1900), an Anglo-Irish benefactor who developed his emigration schemes then turned his attention to national schooling and who was instrumental in founding the INTO in 1868, but also engineered a visit to Glyde Court. This is the ruined Irish ancestral home of the Foster family in Co. Louth, which is badly in need of restoration and redevelopment.

We could see Glyde Court as a working family estate for teachers and students in Ireland, past, present and future, but beyond a democratic interest in educational politics, we had to have a business plan. A debt of gratitude is owed to a group of historically minded colleagues who came to join us and set up the Vere Foster Trust in 2010 with agreement to act as advocates for positive change in educational policy and practice across the island of Ireland: Dr Charlotte Holland (Dublin City University), Professor Joanna Hughes (Queen's University Belfast), Dr Tony Hall (National University of Ireland Galway), Professor Jim Deegan (Mary Immaculate College – University of Limerick), Dr Kevin Davison (National University of Ireland Galway), Dr Bernadette Flanagan (All Hallows College), Dr Rose Dolan (National University of Ireland Maynooth), Dr Finian O'Shea (CICE), Dr Siobhan Cahillane-McGovern (Hibernia College), Dr Joe O'Hara (Education Studies Association Ireland), Professor Marie Parker-Jenkins (University of Limerick), Ms Bernie Judge (Teachers' Union Ireland), Ms Moira Leydon (Association Secondary teachers Ireland), Dr Mags Liddy (University of Limerick); Dr Rory McDaid (Marino Institute of Education) and Dr Deirbhle Nic Craith (Irish National Teachers Organisation).

Gerry Malone, past President of the INTO and Richard Barry, former principal of the Vere Foster National School, Tallenstown, Co. Louth, brought insight to the whole project. We owe particular thanks to Dr Charlotte Holland, who co-developed a proposal to house a world-class conference facility for professional and amateur researchers in educational, social and family history, linking up with major educational institutions across the island of Ireland and internationally. This thanks extends to Shane McEnroe and Francis Duffy of Ecotect Partnership Architects for the first set of architectural drawings, all eco-friendly. For advice in regards the quest to find sponsors hoping they would see merit in a project that would simultaneously stimulate the local economy in Co. Louth and the broader tourist economy, we must thank Dr Denis Cummins, former President of Dundalk Institute of Technology; Andrew Griffin former Chairperson of Dundalk Institute of Technology; Kingsley Aikins, Ireland Fund; Seamus Kirk, Ceann Comhairle (Leader of the Dáil. House of Parliament); Brian Walsh, County Louth Museum; Senator Jim D'Arcy from Co. Louth; Professor Brian MacCraith, President of Dublin City University; Willie Slattery, State Street; Catherine Byrne, former Deputy General Secretary of the INTO; and Aiden Pender of Fáilte Ireland.

We are particularly grateful to Dr Denis Cummins, past President of Dundalk Institute of Technology for his valuable assistance in helping us to further develop the Vere Foster Trust Project. Thanks to Tadhg Mac Phaidín, CEO, and the staff of Club Na Múinteoirí (the Teachers' Club) for their courtesy and generosity in hosting meetings of the Vere Foster Trust and to Michael McHugh and Denise Comerford of Comhar Linn INTO Credit Union for their help and support in providing facilities to hold our own meetings. Thanks too to Paul McArdle for his keen interest in tracing the descendants of the Vere Foster's Assisted Emigration Schemes, John Rountree and the late Brenden Hall for their continued research on Vere Foster and Seamus Bellow from the County Louth Historical Society for the opportunity to lecture on Vere Foster. Also Nicholas Nicholson generously provided a catalogue of the 1981 sale of the Glyde Court Foster family home contents.

While we continue to try to solicit support for the working estate project, which is not easy in the post-recession climate in Ireland, we must give special thanks to Sheila Nunan, Noel Ward, Dr Deirbhle Nic Craith, Peter Mullan and Deirdre O'Connor in the INTO for their unfailingly patient and generous financial and moral support. They share the vision for the Vere Foster Trust to operate as a think tank for like-minded academics, teacher union representatives, practitioners in teaching and teacher education and critical friends. We began by meeting regularly, sharing ideas on networking and discussing educational politics, including the need to foreground research.

Given an interest in histories, we embarked on doing documentary research, so sincere thanks to library and curatorial staff in the PRONI Belfast, but also in the offices of the INTO in Dublin and Belfast, Trinity College Dublin, the National Library Dublin, the National Museum at Collins Barracks Dublin, St Patrick's College, Dublin City University and Queen's University Belfast. It was in the PRONI special collection that we learned of a group with the same name that had been first reported in *The Irish Times* on 12 February 1964. This followed the 1956 INTO Annual Congress in Belfast, which decided to organise a suitable memorial as a tribute to Vere Foster; a committee was set up with INTO President Captain McCune-Reid acting as secretary. This was the committee which recommended the presentation annually in perpetuity of the Vere Foster gold medal to a most deserving student in each of the colleges of education. This gave us some insight into the history of the INTO's interest in Vere Foster, which offers a chance to bring more clarity to the idea of teachers' organising on the island of Ireland.

The Vere Foster Trust also got involved in the work of a public lecture series, so a special thanks for encouragement and support must go to Professors Bob Lingard (University of Queensland), Stephen Ball (UCL Institute of Education), Martin Mills (University of Queensland), Kathleen Lynch (University College Dublin) and Pamela Munn (University of Edinburgh). We would also like to warmly thank the Royal Irish Academy and Dr Marie Bourke, formally Keeper and Head of Education in the National Art Gallery in Dublin, for hosting the first Vere Foster Public Lecture Series and Declan Steadman at ShuttleMedia who did the digital recordings.

We should also acknowledge Dr Joe O'Hara (Education Studies Association Ireland), Professors Joanne Hughes and Ruth Leith (Queen's University Belfast) and Professor Ciaran Sugrue (University College Dublin) for their support and critical constructive feedback on ensuing discussions and debates, inclusive of questions. Their contributions to the public conversations gave us the 'heads up' on the complexities of educational politics not only in the north and south of Ireland, given these lectures were held in Belfast and Dublin, but also in the regional, European and global settings. This was augmented by Paddy Hogan and Kieran Taaffe, who arranged successive meetings at Leinster House with Senator Jim D'Arcy.

Our first foray as co-authors was in successive conference presentations, so we must acknowledge the support from Dr Terence Dooley (National University Ireland Maynooth), who agreed to our presentations at the Irish Country Houses conference, and then Dr Rose Dolan and Dr Joe O'Hara, who accepted our papers at successive Education Studies Association Ireland conferences in Limerick and Athlone. This was followed by a group publication venture led by Professor Joanne Hughes (Queen's University Belfast) and Dr Charlotte Holland who organised an edited collection of articles in *Policy Futures*.

This brought us to Routledge, so our sincere thanks go to Anna Clarkson, Heidi Lowther and Chris Byrne for expert editorial advice on our book proposal to mark the INTO's sesquicentenary in 2018 and for drawing out our ideas about the potential of Irish teachers in their particular international geographic locations. We are also grateful to editors Chloe Barnes, Aiyana Curtis and Will Bateman, and the anonymous reviewers of the book proposal. This extends to Professor Gary McCulloch (UCL Institute of Education), who not only provided us with critical feedback on our ideas but also provided invaluable directions in our response to the reviewers and agreed to write the foreword. Likewise, Professor Bob Lingard (University of Queensland), who shared his work with teacher unions in Australia and provided sensible advice on the eventual revised book synopsis and agreed to write the afterword.

It is also our pleasure to acknowledge Doireann Ní Bhriain (Fuaim Productions) and Nuala Hayes (Two Chairs Productions), who worked on the radio documentaries to bring the Glyde Court restoration project to public attention in the hope that we might attract sponsorship. We should also acknowledge the County Louth Archaeological and Historical Society and the Drumconrath Historical Society, which not only provided opportunities for us to share the project but also stimulating comment. This includes Larry Ward, a notable local historian, and Sarah Jane Ward, a social worker with great insight into contemporary Irish society. We want to give extra-special thanks to Sarah Jane, who opened her home in Dublin to provide a central location for us to meet and the warmest of Irish hospitality. We also want to acknowledge the vital help from Sally Hogg, a lawyer who gave us critical directions on using legal terminology from different justice systems.

We must also recognise the crucial support from Dr Deirbhle Nic Craith and Peter Mullan at INTO not only for their support for the Vere Foster Trust but also for this book project. This includes senior officers for agreeing to interviews and to Ann McConnell for transcriptions, access to archives and work on the photos for copyright permission.

John would particularly like to acknowledge the support of colleagues and friends, particularly Sheila Nunan, Gerry Malone, Richie Barry, Dr Deirbhle Nic Craith, Ruth Warren and Michael McHugh. John would like to give heartfelt thanks to family and friends for their unfailing support and especially to Joan Carr for her steadfast support, encouragement, patience, forbearance and staunch commitment to seeing the book project brought to fruition.

Lori would like to acknowledge and thank colleagues in the Carnegie School of Education at Leeds Beckett University, who all in their own ways provided support for continuing this work. She would also like to give heartfelt thanks to family and friends who unfailingly provide love and support, but especially Lin Williams, Sibyl Fisher, Barbara Eastwood and Annie McClintock, Iain and Margaret Poole and Mary and Steve Roddick, along with those in Australia who not only share a great passion for educational, social and family history in Ireland but also the work of teacher unions: Maurie Mulheron, Joan Lemaire, Sally and Dave McFarlane, Lee and Dave Bell and Judy and Alan Canning.

Last, but by no means least, grateful acknowledgement must go to David Hursh, Tom Collins, Nina Bascia, Stephen Ball, Ciaran Sugrue, Kathleen Lynch, Pamela Munn, Joe O'Hara, Marie Brennan, Terri Seddon, Howard Stevenson and Deirbhile Nic Craith, who agreed to be our critical friends along with Jim Bennett and Amanda Nuttall who read the first draft manuscript and provided invaluable advice and editorial feedback. Thanks also to Tony Doohan and Gavin Byrne for their invaluable help and support.

The book is dedicated to Vere Foster, who deserves never to be forgotten because of his pioneering work to organise teachers and to generate a professional voice.

Figure 0.2 Vere Foster

Source: Reproduced by permission of the INTO.

Endorsements

This is a work that is sure to challenge and inspire in equal measure. It deserves to be read by every teacher – and indeed citizen – who wishes to understand how Irish education has arrived at this particular moment of transition and how this might be used as an opportunity to collectively recommit ourselves to a progressive view of education that values the individual above the system and society above economy. Carr and Beckett are to be congratulated for their exemplary scholarship and rigorous commitment to the truth.
Joe O'Hara, Professor of Education, Dublin City University Institute of Education; President of the European Educational Research Association (EERA); and Irish Universities' nominee on the Teaching Council

As this book ably demonstrates, teacher unions are now more necessary than ever – not just as a defence of teacher's interests and conditions of work but as a progressive voice in the midst of the heat and noise of neoliberal reform. The historical case histories in the collection show unions working in support of families and communities for a fairer and rounded education and bringing sense and reason in the policy process. The focus of the book is on the meaning of the teaching profession and what it means to be educated in Ireland but it has a broad and very important contemporary relevance.
Stephen J Ball, Distinguished Service Professor of Sociology of Education, Institute of Education, University College London

This 150th anniversary book is a tough-minded combination of the history of the Irish National Teachers Organisation and its struggles, put together with political analysis and a strong commitment to education. Carr and Beckett's approach makes fascinating reading, putting the current policy context of teachers in Ireland into sharp relief, linking it to long-term struggles for their professional recognition. Their argument for a strong role for teacher judgement and teacher professional activism in the face of narrow over-regulation of their work is internationally important for teaching as a profession, something the rest of the world can learn from this, very Irish history, politics and analysis.
Marie Brennan, Extraordinary Professor, Stellenbosch University, South Africa; Honorary Professor of Education, Victoria University, Melbourne; Adjunct Professor, University of South Australia

This is a book with an important message. It reminds us that teachers have long organised their work in ways that mediate relations between the governed and those who govern. This organising work sustains teacher's commitments to social justice and resources how they work towards preferred futures. Carr and Beckett trace teacher's organising work with reference to time, showing continuities between past and present. They map teacher's organising work with reference to social movements, revealing the space of intra- and inter-professional negotiation that makes 'occupation' possible. And in pinpointing this interplay between time and space, memory and diverse commitments and claims for recognition and reward, they remind us that, in this present, teacher's organising work is still central to how we remake futures.

Terri Seddon, Director of Research and Graduate Studies,
Faculty of Education, La Trobe University

In the whirlwind of educational policy changes, teacher union histories such as this one provide critical explanations for why teachers are caught in the web of the state apparatus, and how they worked to get out of them. Carr and Beckett have produced a very readable and important contribution to educational history with this work on the Irish National Teachers' Organization.

Nina Bascia, Professor & Chair, Leadership, Higher & Adult Education,
Ontario Institute for Studies in Education (OISE)

Carr and Beckett have created a treasure trove of artefacts, analyses, and articulations of the trajectories of teachers and a teacher union over time that is a major 'glocal' contribution to scholarship on the profession and its union representation. The text is at once empowering and enlightening, as well as a call to arms to teachers and their representatives 'to strive, to seek to find and not to yield', but to pursue and promote an education system that fosters the public good, raises the morale of the profession by releasing its agency and its professional soul from the de-professionalising shackles of 'regimes of control' to the detriment of teaching and learning, by cultivating an enabling sense of professional responsibility. Read it, be empowered and join the effort.

Ciaran Sugrue, Professor of Education, School of Education,
University College Dublin

This scholarly and innovative publication interweaves history, theory and politics to analyse the policies adopted by the INTO and places them in a global context. It takes contemporary issues of accountability, teacher status and professionalism and shows how the Irish experience has relevance for modern debates.

Pamela Munn, Professor Emerita of Curriculum Research,
University of Edinburgh.

All teachers, regardless of their union involvement, will find much in this book to stimulate intellectual and political conversation. Carr and Beckett use the anniversary of the Irish National Teachers Organisation to skilfully tease open connections between history, theory and politics which influence teachers' work today. Of significance in this archival documentary are the accounts of teachers' disquiet, resistance, protests and challenges. These provoke all of us involved in the teaching profession to consider the authors' 'rebuttal' of extant school policies which regulate and sideline teachers' professional work.

Amanda Nuttall, formerly research-active teacher at White Laith Primary School Leeds now Senior Lecturer and Programme Coordinator in Primary Education at Leeds Trinity University.

Foreword

I was greatly honoured to be invited to provide a foreword to this fascinating book by John Carr and Lori Beckett. As we discussed the work in its early stages, I was intrigued by its unusual design and its ambitious aims, and as the authors kindly note, I was able to give some advice. Nevertheless, this was the full extent of my direct involvement in the work, and I played no part in the writing or refereeing.

Reading the work as it reached its final form, I could see that in some ways I was discovering a world that was hitherto scarcely known to me: the life of Vere Foster, the struggles of the Irish National Teachers Organisation, even the broader national politics of Ireland itself. Yet I found myself being drawn into it, admiring the dexterity of the authors as they bound their disparate themes together with their clear commitment to telling the story that had brought them into this project in the first place. And then I saw the connections with my own work: the historical approach; the revisionist perspectives; the links between history, theory and politics; the history of teachers and its relevance to the present day; and the importance of documents of different kinds in illuminating the past. Before I knew it, I was feeling right at home.

I will, then, take this opportunity to summon up briefly the kind of work that has always appealed to me and which helps to shape my appreciation of this present volume from my own vantage point in the United Kingdom. They are closely linked, but I would categorise them as the position of history in understanding teachers, schools and educational systems; the connections between history, theory and politics; the revisionist outlook in the history of education; and the power of the document.

The position and the potential role of history in these areas are beautifully exemplified in the work of the great French sociologist of education Emile Durkheim. It would indeed be difficult to articulate the importance of history for the teacher education curriculum or for supporting the work of teachers any more clearly, or in more eloquent or inspiring tones, than did Durkheim.

Over a century ago, Emile Durkheim, the French sociologist and professor of pedagogy at the Sorbonne in Paris, expressed an expansive vision for the history of education in his lectures on the formation and development of secondary education in France (Durkheim, 1977). This course directly addressed the relationship between theory and practice as it related to educational changes to their longer term historical context. The account put forward in the first chapter of the published version of this great work is a classic formulation of the rationale for history as a part of educational studies in general and the training of teachers in particular.

Durkheim argued that secondary education was in the process of undergoing major reforms, and proposed that if these were to succeed, it was essential for the teachers who were to carry them out to understand them fully and give them life. Thus according to Durkheim,

> It is not enough to prescribe to them in precise detail what they will have to do; they must be in a position to assess and appreciate these prescriptions, to see the point of them and the needs which they meet.

Rather, the teachers had to be familiar with the problems involved in the education for which they were responsible, no less than with the methods by which it was proposed to solve them in order that they might be able to 'make up their own minds with a knowledge of the issues involved' (pp. 3–4).

This kind of initiation, Durkheim continued, could be derived only from a study of educational theory, which needed to be given while the intending teacher was still a university student if it were to be of value. 'This is how the idea emerged that we need to organize through our various faculties the study of education, by means of which the future secondary school teachers can prepare for their functions.' (1977, p. 4). He pursued this key point to develop the potential role of historical study.

First, he suggested, the study of the past was a sound basis for educational theory, especially since, in his view, 'it is only by carefully studying the past that we can come to anticipate the future and to understand the present'. Thus he insisted,

> [O]nly history can penetrate under the surface of the present educational system; only history can analyse it; only history can show us of what elements it is formed, on what conditions each of them depends, how they are interrelated; only history, in a word, can bring us to the long chain of causes and effects of which it is the result.
>
> (Durkheim, 1956, p. 153)

Moreover, he added, history was an indispensable asset in its own right, as a means of illuminating organisations and their ideals and aims over the course of time, and to understand 'man in his totality throughout time' (1977, p. 12). The present was itself merely 'an extrapolation of the past, from which it cannot be severed without losing the greater part of its significance' (p. 15). It was for these reasons, according to Durkheim, that we should carry out historical research into the manner in which educational configurations have progressively come to cluster together, to combine and to form organic relationships.

At the same time, Durkheim linked these concerns systematically with his broader sociological interests. He argued that historical and social studies were 'close relatives' that were 'destined eventually to merge with one another', and that education was bound up with both. For example, he defined education as the methodological socialisation of the new generation through which society renewed itself under the supervision of the State. Moreover, an understanding of psychology was also necessary in order to comprehend the diversity of human intelligence and character.

Despite such powerful insights, since the 1980s, under the influence of a largely neoliberal framework for approaching education policies, the past has come to be widely viewed in negative terms rather than for its potential contribution to providing solid foundations for further development. The past was the problem, to which the solution was the future. This hostile, negative image of educational history tended to mean that it was simplified and telescoped, used mainly to explain problems and failure.

There also developed an ahistorical view of education reform as a 'technical fix'. In this perspective, educational reform was a technical, managerial issue, concerned with addressing particular, narrowly defined problems, and was therefore seen as being unrelated to wider social, historical and cultural concerns. Reform also became subject to the imperatives of the electoral cycle to address perceived needs and problems, and increasingly to the media cycle to respond quickly to events.

In these circumstances, the considered and lengthy, and sometimes rather ponderous, judgements of earlier policy reports were replaced by hurried and often poorly written proposals, and by proposals that rose without a trace to appease a passing mood and win a friendly headline, and regularly reinvented the wheel. The outcome has been that teachers have had little or no opportunity to study the history of educational organisations and aims at a time of major and continuing reforms that they would be expected to put into practice. They have also been rendered unable to engage with the history of their own profession. This historical amnesia is also reflected in government reports on teachers and teacher education, which convey very limited awareness of the past and even less interest in its potential for comprehending current changes. In Durkheim's terms, by severing itself from its past, the policy loses the greater part of its significance.

There were many other radical changes that took place over the same brief period. For many years in the nineteenth and twentieth centuries, teacher education reform was based on ideals of a gradual process leading to greater professionalisation and professionalism for teachers. 'Professionalisation' was conceived as the historical development of a teaching profession with established higher education facilities, training and qualifications. 'Professionalism' was framed around a shared code of ethics in everyday relationships and support based on socialisation into the culture of teaching.

This steady growth of teacher education accompanied the rise of universal primary and secondary education, and the development of a teaching profession which, although it did not attain the high status associated with other professional groups, at least acquired a number of spheres of influence and an element of effective control in their work in schools. These developments were themselves political and ideological in character, betokening the emergence of schooling and teaching as key institutions in modern English society. In political terms, they supported the development of certain types of institutions rather than others, although they were not overtly party-political in nature. They were ideological in promoting a particular kind of social mission for teacher education and for teachers in general.

From the 1970s onwards, such hitherto characteristic approaches were challenged by new political and ideological influences that eventually led to a set of teacher education reforms dedicated to reconstructing the institutions and cultures of teacher education. These new reforms were political both in their support for particular kinds of institutions and thus the focus of public debate. They were ideological in following the lines of market reforms in education designed to promote competition and raise standards, offering a different kind of social mission to the gradual professionalisation and professionalism of teachers (McCulloch, 2011, Chapter 5).

In charting these developments, a newer literature has tried to take over where Durkheim left off to examine the history of teaching itself. Of these scholars, perhaps the one who stands out most, to my mind at least, is the American historian of education David Tyack (see, for example, Tyack, 1989), although there are others such as Larry Cuban and Kate Rousmaniere in the United States, and Peter Cunningham and Philip Gardner in the United Kingdom, who also warrant the most careful attention (e.g. Cuban, 1993; Rousmaniere, 1997; Cunningham and Gardner, 2004). It was Tyack who attempted in a systematic way not only to understand the significance of teachers' history but also to relate this to the present and the future. He pointed out the need to take into account the complexity of the history and to use it neither as 'cheerleaders for the latest fads, affirming the precedents for currently fashionable reforms', nor as 'wet blankets, arguing that those reforms were tried in the past and failed' (p. 410). Indeed, according to Tyack, 'Rarely is the story of reform so simple. History cannot provide policy makers with a list of prescriptions or prohibitions. It can, however, give insights into the trajectory of ideas and events over time' (p. 410).

Tyack spelled out a number of ways in which histories of teaching might be of value. First, no doubt with tongue in cheek, he described this history as a storehouse of experiments on dead people, or a form of evaluation of initiatives that have been tested in the past such as merit pay for teachers. Second, he explained the significance of the dimension of time that history introduces to the study of value conflicts that are often obscured by polemics and politics. Third, he pointed out the long time frame that was available to historians in providing historical evaluations of policies to detect the often unintended outcomes of reforms, Fourth, he proposed meta-analysis to step back from the particulars of reform in a single time and place to ask about the underlying conditions that produce cycles of change and stability – for example, when teachers are categorised as a 'problem', or when teachers become militant or indeed conservative as a group. Further, he suggested three different levels at which such analysis might take place – the macro, the institutional, and the individual – in which evidence of each can complement one another. These insights seem directly applicable to the kind of project on which Carr and Beckett embark in this volume.

More broadly, Carr and Beckett are interested in the connections between history, theory and politics, and here I would put forward another champion who emphasised these connections above all else. For Brian Simon, the most significant historian of education produced in the United Kingdom since at least World War II, there was nothing less than a symbiosis between these three basic elements. Simon identified what he regarded as a 'new function' for the historian of education,

> that of unravelling the social and historical influences which have played so potent a part in shaping both the schools and what is taught inside them; and, most important, of distinguishing the genuine educational theory from the rationalisation which seeks to explain away rather than elucidate.
> (Simon, 1966, p. 95)

He was committed to the central lesson that historical study can and should make a direct contribution to an understanding of the relationship between educational and social change. In a key essay published in 1985, 'Can Education Change Society?', Simon observed that the changed consciousness of individuals and groups that resulted from new circumstances and forms of activity profoundly influenced social development. In the English context, as he maintained, the national system of schooling had been established in order to reinforce existing social and economic relations, but had become itself a site of conflict, with direct theoretical and political implications (Simon, 1985).

Finally, may I also draw attention to the power of the document which Carr and Beckett also affirm in the most uncompromising terms. I am grateful to them for drawing on my own work in this regard, especially since it has long been my view that documentary research has been appreciated far too little in educational research as a whole (McCulloch, 2004). Certainly, there has often been a privileging of certain kinds of documents that lead to top-down accounts of administration and policymaking from the viewpoints of white, male and middle class policymakers. The documents themselves do not always speak for themselves and can often be interpreted in different ways in relation to an understanding of their contexts. Some would argue that an emphasis on documents is itself a form of empiricism based in a naïve and ultimately fruitless search for the 'facts'. In general, it is important to approach historical documents sceptically and with suspicion, alert to what they are trying to persuade their audience and to their own motivations and interests, as one should with any kind of source or evidence in research. And yet it is refreshing to see a text such as this so squarely based on the use of documents as evidence, which may themselves form the site of continuing argument and interpretation.

It is perhaps the rich flavour of debate that I carry away with me when I read the work of Carr and Beckett. This ultimately is the true hallmark of revisionist history: the willingness to engage critically with received accounts that have previously been accepted, sometimes unthinkingly and tacitly, at other times through extensive elaboration. In celebrating the past, in their praise for an anniversary, they also seek to challenge our understanding of it, to shake and scramble it before reassembling it in another way that may be troubling and yet puzzlingly familiar, as we reorient ourselves in a new and different place. There is an inherent intellectual bravery in this struggle that deserves our applause as we prepare to evaluate its contribution to the field.

GARY McCULLOCH
UCL Institute of Education, London

References

Cuban, L. (1993) *How Teachers Taught: Constancy and Change in American Classrooms*. New York: Teachers College Press.

Cunningham, P., and Gardner, P. (2004) *Becoming Teachers: Texts and Testimonies, 1907–1950*. London: Woburn.

Durkheim, E. (1956) *Education and Sociology*. New York: Free Press.

Durkheim, E. (1977) *The Evolution of Educational Thought: Lectures on the Function and Development of Secondary Education in France*. London: Routledge.

McCulloch, G. (2004) *Documentary Research in Education, History and the Social Sciences*. London: Routledge.

McCulloch, G. (2011) *The Struggle for the History of Education*. London: Routledge.

Rousmaniere, K. (1997) *City Teachers: Teaching and School Reform in Historical Perspective*. New York: Teachers College Press.

Simon, B. (1966) The history of education. In J.W. Tibble (ed.), *The Study of Education*. London: RKP, pp. 91–131.

Simon, B. (1985) Can education change society? In B. Simon (ed.), *Does Education Matter?* London: Lawrence and Wishart, pp. 13–31.

Tyack, D. (1989) The future of the past: What do we need to know about the history of teaching? In D. Warren (ed.), *American Teachers: Histories of a Profession at Work*. New York: AERA, pp. 408–421.

Co-authors' introduction
Ireland as a prima facie case

Introduction

The status of teachers, marked by their professional practice as well as the campaigns waged by teachers' unions, is under threat in the present era. They are confronted by demands for the standardisation of teaching, performances from teachers and students and tight accountability. These are in line with local-national versions of what is happening globally, orchestrated by waves of successive neoliberal governments beset by global economic challenges but committed to ideological policy solutions. This is exemplified in a case study of Ireland's national schools – that is, its primary or elementary schools, said to be a key to the nation's socio-economic development and modernisation.[1] Be that as it may, it is crucial to acknowledge the occasions when teachers' voices are sidelined and their unions are relegated. This then exacerbates the ways practitioners are directed and constrained by budget cuts and the shrinking of public funding in this age of austerity and gross inequalities.

Collectively, teachers have seen it all on the island of Ireland in regard to the ways ordinary people live in local school communities north and south. They are witness to the social realities of children and their families living and working or not as the case may be, caught up in particular, if not peculiar, situations, including prosperity during the time of steady economic growth with the Celtic Tiger, then reeling from the fallout of the sudden and devastating collapse of the economy in the Global Financial Crash (GFC) and Troika bailout, and further distressing hardship resulting from austerity policies such as homelessness, lack of food and nourishment and other familial and social problems. Teachers see the stark strains and pressures of daily life, including the lived experiences of inequalities, obscene poverty and cumulative multiple deprivation and how this all takes effect in the classroom.

Much of this has attracted teachers' disquiet, resistance, protests and challenges, but it is important to be politically astute when it comes to the professional responses to these predicaments, especially with the call for 'flipping the system' (see Evers and Kneyber, 2016; Stevenson and Gilliland, 2016). There is much to be gained through policy learning about global neoliberal agendas, free-market capitalism and its push towards profit-making schools but also thinking through what progressive contemporary education politics and policies might realistically look like. To be sure, the teachers' questions posed online[2] provide some directions:

1. Why do we continue to let politicians set the agenda for education?
2. How much longer can teachers stand being overwrought by futile bureaucracy?
3. Are we doing the best by our pupils?

This anniversary book, written for the occasion of the sesquicentenary of the Irish National Teachers Organisation (INTO) or Cumann Múinteoirí Éireann in Gaelic, founded in 1868, has a particular view of teachers' battles for their professional status. This takes into account their professional practice and the campaigns waged by the teacher unions to strengthen the profession, but it also embraces arguments from recent research on teacher unions. As Bascia's (2015) edited volume noted, it is necessarily preoccupied with the rise of neoliberal reform, and she cited recent volumes that addressed the negative effect of neoliberalism on teaching and unionism around the world (McDonnell and Pascal, 1988; Bascia, 2008, 2009; Murphy, 1990;).

However, Bascia's latest volume represented sample studies of teacher union research, said to provide a basis for inquiry and action that could be fruitfully explored. Crucial was a strand of research that showcased teacher unions over time rather than in shorter, episodic snapshots, with a concern to reveal longer patterns of conflict and strife, and the ebb and flow of relations between teacher unions and other entities. This lines up with advice from anonymous reviewers to locate the work of this anniversary book, which aligns with studies that depict the lives and career histories of union-active teachers over time.[3] As Bascia (2015) said, such histories enable us to see how teacher union activities allow teachers to expand beyond the classroom, through informal and non-formal professional learning, curriculum development, political organising and other pursuits. This enables the development of a broader understanding of teachers' work and their contributions to education policy and practice, **but this requires a particular conception of teacher union research in Ireland**.

The main question to be asked is who decides these vernacular forms of global neoliberal ends in Ireland's national schools? This is apparent when we look closely at the press release from the Department of Education and Skills translated as An Roinn Oideachais Agus Scileanna.[4] Dated September 2016, it was for the launch of a major initiative by the Kenny-Varadkar Fine Gael-led minority liberal-conservative and Christian democratic Coalition Government.[5] Minister for Education and Skills Richard Bruton's three-year *Action Plan for Education* (2016–2019) (Department of Education, 2016a) was said to be aimed at making the Irish education and training service the best in Europe by 2026:

> *This plan, which incorporates the Department of Education's Strategy Statement as well as the Action Plan for Education, outlines hundreds of actions*

and sub-actions to be implemented across 2016–2019, with timelines and lead responsibility assigned . . . . Publication of quarterly implementation reports and continuous consultation with stakeholders and members of the Oireachtas will be central to the process.

These myriad instructions from government merit critical analyses of the evidence of the need for such feverish activity, particularly as every year will see the publication of another *Action Plan for Education*. On the face of it, these are set to reform and reorganise Ireland's national system of schooling, which dates back to 1831. As Sharma (2016) intimated in *The Rise and Fall of Nations*, these sorts of initiatives typify the cycles of market euphoria and despair, which is pertinent to Ireland given the rise and fall of its political economy, Brexit and other threats to national and regional stability. He went on to say, 'Every crisis is greeted as a renewed call to action, and the bigger the crisis, the more frantic the action'. This may also have to do with 'hard choices for hard times' (see Hardiman, 2012).[6]

A subsidiary question to be asked is about the provenance of ideas in Bruton's *Action Plan for Education*. The prima facie evidence suggests it takes direction from the Organisation for Economic Co-operation and Development (OECD) Education Directorate, the McKinsey and Company reports (Mourshed, Chikioke, and Barber, 2010), the World Trade Organisation and the European Union (EU). These are compounded by the 'Smart Regulation' agenda advanced at the European level under Ireland's EU presidency in 2013, which took a cue from the National Economic and Social Council (2012) report entitled *Quality and Standards in Human Services in Ireland: The School System No. 129*.

Another twin question to be asked is why and how 'Smart Regulation' has been taken up by Ireland's Department of Education and Skills Chief Inspector Dr Harold Hislop (2012) in a public lecture entitled 'The Quality Assurance of Irish Schools and the Role of Evaluation: Current and Future Trends'. It is currently being rolled out as a new quality framework in terms of external school inspection and school self-evaluation. This has the effect of disrupting the extant edu-political settlement, which followed almost a century of campaigning by the INTO and which brought into being a representative body at the behest of the teacher unions to achieve consensus on a wide variety of professional matters not least the regulation of teaching.

This campaigning resulted in the 2001 *Teaching Council Act*, which has operated reasonably successfully up until the present, where teachers are confronted by Actions 64 and 65 in Bruton's *Action Plan for Education* (Department of Education and Skills, 2016c, 2017, 2018). This seeks to regulate the self-regulatory body: *Comhairle Múinteoireachta* or the Teaching Council. The experience could be called the regulated-regulation of teaching, and this has given rise to teachers' alienation from the Teaching Council, its own representative body, and it has resulted in delays in the development of strategies and policies that should have been realised by a well-functioning Teaching Council. This may yet herald a new era where teachers will most likely be forced to reclaim their professional authority within a new settlement given reflections on the predicament for teachers and democracy in Ireland. It is crucial, therefore, for the INTO to draw from critical research bases so as to engage a critical- interpretive reading of the past, (neoliberal) present and potential (progressive) futures. This should precipitate the evidence for both policy effects of regulating the teachers' own regulation (self-evaluation) and to advocate for research-informed national school policies.

Teacher union research

The argument of this anniversary book is to press for a conception of teacher union research in Ireland that means to interrogate the best way forward for teachers in response to Bruton's *Action Plan for Education* expounding a dominant policy discourse of global neoliberalism in the educational-political arena. This is here abbreviated to edu-politics, where particular attention needs to be given to claims from politicians, power brokers and policymakers about equipping teachers with the right skills for the twenty-first century and improving quality, promoting excellence and increased autonomy for schools and the continuous improvement of the Irish system of education in the interests of international competition.

This is not to forget the matter of teachers' salaries, which has become a mechanism for settling points of contention between the INTO and government, particularly on the ways Bruton's *Action Plan for Education* has reconfigured teacher status tied to a sense of regulated professionalism. This dovetails with Whitty's (2008) typology: traditional, collaborative, managerial and democratic professionalism in England and Stevenson and Gilliland's (2016) reconfiguration of democratic professionalism in Ireland.[7] The notion of regulated professionalism, however, is inextricably intertwined with systems' accountability and performance frameworks. All this has serious implications for the form of the response from teachers and the INTO to the imposition of centrally determined, top-down policies despite being involved in numerous consultation processes.

This has certainly been the case in regard to talks on regulating aspects of the profession, especially in relation to induction, probation and continuous professional development, the *Literacy and Numeracy Strategy*, school self-evaluation, school autonomy and new inspection models, for example. This is not to say that there is total opposition to Bruton's *Action Plan for Education*, because there is little opposition to necessary 'school improvements', for example. In many instances these address non-contentious matters such as improving class sizes and the learning experiences of students notably from areas of poverty and students with special needs.

In effect, this anniversary book is about teachers' research-informed policy advocacy, and it sets out to locate research in the INTO's edu-political activities, so as to marshal evidence on teacher status as it finds expression in, say, 'school improvement'. But it also calls for teachers' own evidence as well as other research evidence so as to respond to the research evidence promulgated by the Department of Education and Skills and its Inspectorate, and to foreground local conditions and social forces operating on teachers' work, so it is marked by professional practices underpinned by democratic principles. It happens that the INTO operates in accordance with its own democratic governance structures,[8] which includes opportunities for critical discussions at the local branch level and in other fora, and which is fertile ground for the promotion of research-informed policy advocacy.

This should include a critical-interpretive reading of the documentary research evidence, which begins here with the teachers in the nineteenth century who moved to form the INTO's forerunner, the Irish National Teachers' Association (INTA).[9] These teachers were at pains to point out their values and customs around concerns for a career, which includes qualifications, rewards and advancement in social standing. Their incredibly significant resolution appeared under the subheading 'The National School Teachers of Ireland' in the inaugural edition of *The Irish Teachers Journal* in 1868.

Indicative of meeting procedure, seemingly a feature of nineteenth-century Irish governance even in edu-politics, it was prescient for teachers' trade unionism not to forget burgeoning Irish nationalism. It was submitted by a local association in Strabane,[10] a town in West Tyrone in what is now Northern Ireland, which had held an adjourned meeting on 5 October 1867, which 'resolved to address' the following:

> *Brethren . . . Under any circumstances or in any country, the office of national teacher is a very grave and responsible one. Under the peculiar circumstances of Ireland it is of transcendent responsibility and importance. To ensure the accomplishment of his arduous and hallowed mission, the Irish national teacher must be not only thoroughly qualified for the discharge of his professional duties, but must also be raised to a position in society which will give weight and authority to his teaching.*

Putting to one side the archaic gendered language with Christian male overtones, it is important to identify the very original arguments about the social significance of teaching. This was clearly tied to the aims and development of national schooling, which assumed a great importance for the teachers and their local communities. It can be seen in the Strabane teachers' mention of their lived experiences and earnest desire to professionalise the teaching workforce, which was brought together with urgings for a new conception of teachers' organising:

> *The objects of the Irish National Teachers' Association will be to stimulate the progress of professional knowledge among its members; to direct fuller attention to the enormous power for good or for evil which lies in the national teachers' hands and to urge upon the Government of the country and the community at large the justice and necessity of elevating to its legitimate position a calling fraught with such paramount and vital interests.*

This resolution articulated teachers' capacity to define the nature of their work and to advocate collectively in regard to the organisation of teaching, given the need for agreed structures, roles and responsibilities that are formalised. This also noted the competing constituencies that need to fall in behind teachers, especially given the call for policies to meet the requisite needs and interests of all concerned. This sort of documentary research is particularly important to scaffold an in-depth understanding of the complexities of teaching, including teachers' qualities, knowledge and skills, but also its contribution to Ireland as a nation then and now.

Throughout these pages, the co-authors recount these documentary case stories because teachers working with each other and with their students, with the support of families and local communities, are a powerful force to be harnessed in the national interest on the island of Ireland. This is all part of the deliberations on preferred forms of professionalism, and so the memory of the battles for teacher status needs to hold in the INTO as it formulates different responses to relevant aspects of Bruton's *Action Plan for Education*. At the heart of it is the INTO's long history of teachers' organising from the time of its establishment in 1868, inspired by Vere Foster (1809–1900) who was part of the Anglo-Irish establishment and who developed his schemes for emigration and education in Ireland's national schools. From the outset, when the need was paramount to combat teachers' lowly status, there have been long-standing battles for recognition of teacher status marked by different notions of professionalism (see Coolahan, 1994; INTO, 1992, 1994, McCormick, 1966; Chuinneagáin, 1998; Carr and Beckett, 2016).

Another useful notion for edu-politics in the present is Brady's (1994) *Historikerstreit* or how to best remember history given so much controversy in Ireland. Here it is well to remember the ways the INTO operated across the generations, even where each generation has had its militant figures. The INTO took root in nineteenth-century, post-famine Ireland, then a colonial outpost, and grew throughout the events that spanned the twentieth century: World War I, the 1916 Easter Uprising and 'votes for women', which coincided with its affiliation as a trade union; it held steady during the turbulence of the civil war, then through Ireland's neutrality in World War II and then when the Republic of Ireland came into being and subsequently became a member of the EU; this was notwithstanding 'The Troubles' and the Good Friday peace accord at the close of the century. The INTO similarly needs to stand firm in this present era of twenty-first century globalisation, compounded by the challenges of Brexit and other threats to stability.

Samples of INTO research activities

The memory of different battles for teacher status and remembering INTO history seems apt given the global push for regulated professionalism, which is a more adequate description of what is happening to teachers in Ireland. There are already reverberations in the INTO in regard to an appropriate professional response to the Kenny-Varadkar Coalition Government's (2016–present) new edu-political orthodoxy. The vernacular forms of global neoliberalism, including the global education reform movement known as GERM (Sahlberg, 2011), which are noted by critical policy scholars, are well documented by the teachers' union. Here it is crucial to look back at the INTO's contributions to credible debates about global neoliberal policies, for example, the INTO Conference on Quality in Education that took place in Armagh in November 2014.

The background paper written by Dr Margret O'Donnell was titled 'Quality Education: Teacher Responsibility and Accountability'. There were keynote presentations by INTO Director of Education and Research Dr Deirbhle Nic Craith (2013–present), General Teaching Council Northern Ireland Registrar Dr Carmel Gallagher and academic Dr Eugene Wall (Mary Immaculate College). As well there were numerous conference workshops by presenters such as Mary Burke (Trinity College Dublin) and Veronica Behan (team leader with the National Induction Programme for Teachers), who led on 'Teacher Professionalism – A Shared Responsibility'. Professor Ciaran Sugrue (University College Dublin) led on 'Professionally Responsible Leadership in a Climate of Performativity: Transformative Resistance through the Zone of Proximal Distance?'.[11]

These debates square with the INTO's support for research, not only with the appointment of a Director of Education and Research with responsibility for the development of research and policy formation on educational issues[12] in tandem with its Education Committee. The INTO also encourages the work of research-active teachers who can be published in *The Irish Teachers Journal*, for example. This annual periodical was re-established in 2013 to provide 'an opportunity to teachers to bring research findings to a broader audience and to stimulate thinking and reflection on current educational issues' as noted in its first editorial.

The INTO also takes seriously critical policy scholars such as O'Sullivan (2005); McNamara and O'Hara (2008a, 2008b); Sugrue (2009a, 2009b); Lynch, Grummel and Devine (2012); Lingard (2012, 2013); Mills (2013); Conway and Murphy (2013); Munn (2014); Stevenson (2014, 2015); Evers and Kneyber (2016); O'Donnell (2017); Gallagher (2017); and Wall (2017). Crucially, Ball (2013a) noted Programme for the International Student Assessment (PISA) is a powerful lever for (negative) change, and poor comparative performance creates a 'policy window' through which ideas, which previously seemed extreme or outlandish, can enter policy discourses and attract attention and support.[13]

The INTO's stance also holds in the Irish Congress of Trade Unions (ICTU). But on this occasion, the INTO, as with the wider trade union movement, is focussed on the wider socio-political circumstances of teaching. This was best described by former ICTU Chief Economist Paul Sweeney[14]:

Ireland, one of the poorest of the poor European countries, had pulled itself up and turned itself into one of the wealthiest European states in a remarkably short period. The Celtic Tiger years of 1987 to 2001 were a 14-year period of stunning economic and social success. A confluence of sound economic policies and prior investment saw a doubling of the net income of average workers, a doubling of living standards and a doubling of employment in just 20 years.

> While there was growth in jobs and incomes in the 7-year period after 2001 until the Crash of 2008, policy was now boosting a massive bubble. It was based on uber-liberal economic policies of de-regulation, privatisation, [and] massive tax shifting from direct to indirect taxes, many of which were based on property, large tax 'incentives' and pro-cyclical fiscal policies.
>
> In the latter years of the boom it may have appeared as if ultra-free market liberalism was working, but it was a gross illusion. We lost almost a decade of economic progress, many Irish businesses closed, all Irish banks collapsed, unemployment and emigration soared and we lost our dignity.

Against this background of austerity, it is important to register that INTO General Secretary Sheila Noonan was recently elected President of the ICTU. This at a time when a significant bloc of Irish teachers are attracted to protest, if not populism, as a response to vernacular forms of global neoliberalism in Ireland.[15] This is a microcosm of what is happening regionally across Britain and Europe and globally. The challenge for teachers is real in this unprecedented edu-political reality, but there needs to be serious research-informed consideration of what all this means when it comes to education, the union movement and the nation of Ireland as a republic, especially in this age of globalisation. As Irish writer and cultural philosopher Desmond Fennell (2016) put it,[16]

> in a time of great political turmoil both within nations and internationally it is not surprising that the terminology of political commentary [PC] in the media is in frantic disarray. . . .What do those most basic terms 'left' and 'right' now mean in PC? In America the Republican right calls the neoliberals (who call themselves 'liberals' and consider themselves 'centre') the Left. In Ireland the nominally left Labour Party has acted to support that identification. In the last election it got virtually wiped out because in government, instead of appealing to the working class that it existed to serve, it went for respectability in Dublin 4 by pursuing the neoliberal agenda.[17]

The bigger challenge for the INTO in the present is not to gloss over the widespread disquiet among Irish teachers on the policy directions for teaching nor to ignore the levels of resistance, protest and challenge in the INTO about the directions the teacher union should adopt. This is all the more urgent if teachers are of the view that they are not being given an opportunity to dispute the facts of the case as laid out by Bruton's *Action Plan for Education* much less participate in Ireland's democracy.[18] The twin task here is to underline the INTO's strong record of teachers' organising to provide directions on ways to articulate research-informed policy advocacy that is both reactive and proactive (see O'Connell, 1968; Coolahan, 1981; O'Buachalla, 1988).

This is intended to help counter misguided policy directions in the present to re-configure Ireland's system of national schools. Is it any wonder Fennell (1993) subtitled his book *Heresy. The Battle of Ideas in Modern Ireland*, a notion that could easily apply to edu-politics and the INTO as it faces significant challenges from within and without? As Bascia (2015, citing Bascia and Osmond, 2012) said,

> *Teacher unions have become key defenders of public education at exactly the same time that they face significant challenges: their marginalization is in fact a goal of many reform efforts, and this marginalization, in turn, may lead to teachers' inability to recognise the importance of organised action.*

This 'battle of ideas' echoes INTO General Secretary Joe O'Toole's (1994) claims in the foreword to the booklet titled *Comhairle Múinteoireachta. A Teaching Council*, which outlined the INTO position:

> *Today there is a growing demand for transparency, accountability and quality from those who give service to the public. The delivery of an education service is the responsibility of Government and the ultimate shape of the educational service must always reflect the democratically expressed preference of the people.*

This required recognition of three major issues: the control of the profession, modern demands of transparency and the responsibilities of government in education, which exemplified the teachers' union approach to operate politically and strategically at the time. These arguments were marshalled in a proactive effort at research-informed policy advocacy to establish a Teaching Council, said to be a body that would give greater say to teachers, a greater accountability to the community and an invaluable resource to government.

Crucially, a Teaching Council was guaranteed to enjoy support from all partners, and the booklet was the result of one year's of consideration, discussion, research and redrafting. Moreover, it outlined a detailed and comprehensive Bill following advice of legal Senior Counsel to provide a necessary statutory base for the establishment of a Teaching Council. The INTO campaigned to have the proposal accepted among its members, but also accepted by John Bruton's Fine Gael, Labour and Democrat Left 'Rainbow' Coalition Government (1994–1997) and the Ahern-Harney Fianna Fáil and Progressive Democrats Coalition Government (1997–2002).

This backstory for *An Comhairle Mhúinteoireachta* or a Teaching Council needs to be featured for two reasons: it was a deft edu-political strategy and a case study of social partnerships that was specifically engineered. During the social partnership talks on the *Programme for Economic and Social Progress* (1991–1994), INTO General Secretary Gerry Quigley (1978–1990), with the support of his trade union colleagues in the Irish Congress of Trade Unions, convinced the Haughey Fianna Fáil Progressive Democrats Coalition Government (1989–1992) to underpin primary education with legislation. The promise was for a Green Paper on Education in 1991 to be issued, followed by a white paper soon after. These were to set out government policy on education, and in turn, they were to be subsequently followed by an Education Act. Although proceedings did not follow the agreed timelines, in 1995 the white paper on education,

Charting Our Education Future, contained a commitment to 'publish a draft legislative framework for the operation of the (Teaching) Council'.[19]

Co-author John Carr, the immediate past General Secretary of the INTO (2001–2010), was central to this initiative, given his 'work' interest in teachers as professionals coupled with a personal interest in the Irish language, as he hails from Rosguill Gaeltacht in Donegal. As Carr (1991a) put it in *A Teacher's Perspective on Professionalism*, written when he was Assistant General Secretary INTO (1992–1995),

> *Teaching appears to achieve some, but never all, of the criteria required to become a 'true' profession. It is this constant resistance towards according teachers true professional status which prompted me to challenge many of the prevailing, value-laden assumptions about professions that continue to influence the current literature on teaching.*

Carr (1991b) then squarely addressed the question of professionalisation for the INTO at the time of the work to establish *An Comhairle Mhúinteoireachta* or a Teaching Council in his contribution entitled 'Issues of Provision, Access, Participation & Incentives: The Profession's Response in Swan's (1991) edited booklet *Teachers as Learners*. He acknowledged the role of the State in continually resisting attempts by teachers to establish occupational self-government by placing insurmountable obstacles in the way of *An Comhairle Mhúinteoireachta*. However, it eventually came to fruition with the 2001 Teaching Council Act, which precipitated the development of a worthy representative body that enjoyed support of successive governments. This showed the importance of social partnership to progress the trade union agenda, despite experiencing fervent criticism of social partnership from critics in the opposition parties most notably from Richard Bruton (Sheehan 2008, 2015).[20] As he put it, it was 'a Byzantine institutional environment that has slowed down rather than accelerated much needed reforms' and a 'phoney and polite consensus that has sheltered government from tough questioning on the role and focus of government deals'.

This only serves to highlight Seddon, Billett and Clemans's (2004) 'The Politics of Social Partnerships', reprinted in Lingard and Ozga's (2007) edited collection, *Education Policy and Politics*. Seddon et al. argued that the then-emergent structures for governance and learning within the broad field of education and training were characterised by certain features, dynamics and controversies. Their concerns about critical moments of overt conflicts or implicit conflicts, especially the structural tensions evident within the organisation and operations, are of particular interest to a study of teachers organising in Ireland.

Bruton's (Sheehan 2008, 2015) criticisms also speak to Bascia's (2015) revelation about continuity and change in relationships between teacher unions and teachers, the public and government. She made the point that in more recent decades, when governments have constitutional authority over educational policy, there has been a tendency to centralise and standardise many of the decisions affecting teachers' work. A consequence has been teacher unions' abilities

Co-authors' introduction

to negotiate have been restricted to an ever shrinking range of issues. This includes support for the professional self-regulation of teaching in Ireland, but, ultimately, it was acceptable to consecutive governments: Ahern-Harney Fianna Fáil and Progressive Democrats Coalition (1997–2002), which was followed by the Ahern Fianna Fáil and Progressive Democrats Coalition (2002–2007), the Cowen Fianna Fáil Government (2007–2010), the Kenny-Gilmore Fine Gael-Labour Coalition (2011–2016) and up to the Kenny-Varadkar Coalition Government (2016–present).[21]

This anniversary book project

Carr's collaboration with co-author Lori Beckett came by chance[22] to work in the Vere Foster Trust with colleagues who shared similar concerns about the slow dawning of vernacular forms of global neoliberalism in Ireland. They also shared a vision for the ruins of the Foster family home, Glyde Court, in County Louth to be reclaimed and rebuilt as a world-class research facility, inclusive of a digital library that connects with university libraries and the National Library.[23] Carr and Beckett (2016) publicly promoted the potential of Glyde Court as an intellectual home with conference and residential facilities for teachers and academic partners. They exemplified a calendar of events with the inauguration of the Vere Foster Public Lecture Series with invitations accepted by Bob Lingard, Stephen Ball, Kathleen Lynch, Martin Mills and Pamela Munn.[24] Significantly, Pamela Munn helped produce Sahlberg, Furlong and Munn's (2012) *Report of*

Figure Intro.1 Glyde Court
Source: Publishers David & Charles, now F&W Media International Ltd.

the *International Review Panel on the Structure of Initial Teacher Education Provision in Ireland*. This continues to be an inspiration in a critical consideration of the INTO's practitioner research activities.

This anniversary book builds on Carr and Beckett's (2016) article 'Analysing the Present' for *Policy Futures* and outlines a sample of documentary research projects using select INTO archives to shed light on teachers organising on the matter of teacher status tied to their professional standing. The selection is intended to build teachers' 'case for the defence' against politicians, power brokers and policymakers who are apt to distort 'truths' about teachers' work for ideological purposes. It is envisaged that these samples, foreshadowing teacher union research on teachers' organising in Ireland, could be developed under the direction of the next generation of research-active teachers working with academic partners with allegiance to the INTO and making available their research intelligence on policy and practice to the INTO. Of necessity, in view of teachers' disquiet, resistances, protests and challenges to aspects of Bruton's *Action Plan for Education*, it is envisaged that this would be to inform INTO policy debates about national schools harnessed to the future of Ireland.

That said, it must be acknowledged that documentary research needs to be supplemented with other research strategies and methods (see McCulloch, 2004). Accordingly, this sample of documentary research is augmented with some qualitative data using Carr's recollections, which are a central part of memory work as a method,[25] and interviews with past and present senior leaders of the INTO and school principals. There was certainly a strong sense of responsibilities for teachers' representatives to ensure research-informed policy advocacy in the interview with INTO General Secretary Sheila Nunan (2011–present):

> *[It is vital] being clear about the key things we want: the key principles, be it equity in education or good outcomes for all children, or those broad principles of holistic education; but being researched [informed] on the matters. When we have our representative going (into talks) [we need them well briefed] because in fairness to the other side, they have got much better on the research. They are constantly quoting [sources]; Ministers are much more reliant on the OECD. This is what [our] people say, so we do need to invest in [research thus] ensuring that everything isn't just simple. If we had more money we could do this.*

This recognition by the INTO's most senior executive leader of the complexities of the negotiations with 'the other side' – that is, government and other stakeholders – was a crucial signpost to tease out the worth of research. It showed that it is not enough for INTO representatives to broach education and national school policy, nor go into high-level talks unprepared, especially on the Teaching Council. In effect, this means their 'stories from the field' needed to embrace narrative accounts of research studies, which meant familiarity with research design and methods on particular problematic issues (see Somekh and Lewin, 2005). Nunan then highlighted the difficulties that can be experienced in INTO negotiations, not on the Teaching Council per se, but with reference to past experiences over the

Kenny-Gilmore Fine Gael-Labour Coalition Government (2011–2016) Minister for Education Ruairí Quinn's Literacy and Numeracy strategy. As Noonan said,

> [That] was a bolt out of the blue. Ministers will have a notion what they want to do [while] you are trying to anticipate the trend in the first instance; and then you are trying to do a small piece of research for discussion or debate; or bring in a sub-group of people; or maybe commission somebody. [This could be] one of your members who are good at research to do a paper, which we can then tear apart to do a little bit of preparatory work. But I think the harder part is trying to anticipate the curve of where education is going next and how much we are going to be able to influence that.

Nunan was alluding to an overarching practitioner research question about 'where education is going next' (Whitty, 2008). Her critical reflections on the development of policy knowledge and understandings in the INTO, as for the Teaching Council, coupled with the use of the pronoun 'we' bear witness to the democratic ways the teacher union works. There has seemingly been consistency on the ways polices need to be developed reflexively and critically, drawing on professional knowledge from critical discussions at local branch level through to the senior Central Executive Committee (CEC). This was evident in the interview with former INTO General Secretary Joe O'Toole (20 July 2017):

> I think the role and function of a teacher union has to begin with the role and function of the profession, and the profession must be focussed on the child/pupil/student . . . . The logic is very clear: the teacher is there to do his or her best for the pupils under their care and the teacher union is there to ensure that the conditions nationally and locally and within the school allow that . . . . In other words the teachers should be able to focus full-time on his or her profession in their role as a teacher in the confidence that his/her union will be looking after the big issues, the national issues, the legislative issues, the professional issues and philosophical issues.

Taking these emphases on research-informed policy advocacy forward, the co-authors of this anniversary book work together as a prototype teacher and academic partner in the Vere Foster Trust.[26] They share common personal and professional backgrounds and views about how these inform respective outlooks on the tasks at hand (see McCulloch, 2004). Beckett's (2013, 2014, 2016) work in the north of England was marked by certain personal and political interests in disadvantaged schools, which began with teacher partners in Sydney in the New South Wales Priority Action Schools Project (see Beveridge et al., 2005; Groundwater-Smith and Kemmis, 2005) before her appointment as professor of teacher education in Leeds. Whitty's (1985, 2002, 2008) and Mortimore and Whitty's (1997) advice was central to her work, which traces work supporting and mentoring teacher partners to become research-active in order to confront anxieties about GERM and the dismantling of national systems of schooling.

These warnings from the United Kingdom are timely in Ireland in view of government moves underway to amend arrangements on school patronage or sponsorship apropos the decline of the Catholic Church's long-standing control of Ireland's national schools. The emphasis at present is on pluralism in schools, but the old adage 'forewarned is forearmed' holds in regard any likely Anglo-American corporate system reforms and actions by consecutive neoliberal governments. Minister for Education and Skills Ruairí Quinn in the Kenny-Gilmore Coalition Government (2011–2016) and now Minister for Education Richard Bruton in the Kenny-Varadkar Coalition Government (2016–present) both pressed for major reforms to governance among other significant matters.

Following advice from Chief Inspector Hislop (2012, 2013, 2017), the plan has seemingly been to enforce forms of accountability said to be distant from performativity. However, this seemingly still entrenches a responsive regulatory framework. The concern here is with performativity, especially if/when it is aligned with sanctions and, as in England and the USA, punitive measures could be used to set up so-called failing schools in communities already suffering the devastating effect of austerity compounded by uncertainties about Brexit. This is the mechanism for marketisation, corporatisation and, ultimately, privatisation (see Ball, 2013a, 2013b; also Hursh, 2008, 2015; Beckett, 2014, 2016).

The INTO, with the support of research-active teachers and academic partners, is indeed well placed to coordinate research-informed responses both reactive and proactive to Bruton's *Action Plan for Education*. This is among other centrally imposed policies in the foreseeable future, which requires historically sensitive practitioner research intelligence, which sits well with Hardiman's (2012) advice on Irish governance given a plethora of interests: religious, civil society and corporate interests. This is not to forget teachers' and children's civic interests. In turn, this requires sensible and sensitive teacher influence on national school policy and practice, which is the substance of the argument posited in this anniversary book for teachers' voices in Ireland's democracy: in national schools, in the INTO and in wider edu-political arenas.

The INTO's battle for national schools

It was exemplary on the part of the INTO to have invited Irish historian Diarmaid Ferriter to deliver the keynote address to the 2016 INTO Annual Congress[27] on the occasion of the centenary of the 1916 Easter Uprising. A key point was to look at the republican focus on the education of children over the course of the last 100 years or so: 'Look at the promises of 1916 and the promises of the Proclamation'. In effect, this was a call to look at watershed moments in Ireland's history and teachers' roles in that history. It was fortuitous that Ferriter came to promote this sort of documentary research by teachers for two reasons. It drew attention to 'history from below' (Ferriter, 2015; D. Thompson, 2001; E.P. Thompson, 1966/2001), which shows grassroots forces at work in any given period and which complement more traditional 'top-down' accounts. Secondly, it lends itself to policy learning about different governments' plans over the years for teaching and teacher education, whatever their persuasion.

Ferriter gave renewed prominence to neglected collections of INTO archives, which dovetail with this anniversary book, to give practical expression to the idea that research needs to be a mark of the teaching profession: see Stenhouse in *Research as a Basis for Teaching* (edited by Rudduck and Hopkins, 1985); Lingard and Renshaw (2010) on teachers' 'researchly' dispositions; McCulloch (2004) on documentary research and Punch (2009) on policy research. That said, it is crucial not to exaggerate research and its influence, never mind resistance, protest and challenge, and heed advice from Mills and Morton (2013) in their discussion about ethnography when it comes to work with teacher partners building school-community-based evidence about teaching practices:

> *'Collaboration', 'participation', 'engagement' and 'impact' are the current buzzwords.*
> *Their implications for research strategies are still being worked through. It is much easier to talk about participatory research than to put it into practice; much easier to take a strong political stand than to stay attuned to the complexities of power.*

This not only requires a keen historical sense of teachers' organising, given the INTO's role in Irish edu-politics in relation to intellectual and national traditions, but also the international circulation of ideas. This is where Lingard and Ozga's (2007) advice on reading education policy and politics is crucial because teachers organising requires a critical understanding of power and its arrangements. In Ireland, this includes the INTO, consecutive neoliberal governments, the bureaucracies of the Department of Education and the Inspectorate, and underlying patterns of governance (see Hardiman, 2012).

The INTO could be viewed as part of 'networked' state power or 'governed interdependence', which needs to acknowledge the INTO's record on 'The Managerial System' (see O'Connell, 1968) and 'The New Managerialism' (Lynch, Grummell, and Devine, 2015). This facilitates teachers' critical understanding of the Catholic Church's waning power but also the structural forces now operating nationally as well as regionally and globally with Brexit and the EU. These matters need to be debated and then resolved to the satisfaction of teachers in the INTO in the face of widespread disquiet about policy directions for teaching apropos aspects of Bruton's *Action Plan for Education*. It is posited here as one way to address the levels of resistance, challenge and protest in the INTO about the directions of the teachers' union.

This is not to idealise or romanticise the INTO, but instead to recognise its history, its limitations and the necessity for renewal because, as Hardiman (2012) said, 'The complexity of the policy mix in place at any one time can make it particularly challenging to characterise the Irish state with reference to a single underlying dynamic'. As teachers and academic partners with an allegiance to the INTO channel their research intelligence into the teachers' union, the elected leaders together with members need to be savvy about the Irish state as a structure of power with a set of policy capacities amenable to comparison with those of other advanced industrial societies. As Bascia (2015) p. 2 said, it is crucial to recognise the important role teacher unions must play in defending public education and in minimizing the damage caused by ill-thought-out educational policies.

These concerns are expounded in this anniversary book, constructed in three sections each with two chapters that chart a sample of documentary research to encourage research-active teachers and to enhance teacher union research:

- **The histories of teachers organising** highlights union-active teachers' struggles over time for teachers' status and professional standing, and develops capacity for historicising teachers' organising or tracing its development.

Chapter 1 begins with critical reflections on 'analysing the present' and homes in on the history of some contentious policy ideas such as 'Smart Regulation' to institute the regulated-regulation of teaching:

- 2012 Hislop's lecture on Quality Assurance of Irish Schools
- 2016 Department of Education and Skills *Minister's Briefing*
- Bruton's *Action Plan for Education*:

    Select item:

    1   the Inspectorate

These samples of documentary research provide crucial scaffolding for a critical understanding of aspects of Bruton's three-year *Action Plan for Education* (2016–2019), but also the battles for teachers' status, including their professional practice and the INTO.

Chapter 2 proceeds with backward mapping to Vere Foster (1819–1900), who helped found the INTO and promoted teachers' professional career development and his compatriots such as the proprietor and editor Robert Chamney, but also activist teachers in the mid-late nineteenth century:

- 1868 letter from Vere Foster in *The Irish Teachers' Journal*
- 1868 Chamney's inaugural editorial in *The Irish Teachers' Journal*
- 1869 teachers' evidence to the 'Primary Education Commission' (Ireland)
- 1878 newspaper report on teachers' protests on performance-related pay

Taken together, these documents bring texts together with contexts and consequences (see McCulloch, 2004; also Henry et al., 1988; Taylor et al., 1997). The battles for the recognition of teacher status were tied to more traditional notions of professionalism as they developed, which shed light on similar battles over the regulated-regulation of teaching in the present.

- **The theories of teachers organising** concentrates on teacher activism as it finds expression in efforts to raise the status of teachers but also in support of Ireland's modernisation, albeit in different guises in some watershed moments in the early twentieth century.

Chapter 3 looks at landmark moments in the era of revolution that struck for independence through to the time of the Provisional Government and beyond when cultural revival was central:

- 1916 Padraic Pearse's (1916) pamphlet titled *The Murder Machine*
- 1916 Catherine Mahon and women's struggles
- 1922 National Programme of Primary Instruction
- 1941 INTO Inquiry into the Irish language question

Chapter 4 homes in on some specific instances of teachers organising with landmark INTO initiatives, which together draw attention to the idea of progress as it relates to the idea of Irish development and modernisation:

- 1946 Teachers' Strike
- 1947 INTO Plan for Education
- 1957 INTO presidential address by Margaret Skinnider
- 1968 INTO centenary history book *100 Years of Progress*

These samples of documentary research align with Ferriter's (2016a) INTO keynote on the occasion of the centenary commemorations of the 1916 Easter Uprising, notably his counsel to look at the republican promise for a nascent independent Irish nation, but also to maintain the link between education and society.

- **The practical politics of teachers' organising** comes full circle back to teachers' critical understandings of edu-politics in the twenty-first century, in effect their politicisation about what it means for the INTO to stand up for teaching as an intellectual activity and participate in power struggles.

Chapter 5 spans co-author John Carr's term as a teacher (1967–1989) with a particular focus on his designated work as a branch officer: secretary then chair of branch in the years (1975–1981) and on the CEC in 1982, prior to his appointment as INTO education officer in 1989:

- 1969 INTO submissions to the Tribunal on Teachers' Salaries
- 1970 INTO Comments on Higher Education Authority (HEA) Report on Teacher Education
- 1971 curriculum
- 1988 INTO position paper on curriculum prescription

Chapter 6 continues to span co-author John Carr's term as trade union official in the INTO (1989–2010) with a particular focus on his designated work towards *Comhairle Múinteoireachta. A Teaching Council*. This was on the strength of social partnerships that coincided with an unwitting slow embrace of Thatcherism and vernacular forms of global neoliberalism, which culminates in initiatives since Carr's retirement:

- 1990 INTO letter on the Teaching Council
- 1994 *Comhairle Múinteoireachta. A Teaching Council*

- Bruton's *Action Plan for Education* (Department of Education, 2016, 2017):

Select items

1 School self-evaluation
2 *Droichead* or induction
3 *Cosán*, the first national framework for teachers' learning

These samples of documentary research showcase the necessity of teachers' historically sensitive research-informed responses to the current wave of successive neoliberal governments' centrally imposed policies. Such responses would be ideally underpinned by practitioners' policy intelligence (about England) and developments in global neoliberalism.

The co-authors' closing chapter revisits the work of this anniversary book to encourage research-active teachers and to enhance teacher union research where teachers and academic partners with allegiance to the INTO are intellectually and politically engaged in teachers organising. It distils the lessons to be learned from the samples of documentary research insofar as these shore up the INTO in the present so that it can operate politically and strategically – that is, professionally. The 'rebuttal' is a euphemism for the tasks at hand, which is to confront threats to teacher status and their professional standing that come not only from politicians, policymakers and power brokers but also from ill-considered forms of teacher activism. This is exemplified in regard to the pressing matter of school autonomy in Bruton's *Action Plan for Education*.

Notes

1 This is a major theme for historians and social commentators in Ireland; see J. J. Lee (2008) *The Modernisation of Irish Society 1848–1918*; also Garvin (2004) *Why Was Ireland so Poor for so Long?*
2 See www.flippingthesystem.co.uk. Evers and Kneyber (2016).
3 It is important to clarify the meaning of union-active teachers, especially in Ireland where the notion of union-activity means engagement in politics mostly to do with Northern Ireland and its union with Great Britain, marked by loyalty to the monarch.
4 See Department of Education and Skills 2016b
   https://www.education.ie/en/Press-Events/Press-Releases/2016-Press-Releases/PR2016-09-15.html
5 The two main political parties in Ireland, Fine Gael and Fianna Fáil were formed as a result of the split which occurred in in 1922–1923 with Cumann na nGaedheal, a political party that formed the government in the Irish Free State with independence. Fine Gael supported the 1921 Anglo-Irish Treaty and Fianna Fail opposed the settlement. The ideological differences between the parties today are minimal with Fine Gael being variously described as a Liberal-conservative and Christian Democratic Party and Fianna Fail as a centre-right Republican Party. The Labour Party, formed in 1912, is a social democratic party with left of centre leanings. Sinn Fein, although first founded in 1905 as an Irish political and cultural society to promote political and economic independence from England, arose as a party contender after a split in the republican movement in 1969–1970;

it is regarded as a left wing Irish Republican Party. A number of smaller parties have emerged on the Irish political landscape in recent years: People before Profit, a socialist workers party formed in 2005; Solidarity, formally known as Anti-Austerity Alliance, reformed as a socialist party in 2015; and the Social Democratic Party, committed to the Nordic Model of social democracy launched in 2015. The Green Party, which associates itself with environmental issues, is formally in existence as a political party since 1987. Two further political grouping have been established in the recent past: the Independents 4 Change registered as a political party in 2014 while the Independent Alliance formed as a political grouping rather than a political party in 2015.

6 See Hardiman preface and ch.1 on the economic reasoning for Ireland and education commentators on the effect of globalisation such as Ball, 1990/2012; 2012; Rizvi and Lingard, 2010.

7 Though co-author Lori Beckett worked long enough in England (2006–2017) to know that democratic professionalism is wishful thinking, in developing an appropriate professional response in England as elsewhere, she encouraged teachers' research, given mentoring and support from academic partners, which coupled with their politicisation (see Ghale and Beckett, 2013). But in the face of resistance to such professional practice, she resorted to promoting the strategy of a 'choreography of policy conflict' (see Beckett, 2016).

8 The INTO is structured as follows under Rule 4 of INTO Rules and Constitution: Congress, the supreme governing body, 7 National Committees, CEC 22 members with responsibility to carry out the orders of Congress to report on the progress made on the implementation of Congress resolutions and managing, superintending and directing the affairs of the organisation between Congresses; Benefit Funds Committee (BFC) 7 members with responsibility for administering various funds of the organisation, in particular the Benevolent Fund and the Illness and Mortality Fund; Northern Committee (NC) 16 members charged with managing the affairs of the INTO in Northern Ireland; Education Committee (Ed.C), 18 members who advise the CEC on educational issues; Equality Committee (Eq.C), 18 members who advise the CEC on equality matters; Principals' and Deputy Principals' Committee (PDC), 18 members who advise the CEC on school leadership issues; (PDC); 16 Districts/ District Secretaries; 180 Branches/Secretaries and 40,615 members: see www.into.ie/ROI/InfoforTeachers/Downloads/StaffRep_handbook.pdf.

9 The INTA was the forerunner to the INTO. It was an amalgam of 72 previously existing local teachers' associations. Its establishment coincided with the National Association for the promotion of Social Science Conference, which was held in Belfast in 1867 at which Vere Foster addressed the delegates on the Status of the Teacher and later encouraged the formation of a national association in the first edition of the *Irish Teachers' Journal* in January 1868 in correspondence he submitted on the status of the teacher. Vere Foster was invited to become president at the INTA's full-scale Congress in December 1868 attended by 42 delegates. The INTA operated on an ad hoc basis for the first year before a CEC of eight members was appointed in 1869 with Vere Foster as President: see Doyle (1914).

10 According to INTO historian T. J. O'Connell (1968), the Strabane Association was a very active Association who 'had more than once urged some form of coordination for the separate associations'.

11 These conference proceedings were finally published by the INTO in 2017. The conference programme, conference background paper, keynotes, presentations and workshop details are to be found online at www.into.ie/ROI/NewsEvents/Conferences/EducationConsultativeConference/EducationConsultativeConference2014/.

12 In 1978, the INTO appointed a full-time education officer with responsibility for education and research. In 2014, this position was upgraded to director of education and research as part of the senior management team in the INTO. The remit was to develop INTO policy and conduct research on education issues including curriculum and assessment, special education, social inclusion, early childhood education and Gaeilge (Irish language).
13 A case in point in Ireland was the launch in 2011 by the Kenny-Gilmore Fine Gael-Labour Coalition Government Education Minister Ruairi Quinn of the National Strategy to Improve Literacy and Numeracy among Children and Young People 2011–2020, which was developed by the Department of Education and Skills following the disappointing PISA results in 2009 among 15-year-old children, thus bypassing the NCCA. See The National Strategy to Improve Literacy and Numeracy among Children and Young People 2011–2020.
14 This can be accessed online: www.socialeurope.eu/2015/02/experience-troika-ireland/ (last accessed 28 April 2017).
15 For example, challenge and protest came to mark the INTO presidential campaign in 2016 when Vice-President John Boyle was challenged by a Dublin teacher candidate Gregor Kerr without INTO executive experience, who based his campaign on allegations of a growing divide between members of the INTO and the INTO leadership. The election for INTO president was conducted by postal ballot between 27 March and 12 April 2017 among an electorate of 43, 262 INTO members. The total valid poll was 12,381, of which Vice-President John Boyle received 12,381 votes and Gregor Kerr received 9436 votes. Accordingly, the challenging candidate lost by a margin of 2,945 votes to the vice-president elected at the previous Annual Congress. As is usual procedure, he then stepped up into the office of INTO president.
16 See Desmond Fennell's (2016) article, In defence of populism, none of the populist movements in the west have declared democracy to be their enemy, *The Irish Times*, 23 December: www.irishtimes.com/opinion/desmond-fennell-in-defence-of-populism-1.2912713 accessed 2 May 2017.
17 This reference to Dublin 4 lines up with Fennel's (1993) book chapter, 'Getting to Know Dublin 4' about the more affluent side of the city south of the river Liffey, in *Heresy. The Battle of Ideas in Modern Ireland*.
18 The notion of liberal democracy best expresses the dominant thinking about European societies; however, it must be said our preference is for social democracy.
19 See, too, Fintan O'Toole: www.irishtimes.com/opinion/fintan-o-toole-why-social-partnership-needs-to-be-revived-1.2848959.
20 It needs to be noted that Richard Bruton was previously Minister for Enterprise and Employment (1994–1997) in his brother Taoisearch John Bruton's 'Rainbow' Coalition Government (1994–1997). Richard Bruton was then Fine Gael Opposition spokesperson on education when the Ahern-Harney Fianna Fáil and Progressive Democrats Coalition Government (1997–2002) Minister for Education and Science was Micheál Martin (1997–2000).
21 Enda Kenny, credited with bringing Ireland back from the brink of economic ruin and described as a 'statesman' and a 'patriot', finally announced his resignation after 15 years as leader of Fine Gael and head of two governments, following several delays and a series of political setbacks. He was succeeded by Leo Varadkar, the son of an Indian immigrant, the first from an ethnic minority and the country's youngest leader. He makes known his conservative right wing values and his homosexuality.
22 This backstory is such that co-author Lori Beckett's family history quest at that point was searching for answers to burning questions about her Irish maternal lineage in Co. Meath: ostensibly, research questions about how her great grandmother

aged 20 with her sister aged 19 came to immigrate to North Queensland in the late nineteenth century and why it was they could read and write English. The advice from Sean and Aggie Halpenny was to investigate Vere Foster and visit the Foster family home, Glyde Court, in neighbouring Co. Louth. Lori made contact with the INTO to make inquiries and was directed to John Carr.

23 This was the substance of our contribution to two radio interviews, which also included contributions from John Coolahan and Diarmaid Ferriter on Vere Foster; see https://www.rte.ie/lyricfm/the-lyric-feature/programmes/2014/0502/614976-the-lyric-feature-friday-2-may-2014/ (last accessed April 2017).

24 Professor Bob Lingard (University of Queensland) did the inaugural public lecture on 10 September 2012 entitled 'Schooling and Pupil Progress: What Needs to Be Done in Policy, Schools and Classrooms'. Then came Professor Stephen Ball (UCL Institute of Education) with 'Neoliberal Education? Confronting the Slouching Beast' on 26 February 2013. Professor Kathleen Lynch (University College Dublin) delivered 'New Managerialism in Education' on 27 September 2013. Professor Martin Mills's (University of Queensland) lecture was entitled 'Challenging the 'Tyranny of No Alternative'. Teachers and Students Working Towards Socially Just Schooling' on 7 November 2013. Finally, Professor Pamela Munn (University of Edinburgh) delivered 'Taking Research-Informed Teaching Seriously: From Aspiration to Reality' on 11 September 2014.

25 See Frigga Haug (n.d.) Memory-Work as a Method of Social Science Research: A Detailed Rendering of Memory-Work Method, accessed online 14 June 2017: www.friggahaug.inkrit.de/documents/memorywork-researchguidei7.pdf.

26 We acknowledge this idea of teachers and academic partners working together under the auspices of the teachers' union is not new; see Groundwater-Smith and Kemmis (2005) on an initiative inaugurated by the New South Wales Teachers Federation in Australia, Stevenson and Gilliland (2016) where the latter works in the INTO and edited collections by Compton and Weiner (2008) and Bascia (2015), who feature contributions from academics and teacher unionists.

27 See the online link to Ferriter's 2016a keynote: www.into.ie/ROI/NewsEvents/Conferences/AnnualCongress/AnnualCongress2016/WebcastArchive/Tuesday29March/.

Part 1
The history of teachers' organising

Section essay: the history of teachers' organising

This section highlights the histories of union-active teachers engaged in INTO struggles over time for teachers' status and professional standing, and develops a capacity for historicising teachers organising or tracing its development. This historicising is crucial to scaffolding towards teachers' 'case for the defence' against regulated professionalism. It means to engage in a critical-interpretive reading of teachers' engagement in edu-politics as a product of the INTO's historical development. Bascia (2015) proved insightful in regard to the history of teacher unionism, emphasising the emergence of teacher unions, recent governmental relations and career histories of teachers who carried out their social activism within their union's organisational frameworks. Interestingly, she cited the United States, Canada, England and Australia, where teacher unions found their organisational footing around the turn of the twentieth century in relation to their emerging systems of mass education.

Teacher organising in Ireland is different given the foundation of its mass education system in 1831 and the INTO's sesquicentenary history dating back to the mid-nineteenth century in the post-famine era. This difference carries into the present where research-active teachers have been encouraged by the INTO over the years but also more recently given Ferriter's keynote to 2016 Annual Congress in Wexford. He exemplified what it means to showcase the sources of teachers' history, in effect the 'common people' in Irish national schools. As the evidence shows, the INTO provides material support for the publication of practitioner research activities in the *Irish Teachers' Journal*, both early and later editions, and through INTO publications. There is much to be found in these INTO archives on Irish governance and edu-politics, not least its complexities and ways to operate politically and strategically.

In this section, we begin with 'analysing the present' to provide some samples of documentary research that set the stage to sketch some traditional 'top-down' accounts of national schools followed by some 'history from below'. Dorothy Thompson (2001), in a reference to the difference between the people's history and 'English History Proper', called it a populist tradition in history. This is a unique approach because it searches the INTO archives for evidence of

Ireland's teachers' career histories insofar as their status and professional standing demanded activist responses. The idea of 'history from below' has a participatory relationship with its audience, in this case teachers, but it must be said that the sample of documentary research projects in this anniversary book are selective. The archival data was chosen to develop a thesis about teacher status tied to notions of professionalism. It was not intended to be comprehensive, and this anniversary book project cannot replicate the world-class research required for a comprehensive history of Irish education (see Coolahan, 1981; O'Donoghue and Harford, 2016; Coolahan, 2017; Puirséil, 2017).

Chapter 1 begins in the present and homes in on Bruton's predecessors in the Ministry of Education and Skills but also Chief Inspector Dr Harold Hislop's (2012, 2013, 2017) efforts at regulatory governance to institute regulated professionalism. It then embarks on critical analyses of the issue of quality in Hislop's (2012) lecture on Quality Assurance of Irish Schools and the Department of Education and Skills' (2016) *Minister's Briefing* document on Ireland's system of education. This was prepared for Bruton as he took office as Minister for Education and Skills in the Kenny-Varadkar Coalition Government (2016–present). It provides useful insights into Bruton's *Action Plan for Education*, which has the capacity to re-shape edu-politics, national schools & social life with consequences for democracy, human affairs and citizenship in Ireland. This is stark in the light of the histories of teachers' organising.

Chapter 2 proceeds with backward mapping to Vere Foster (1819–1900), who helped found the INTO and promoted teachers' professional career development. It charts the uses made of the first edition of *The Irish Teachers' Journal*, not only as a business venture for Foster's compatriot the proprietor and editor Robert Chamney but also as a voice for teachers. It then charts the work of Foster in concert with teachers, who learned the value of research activity with questionnaires sent out to solicit responses for some major consultations. Finally, it charts Foster's demise, which is closely linked to the fate of the Anglo-Irish in late nineteenth-century Ireland.

These efforts at historicising in the course of this sample of documentary research about teachers' struggles are necessary to inform contemporary teachers' reactions to aspects of Bruton's *Action Plan for Education*, which represents one of the priorities of the Kenny-Varadkar Coalition Government (2016–present). It is an argument of this anniversary book that the INTO consultations and negotiations on regulated professionalism will benefit from such historical understanding, which will enable teachers representing the INTO in the present to exert better influence. As McCulloch (2004) said,

> *Documentary studies need to come to terms with alienation from history and to find ways of reconciling the historical with the contemporary.*

McCulloch's advice points to the need to understand the documents as their contemporaries would have understood them, not just as they might be understood today (McCulloch, 2004, citing Marwick, 1981). This squares with counsel from Irish civil servant Sean O'Connor's (1986) reflections on the Irish educational scene in the mid-twentieth century when he said his work provided a view of education from near the Minister's seat rather than a comprehensive history of Irish education. This requires attention to the historical texts but also the contexts and consequences (see McCulloch, 2004; Henry et al., 1988; Taylor et al., 1997), which has to do with education, economy and society as they relate to a peculiar understanding of the nation in the regional and global setting (see Hardiman, 2012; Sharma, 2016).

1 Historical revisions

Introduction

In order to showcase the work that could be done by teachers and academic partners working in collaboration, ideally using Vere Foster's family estate, Glyde Court, reclaimed and rebuilt as a world-class research centre with residential facilities, it is crucial to exemplify some samples of work. Having brought together a network of research-active practitioners[1] who agreed one strategy was to put together a collective contribution to *Policy Futures*, Carr and Beckett (2016) began with a framing 'analysis of the present'. In keeping with the vision for the Vere Foster Trust, the inspiration to provoke a public policy debate on the future of schools that resonated with practitioners on the island of Ireland came from Hall, Massey and Rustin (2015), published online as the *After Neoliberalism?The Kilburn Manifesto*.[2] This helped broach neoliberal education policies in Ireland, although it was never intended as a synopsis of the suite of policies that have been incrementally introduced.[3]

From the outset, it is important to share some critical reflections on working together as a prototype teacher and academic partner in the Vere Foster Trust. This could be a first approximation towards historicising teachers organising, taking seriously practitioners' critical inquiry after Stenhouse (1976) and Cochran-Smith and Lytle (2009). Carr and Beckett (2016) focussed on the Kenny-Gilmore Fine Gael-Labour Coalition Government Minister for Education and Skills Ruairí Quinn's (2011–2014) published reform agenda, 'The Future Development of Education in Ireland', and Chief Inspector Dr Harold Hislop's (2013) paper 'Applying an Evaluation and Assessment Framework: An Irish Perspective'. A democratic impulse was to spark critical commentary.

With the benefit of hindsight, maybe Carr and Beckett's (2016) *Policy Futures'* article was too preoccupied with Quinn and Hislop's initiatives, and needed to home in more on the provenance of their ideas[4] and then come to practitioners' efforts at reproach. Quinn and Hislop took direction from transnational agencies such as the OECD Education Directorate, the McKinsey and Company reports (Mourshed, Chikioke, and Barber, 2010), the World Trade Organisation, the World Bank and the EU. Concurring with Ball (2013a), these are very powerful and very persuasive agents and organisations that legitimise, disseminate and sometimes enforce neoliberal reform. Such a focus on the major players such as the Minister and Chief Inspector at the expense of the force of their ideas and censure was ironic. The interest, as it happens, is in teachers' organising to assert their effects at the micro-political levels and impel the INTO in a variety of possible directions, often simultaneously (see Bascia, 2015).

This anniversary book builds on lessons learned from that early co-authored work, which was also given some public airing at different conferences.[5] The intention here is to maintain a tight focus on teachers' organising and what they do to secure teacher status in terms of teachers' place, role, function and professional standing. This requires thinking through changing notions of professionalism as it is espoused by government and teacher unions but also in research. We are inspired by Bascia (1994, 2008, 2009, 2015) on teacher union research in concert with Whitty's (2008) traditional, managerial, collaborative and democratic modes of teacher professionalism, and the changes that vary across time and place, though he was writing in the English context. We also acknowledge the work done in Ireland by Stevenson and Gilliland (2016) in regard to their vision of a new democratic professionalism in Ireland with teacher unions at its heart: that mobilising teachers requires unions to renew themselves but also to create the conditions for renewal itself. The point of departure for the co-authors of this anniversary book is that much more is required than a positive vision of teaching, asserting teachers' professional voice, challenging orthodoxy and 'flipping the system'.

Broaching forms of professionalism in Ireland requires contextual and historical sensitivities in regard to the INTO's long-standing preoccupation with teacher status tied to notions of professionalism that found different expressions over time. This is in effect the INTO's raison d'être, which is sorely tested in the present, given moves towards regulated professionalism. To this end, the aim is to identify current neoliberal policy challenges for the INTO, some of which are familiar even if the responsive strategies are not always well developed, while others are embryonic and developing.

For example, the Department of Education and Skills (2016e) introduced a new Quality Improvement Framework, *Looking at Our School: A Quality Framework for Primary Schools*, designed to underpin both school self-evaluation and school inspection. According to the accompanying *Circular 0039/2016*, schools were to be charged each year with producing a short self-evaluation report and school improvement plan in a single document. The structure and application of the Quality Improvement Framework contained two dimensions of teaching and learning, leadership and management, divided into a number of domains, with standards for each domain consisting of statements of practice given at two levels: statements of effective practice and statements of highly effective practice.

In reply, the INTO issued two directives to members on non-co-operation with school self-evaluation in March and again in April 2016. The INTO took this action in order to progress a demand for the restoration of promoted posts and to address the issue of increased workload for primary teachers, but this is not to ignore an opportunity for critical discussions about the quality of teaching, which may well be distinct from the government policy discourse. The INTO took further action when the Central Executive Committee (CEC), at its meeting on 5 January 2018, decided to lift the INTO directive on school self-evaluation in effect from 19 February 2018. This was a necessary compromise for the negotiations on teacher salaries in order to ensure that all INTO members receive the benefit of pay restoration measures.[6] The CEC also reiterated the INTO's determination to pursue additional posts of responsibility and to intensify discussions with the Department of Education and Skills on workload issues.

This was one instance where teachers' salaries had become a mechanism for settling points of contention between the INTO and government, particularly on the ways Bruton's *Action Plan for Education* has reconfigured teacher status tied to a sense of regulated professionalism. This sort of neoliberal policy challenge for the INTO lends weight to the concern about the so-called politicisation of policy where politicians and power brokers assume control of partisan policymaking. This is despite engagement in the processes of consultation with relevant stakeholders as required under the Education Act (1998), which calls into question the government policy discourse about external standards of quality and performance as a yardstick for benchmarking. Perhaps there needs to be more responsive consultation about the quality of teaching, the research evidence, and the lived experiences of Ireland's political economy, given that collectively teachers have seen it all.

Teacher union research in Ireland

Teachers' 'history from below' needs to be fleshed out, which begins in this chapter with samples of documentary research into traditional 'top-down' accounts and augmented by personal recollections and memory work. For instance, co-author John Carr had much to say about Whole School Evaluation and the INTO's work, including reactive and proactive policy advocacy. As he described it, prior to the introduction of a new Whole School Evaluation inspection system in 2004 (replacing the old School Reports system, which was designed to be carried out on schools every seven years), the Inspectorate worked on a collaborative and advisory basis with teachers. In 2006, the Department of Education issued guidelines to schools setting out the practices and procedures that were to be followed, including the publication of school reports on the Department of Education website. Despite objections from the teacher unions to the publication of school reports, the Department went ahead and posted the reports on its website following inspections carried out in individual schools. In addition, the Department rejected teacher objections to the issuing of questionnaires to parents during inspection visits, but, ironically, it did not proceed at that time.

However, two years later in 2008, the Inspectorate initiated a review of the guidelines in consultation with a new configuration of partners in education, notably management, parents and teachers. An objective was to shorten the notification period of the six weeks, which in the Inspectorate's view allowed schools too much time to prepare for Whole School Evaluation in advance of inspection visits. The perceived excessive run-up time was also considered opportune to solicit the support of parents' representatives and management authorities for the issuing of questionnaires to parents. The rationale put forward by the inspectorate was that the schools were producing too much paperwork (which they were obliged to evaluate) and that the information that they were receiving from parents' representatives did not, in many cases, reflect the work going on in the schools that they had inspected. While welcoming the reduction in paperwork being proposed by the Inspectorate following the review, the teacher unions did not accept the argument that the parents' representatives did not adequately reflect the operation of the school.

Then without prior consultation, the Inspectorate announced as part of its own reform agenda in 2009 that incidental inspections, which had not been a common feature of the evaluation process since the introduction of the Whole School Evaluation system, would be resumed, claiming that both forms of inspection existed in complementary fashion within the inspection regime. The Inspectorate also invoked its entitlement under the 1998 Education Act to decide on the appropriate forms of school evaluation following consultation with the education partners. The INTO raised concerns regarding the reintroduction of unannounced incidental inspections, but following consultation with members, who expressed reasonable satisfaction with their experiences with incidental visits, did not pursue the matter further.

This narrative from memory work, expounding teacher union research, provided a springboard to study the INTO archives. This was to glean evidence about the various conflicts, negotiations, resistances, mediations and settlements, which characterised INTO engagement in edu-politics, not to forget the changing nature of inspection systems. This draws attention back to the politics of social partnerships and the contradictions and conflicts they call forth (see Seddon et al., 2007), but this is not to shy away from necessary school improvements, including quality of teaching. As INTO General Secretary Senator Joe O'Toole said in the foreword to an INTO publication *Professionalism in the 1990s* (INTO 1992):

> *Change is an integral part of the education process. The problem facing the teaching profession is to recognise its acceleration and direction and to develop new ways in which teachers can exert greater influence and control over their professional activities. Primary teachers have been subjected to both State and Church control since the inception of the national school system.*

This squares with Bascia's (2015) more recent advice that as the educational environment continues to change, teacher unions need to evolve. So it is with the INTO over its sesquicentenary history and its teacher union research, always rich and varied, but also how it might evolve topically, methodologically and conceptually. This is not to ignore teachers' disquiet, resistances, protests and challenges, which pre-supposes teachers' politicisation when it comes to actively insisting on an education system that recognises teachers' status tied to professional standing and how this was/is the subject of struggle over time (see Ghale and Beckett, 2013).

This chapter charts a sample of documentary research to encourage research-active teachers and to enhance teacher union research: a first tranche of documents homes in on the more contentious policy ideas amenable to critical policy analyses[7] and includes the following:

1. Hislop's (2012) lecture on Quality Assurance of Irish Schools;
2. Department of Education and Skills (2016a) *Minister's Briefing* document on Ireland's system of education;
3. Bruton's *Action Plan for Education*.

- Select item:
    i the Inspectorate

The first two documents provide crucial scaffolding for a critical understanding of Bruton's initial three-year *Action Plan for Education* (2016–2019). This needs to be synchronised with the more specific *Action Plan for Education* for 2017 launched in February of that year, incorporating over 400 actions and sub-actions, and any subsequent plans. All these invite critical-interpretive readings of the texts in relation to their contexts and consequences (see McCulloch, 2004; Henry et al., 1988; Taylor et al., 1997), keeping in mind McCulloch (2004) on explanatory points:

- Who were the authors and what were they seeking to achieve?
- How/why were the documents produced and how were they received?
- What are the potential links between past/present/historical context?

Such a political orientation informs efforts to flag the edu-politics in the battles for teacher status marked by deliberations on notions of professionalism, including the regulated-regulation of teaching in the present. In linking the past, present and future, hopefully, this sample of documentary research will be supported and sponsored by the INTO and subsequently developed under the direction of the next generation of research-active teachers and academic partners plugging their research intelligence on policy and practice into the INTO. With any luck, by then, its archive will be situated in the reclaimed and refurbished Glyde Court in County Louth with a digital library that interlinks with university libraries, national libraries and museums on the island of Ireland and internationally. In this way, we all follow Bascia's (2015) lead to provide a fine-grained picture of how groups, sub-groups and individuals identify and pursue different strategic directions, often simultaneously.

Hislop (2012) lecture on quality assurance of Irish schools

Dr Harold Hislop, chief inspector Department of Education and Skills, delivered the Professor Seamas Ó Súilleabháin Memorial Lecture entitled 'The Quality

Assurance of Irish Schools and the Role of Evaluation: Current and Future Trends' at National University of Ireland (NUI) Maynooth. In introductory remarks, transcribed in Gaelic and English, Hislop described the parameters of his lecture, which could be read as the terms of a debate on quality. Firstly, that his comments and reflections were about the first and second-level education systems – the Irish terms for primary and secondary education. Secondly, his focus was to be on developments regarding the quality assurance of Irish schools and centres for education. Significantly, Hislop acknowledged the 'many actors that have a role in ensuring that children and young people have the opportunity to engage in effective learning experiences in schools' and drew attention to the quality of the curriculum, the quality of the professional education, the quality of the facilities and resources available to schools and the supports given to school management to ensure the quality of the educational experience for learners. Hislop then named the actors:

> *The National Council for Curriculum and Assessment (NCCA), State Examinations Commission, the Teaching Council, the school support services including the Professional Development Services for Teachers (PDST) and the National Induction Programme for Teachers (NIPT), providers of initial and continuing education for teachers, the Department's Schools Division, as well as management authorities, teacher unions and bodies representing parents and students.*

Even a cursory glance suggests Hislop takes an inclusive approach to quality assurance, which is evidently research-informed given the lecture runs to 11,324 words over 30 A4 pages and incorporates references to relevant policies and research in extensive footnotes. It is beyond the scope of this anniversary book to engage in-depth critical policy analyses of quality assurance ably done elsewhere (see Conway and Murphy, 2013), but it is a sample of documentary research that can shed light on what a more defensible notion of what 'teaching quality' might mean (see Carr, 1989). Hislop's (2012) lecture could be described as an institutional record of the Inspectorate in the immediate aftermath of the latest Global Financial Crash, which once again hit Ireland hard. The GFC, as it came to be called was a continuation of Ireland's 'economic suicide' well documented in O'Toole's (2009) *Ship of Fools. How Stupidity and Corruption Sank the Celtic Tiger.*

Against this background, it is crucial to tease out some salient points in Hislop's concentration on the role of the Inspectorate and its work in external quality assurance and on the role of the school itself. This draws attention to teachers' understanding of teaching quality in view of their values, ideas and arguments, and to the matter of constructing quality evidence about teachers' practices. Hislop's themes are consistent with the government discourse foreshadowed by Richard Bruton when he was Opposition Spokesperson on Education and Science (1997–2000). They are also consistent with former Kenny-Gilmore Fine Gael-Labour Coalition Government Minister for Education and Skills Ruairí Quinn (2011–2014).

Hislop (2012) began with a rationale for the emphasis on the quality of outcomes, posed the question, 'Why now?', and then provided a qualified answer: 'It is fair to say that at this juncture in the history of our educational system, we are increasingly concerned with the quality of the learning in which young people are engaged in schools and centres for education'. Presumably, the pronoun 'we' referred to the Inspectorate if not the main actors, although Hislop hastened to add, 'Ireland is not alone in having this heightened level of public interest in the quality of educational outcomes', which was indicative of interconnectedness in wider regional and global arenas. Beyond his appeal to consensus, he laid out a main argument, which started with a look back to the late 1990s and which should be noted as a watershed moment for Ireland given what happened to its tiger economy (see O'Toole, 2009).

Hislop's focus was tactically on the quality and effectiveness of provision, pointedly

> asking ourselves whether our efforts have achieved the objectives we desired, particularly regarding equality of opportunity and the effectiveness of interventions to address educational disadvantage. We have been able to move from a focus on inputs and supply to a focus on outcomes and achievement.

The pronoun 'we' notwithstanding, these questions were seemingly glossed over without any regard for professional debates about quality of teaching much less quality of evidence about teachers' practice (Groundwater-Smith and Mockler, 2007). For example, the renewed emphasis on outcomes as part of a quality assurance framework heralds a key policy shift away from whole school development towards whole school improvements with emphasis on internal accountability and external evaluation. Hislop then adumbrated a series of issues: the professionalisation of teaching, a focus on quality in human services, the drive for value for money, market mechanisms and school autonomy, globalisation and international comparisons, an aside about PISA and a combination of factors. These assumptions, which begin to acquire 'the status of a literal truth' (Carr, 1989), are all worthy of close study to develop a deeper understanding of the embrace of dominant neoliberal discourses. Two stand out, given their significance for the INTO's ongoing struggle for teacher status and teachers' deliberations on notions of professionalism:

1. The professionalisation of teaching, said to be tied to 'an increasing willingness of teachers and school leaders to set professional standards, to lead their own professional development and to seek to improve the educational experience for learners'. A note was made of constructive criticism of schooling and education, strategically attributed to teachers themselves engaged in studies and research.
2. A combination of factors, said to underline the reasons for the current focus on quality in our school system, summarised in terms of 'the stage of development of our school system, the concern to ensure equity in the system, the

desire for value for money, a move to school autonomy, and the impact of international comparisons'. It was noted that this was not a definitive list of the reasons for the focus on the quality of Ireland's school system, given further factors could be suggested, presumably open to teachers' concerns about those children and young people 'left behind' across the island of Ireland.

Hislop was seemingly driving for consensus as he indicated, 'These factors are among those that are shaping the ways in which quality assurance of schools has and is developing'. He turned to those developments under the major subheading 'A Framework to Consider the Quality Assurance of Schools'. Immediately, he cited the National Economic and Social Council (2011, 2012) on the quality of human services in Ireland, notably the body of research on the approaches used to enforce or assure quality in service provision. These documents, too, require close study because they are significant in a number of ways; notably, they are one step removed from the teaching profession's research literature on quality of teaching; they foreground the regulated-regulation of teaching and the ways this was to be instituted. This raises questions, especially as Hislop noted the description of 'a possible continuum of approaches ranging from regulation and control at one end to complete self-regulation at the other', and 'an approach to quality assurance which it terms "smart regulation" or "responsive regulation" in which elements of both regulation and self-regulation are combined in order to encourage and embed improvement in the delivery of services'. He went on 'to consider where quality assurance of Irish schools, through external inspection and school-based self-evaluation, might fit on the continuum between regulation and self-regulation and how the balance between the two has altered and may continue to develop'.

This was the substance of the remainder of Hislop's lecture, expounded under the following subheadings that show an extensive amount of detail to inform any new government policy discourse:

- Quality assurance and the Education Act 1998;
- The Inspectorate and external quality assurance in the 1998 Act;
- Self-evaluation of schools in the 1998 Act;
- But effective "smart regulation" is not yet realised;
- A wider range of efficient inspection models;
- Intelligent planning of the inspection programme;
- Defining and articulating standards for the school system;
- Using data to inform school evaluation and improvement;
- Using data for system-level monitoring and improvement;
- Reforming the rules and regulations that govern schools;
- Embedding a culture of robust self-review and professional accountability in schools and school communities;
- Utilising strong feedback loops;
- Dealing with teacher appraisal;
- Following up inspections and dealing with under-performing schools.

Historical revisions 35

The details demand a search for the evidence of the need for such feverish activity, but again, for the purposes of this anniversary book, two features of the institutionalisation of the regulated-regulation of teaching stand out. These are significant for the ongoing struggles for teacher status and deliberations on notions of professionalism including regulated professionalism:

1. Self-evaluation of schools in the 1998 Act:

   This was a reference to the 1998 Education Act, invoked by Hislop (2012) in support of his rationale for introducing self-evaluation or, to use his preferred term, the 'self-regulation at the other end of the spectrum'. This, too, requires a close critical – interpretative reading to ascertain shared knowledge about the legislation. Hislop stated that the Act clearly placed the 'primary responsibility for the quality of education provided to students on the school's Board of Management' in accordance with Section 15 of the Act, while it envisaged that the school principal would have a major role to play in leading good practice and in monitoring the achievements of students in the school under Section 22 of the Act. In support of his argument for the introduction of self-evaluation, he also cited Section 20 of the Act, which included the provision that Boards of Management should 'establish procedures for informing the parents and students in the school of matters relating to the operation and performance of the school'.

2. But effective 'Smart Regulation' is not yet realised:

   This was a reference to the progress on achievements to date in both the areas of external evaluation and school self-evaluation, which similarly requires a close critical, interpretative reading to establish agreement. Hislop (2012) maintained that there was still a considerable amount of work to be done to achieve the envisaged quality assurance system in Ireland's schools: 'Such a system, if it is to conform to the ideals of 'smart regulation' or 'responsive regulation' must use a judicious combination of robust self-evaluation and external school inspection to assure quality and to promote improvement in individual schools'.

Hislop's conclusion was telling insofar as he brought attention back to inspection systems and processes, and offered an ostensibly official assurance that this was all to be in the favour of 'young people to enjoy a rich, challenging and fulfilling educational experience', but with the proviso only 'when we harness the enthusiasm and commitment of professionals'. It would be extremely worthwhile if teachers and academic partners, supported by the INTO, were to take up the challenge and develop some practitioner research projects on student voice. This could be complimentary to the consultation with students undertaken by Ireland's National Council for Curriculum and Assessment (NCEA) or an Chomhairle Náisiúnta Curaclaim agus Measúnachta about its work in early childhood, primary and post-primary education.[8] As the brief online said, 'Students are best placed to provide informed perspectives about what it is like to be students at different stages of their education'. Two projects were listed: Student Voice Forum on Assessment, dated October 2015, where 'Students and teachers met to talk about assessment, what works and what does not and how it can support learning', and a Student Voice Forum about Wellbeing, dated March 2016, where 'Students and teachers met to talk about how schools can support student wellbeing'.

This focus on consultation with students would not have been lost on Hislop (2012), while his lecture on Quality Assurance of Irish Schools, in the form of an institutional record of the Inspectorate, was an interesting example of interaction between the State, social institutions and professional identities (see McCulloch, 2004). As Hislop put it,

> *The Inspectorate relishes the challenges before us and we look forward to continuing the strong, professional collaboration that we enjoy with stakeholders to achieve this vision of 'responsive regulation' and high quality education services for young people. If we achieve our collective goal, I think the Irish school system will have served our young people well.*

This is so far removed from teacher voice and indeed student voice, in effect 'history from below', and simply raises alarm bells. Firstly, because of the definitions on 'Responsive Regulation', 'Meta-regulation' and 'Smart Regulation' provided by the National Economic and Social Council (2012) report entitled *Quality and Standards in Human Services in Ireland: The School System No. 129*. Secondly, because the 'Smart Regulation' agenda was advanced at the European level under Ireland's EU presidency in 2013,[9] which took a cue from the National Economic and Social Council (2012) report. This put forward the view that 'Regulation is one of a number of quality-enhancing mechanisms that can improve the quality of services', but warns that 'regulation is not always effective when there are only two extreme options applied: rules and regulations implemented through a top-down approach directed by a central regulator' and 'a bottom-up approach where service providers and professionals self-regulate.' (NESC, 2012, p. 3). Consequently, the proposal in the report urged the adoption of the concept of a Responsive Regulation, which aims to combine both approaches in the following lock-step:

- Responsive Regulation: aims to combine a top-down 'command and control' approach containing rules and regulations with a bottom-up system, where service providers and professionals engage in a process of self-regulation. Often depicted as a 'regulatory pyramid of approaches, with self-regulation and voluntary approaches at the base and sanctions at the top' (Braithwaite, Makai, and Braithwaite, 2007), the oversight body ensures that standards are met by beginning 'at the bottom of the pyramid with information and persuasion, but with the capacity to escalate towards punishment if persuasion fails, sometimes referred to as "the gorilla in the closet". Regulators will seek to persuade but will act further if matters do not improve' This process has

been refined further by Seddon (2008) who 'focuses on increasing purpose and *performance* in services rather than relying on compliance with regulators, and who sees frontline staff heavily involved in driving improvements' (NESC, 2012, p. 3).
- Meta-regulation: one of the main mechanisms within a Responsive Regulatory framework 'where organisations establish systems of self-regulation themselves and regulators then seek to assure themselves that these systems are adequate and being followed, i.e., it is the regulation of self-regulation' (NESC, 2011, cited by NESC, 2012).
- Smart Regulation: the second-most common mechanism which is usually deployed under a Responsive Regulatory framework (Gunningham and Grabosky, 1998) 'where a range of non-State bodies are involved in supporting regulation, for example professional organisations, trade unions and NGO's. These groups may be able to act as 'quasi-regulators, for example, NGO's that provide supports to implement standards. It may be necessary, however, for the State to enforce such standards with organisations who do not respond to the persuasive work of NGO's or third parties' (NESC, 2012). The bodies concerned with primary education in Ireland are the Irish National Teachers' Organisation (INTO); the Irish Primary Principals Network (IPPN); Management Bodies and Patrons; Inspectorate and Teaching Council; state agencies such as National Council for Curriculum and Assessment(NCCA), National Certificate of Educational Achievement (NCEA) and National Education Welfare Board (NEWB); parent and students councils; and Internal and International Assessment Agencies (e.g. Education Research Centre, PISA, Junior Cycle Framework).

As it happens, this feeds into the current Kenny-Varadkar Coalition Government (2016–present) policy discourse about quality of teaching. The Department of Education and Skills, as the overseeing body, is charged under Bruton's *Action Plan for Education* with adopting a 'Meta-regulation' approach by assuming responsibility for regulating the Teaching Council. This amounts to the regulation of the teachers 'self-regulatory body or the regulated-regulation of teaching. The Inspectorate is also charged under Bruton's *Action Plan for Education* with adopting a 'Smart Regulation' approach by setting standards of teaching and learning (to be followed later by standards of leadership and management and standards for student supports) through the promulgation of school self-evaluation procedures and by the introduction of appropriate external inspection models. This similarly amounts to regulated professionalism. This points to a more in-depth understanding of the predicament for teachers, given the INTO needs to marshal the evidence for both policy effects and policy advocacy.

Department of Education and skills (2016)
Minister's Brief Overview

This four-part briefing paper, nearly 80 A4 pages in length and published online,[10] could also be described as an institutional record that consolidates the new government policy discourse. It contains particularly significant advice on the Department of Education and Skills translated as An Roinn Oideachais Agus Scileanna. Titled *Minister's Brief Overview* and without an identified author, it provides fascinating insight into the workings of government in this era of Brexit, which has witnessed the two Fine Gael Taoisigh,[11] Enda Kenny and Leo Varadkar, at the centre of negotiations in Belfast, London and Brussels, and Bruton's portfolio as Minister for Education and Skills:

- Part 1 Context with ten subheadings
- Part 2 Schools: Early Childhood Education with Two and Schools Sector 19 sub-subheadings
- Part 3 Further Education and Training and Higher Education with 15 subheadings
- Part 4 Infrastructure with six subheadings

There is much to celebrate in each of these parts, but the content is worthy of close scrutiny to tease out the rhetorical phrases, slogans and metaphors, not least the goal very early in Part 1: Supporting Inclusion and Diversity:

> *We want an education and training system that welcomes and meaningfully includes learners with disabilities and special educational needs, learners from disadvantaged communities/backgrounds, and those with language, cultural and social differences.*

This is followed by another goal: Building the right systems and infrastructure:

> *We want a modern, flexible education and training system which makes the best use of available resources.*

Yet again, the pronoun 'we' notwithstanding, given who is included under the departmental umbrella, the details provided interesting census data:

> *In all, there are over 1 million full-time learners across the system. These include the following:*
>
> - *Over 67,000 pre-school children;*
> - *916,000 children in over 4000 schools;*
> - *270,000 in further education and training; and*
> - *173,000 full-time students and 38,000 part-time students in 31 state-funded higher education institutions.*
>
> *The Education and Skills sector is a major employer, accounting for one third of public sector employees. This includes over 59,000 teachers, 12,000 special needs assistants (SNAs), 23,000 staff in higher education institutions and approximately 4000 staff working in the further education and training sector ...*

> *The staffing of the Department at end December 2015 totalled 1289 (1206 whole time equivalents) ... The overall staffing complement of the Department has been reduced by 114 whole time equivalents (9%) since the introduction of the moratorium on public sector recruitment in March 2009.*

In Part 2, under 'Schools Sector', 3 of the 19 major subsections entitled 'School Patronage', 'Autonomy and Accountability Consultation' and 'Developments in Inspection of Schools, Including School Self-Evaluation', all located more or less half way through the briefing paper, proved to be of great value to understanding the ways quality in teaching comes to be expressed in certain ways. School patronage might seem peripheral to our concerns about Bruton's *Action Plan for Education*, teachers' status and deliberations on democratic professionalism, especially when it comes to the regulated-regulation of teaching. Of particular interest are the moves towards the establishment of new schools on the strength of an argument about diversity, given concerns about areas with population growth, opportunities for consideration of new schools and different types of schools with provision for Irish medium and multidenominational education. But professional definitions of teaching quality with evidence to the fore!

While it is welcome to see direction on the reconfiguration of existing primary schools to accommodate different and diverse interests in education, it is necessary to be mindful of Bruton's (1999) concern with the UK quality control approach and any hint of back-tracking.[12] It is the case England's Ofsted inspection system is engrossed with school performances and ever ready to name 'failing schools' in the State system to affect marketisation, corporatisation and semi-privatisation (see Ball, 2013a, 2013b; Beckett, 2014, 2016). While not an issue in the current debate on diversity of school provision in Ireland, school patronage could readily become a mechanism for any possible Anglo-American style school reform. This would be inviting corporate sponsors or multinational companies to take over national schools in Ireland, especially given the *Minister's Briefing* indicated,

> *At primary school level, 90% of schools are under the patronage of the Catholic Church. The Catholic Church has itself highlighted the necessity for a greater plurality of provision to respond effectively to the changing social needs. The possibility of the Catholic Church divesting itself of the patronage of certain primary schools was raised by Catholic Church authorities initially.*

This alluded to a Forum on Patronage and Pluralism in the Primary Sector, established in 2011 by former Minister Ruairí Quinn (2011–2014).[13] Officially, it was to make recommendations on what steps could be taken to ensure that the education system at primary level could provide a sufficiently diverse number and range of primary schools to cater for children of all religions and none. This has major implications for teachers, effectively controlled by the Catholic Church since the inception of mass education when it had become increasingly clear to Westminster that the voluntary proselytising society model of school provision was no longer going to be tolerated by the Catholic population. According to

Akenson (1970), in 1831, the chief secretary for Ireland Lord Stanley took the initiative and wrote to the Duke of Leinster, a member of the Privy Council of Ireland and Lord High Constable of Ireland, informing him of the government's intention of constituting him as president of 'a board for the superintendence of a system of national education in Ireland'. The Board of Commissioners for Education was established in that same year to provide aid to schools.[14] As the majority of the population were Roman Catholic at the time, over 90% of schools were established by the Catholic Church. It remains to be seen what any mooted changes to such long-standing patronage might be, particularly with contemporary parents articulating demands for alternative school provision either through state community schools, non-denominational or multidenominational schools, but whatever transpires, it will reverberate down the twenty-first century.

The Department of Education and Skills (2016a) *Minister's Briefing* continued, under the major subheading 'Autonomy and Accountability Consultation', with a description of the departmental research being carried out. This was at the behest of the Cabinet Committee on Social Policy and Public Service Reform, which requested some investigation of a trend across many developed countries 'towards devolving greater autonomy away from central government to lower levels of the education system'. It was indicated that

> *in Ireland, schools have a good degree of autonomy over many aspects of their work, although they are not completely autonomous . . . that schools must have the capacity to exercise autonomy granted to them if the policy is to improve education outcomes [which] ties in with the initiative under way to build the leadership capacity in schools.*

There was acknowledgement that 'changes to school autonomy must be carefully planned and delivered and are best preceded by an engaged policy debate on how autonomy can work best in an Irish context'. Presumably, with quality of evidence at issue, a consultation paper was prepared and circulated to seek 'views from all interested parties on the issue of advancing school autonomy' on the items of governance, management and ethos; curriculum, pedagogy and assessment; and budgets and funding.

Pointedly, there were evident concerns about Anglo-American style school reforms that found expression among the 60 submissions received from so-called interested parties, given the departmental briefing reported,

> *A preliminary analysis of the submissions shows that there is some hostility to the concept of autonomy, with many submissions criticising the importation of a concept from England and the USA which does not take account of the different features of the Irish education system.*

Under the third major subheading selected for critical discussion here, 'Developments in Inspection of Schools, Including School Self-Evaluation' the sub-subheadings require close study because they too are significant to the regulated-regulation of teaching and the ways this was to be instituted. The first was presented in capital letters, followed by sections with subheadings that developed the departmental rhetorical argument that can be readily identified with dominant neoliberal discourses:

- Information, Monitoring and Quality in Early Years and Schools
  - Research-informed approach to quality
  - Education-focussed inspections in early years' settings
  - Inspection of schools
  - Using a range of inspection models, including follow-up inspections
  - New inspection models for schools
  - Publication of 'A Quality Framework for Schools'
  - School self-evaluation
  - Information on schools and school performance

It is worth pausing here on two significant points: the first is in regard to a research-informed approach to quality because we are struck by the claim in this briefing paper that 'the Department's approach to quality assurance of provision in the schools sector is informed by international research, much of it produced under the auspices of the OECD'. This raises questions about whose research and evidence is preferred when it comes to bringing scholarly knowledge and practical wisdom about Ireland's schools to policy deliberations. Here it is important to be alert to the policymaking processes and those operating inside and outside of government, not to forget Irish teachers with historically informed professional interests to engage with policy. Following on, a profound concern remains about the relationship between education policy and research, and as Saunders (2007) decried, what might be involved practically and intellectually in creating environments where research can have a realistic and beneficial influence on the development of particular policies.

The second significant point relates to information on schools and school performance, especially the type and collation of information, and what this means in regard to evidence for claims, given that in 2015, 'the Minister for Education and Skills and the Cabinet Committee on Social Policy asked the Department to begin examining issues concerning how information on schools could be made more easily accessible and this work has commenced'. Another profound concern is that this foreshadows a major problem for Irish teachers, as for teachers in England and elsewhere burdened by highly restrictive curriculum, teaching methods and assessment practices that ultimately result in pressures to meet unrealistic benchmarks set by government. Moreover, it gives way to phenomenal tensions and challenges for teacher partners who seriously struggle to find their professional voice on quality teaching along more democratic lines (see Beckett, 2014, 2016), which is at the heart of this anniversary book project.

Bruton's *action plan for education* 2016–2019

As Minister for Education and Skills in the Kenny-Varadkar[15] Coalition Government formed after the 2016 general election, Bruton was ready for the

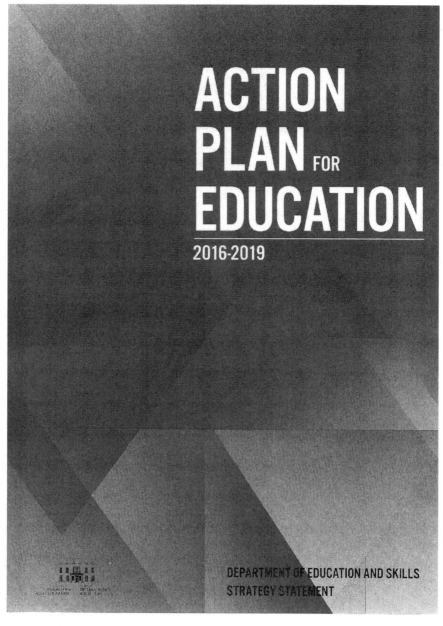

Figure 1.1 Action Plan for Education, 2016–2019

Source: http://www.education.ie/en/Publications/Corporate-Reports/Strategy-. Reproduced courtesy of the Department of Education and Skills.

Department of Education and Skills (2016b) to release his three-year *Action Plan for Education* (2016–2019) in September of that year.[16] The 65 A4 page document, most likely authored by a team of civil servants, dovetailed with his long-held ideas about quality (see Bruton, 1999). In turn, these sat well with consecutive neoliberal government Ministers[17] and most importantly with Chief Inspector Dr Harold Hislop (2012, 2013, 2017) as well as departmental Secretary General *Seán Ó Foghlú*.

This institutional record replicated a similar *Action Plan for Jobs* Bruton pioneered as Minister for Jobs and Enterprise in 2012, which followed his earlier stint as Minister for Enterprise and Employment (1994–1997). The government press release dated 15 September 2016, indicated top-level support at the time of the launch of the *Action Plan for Education*. According to Taoiseach Enda Kenny, the actions were deemed 'to be the way to ensure equality of opportunity, success, and hope and break the cycle of disadvantage'. Further, publication of quarterly implementation reports and continuous consultation with stakeholders and members of the Oireachtas Éireann, the legislature of Ireland would be central to the process.[18]

In an accompanying memo, the Department promised that in each subsequent year it would publish an updated annual *Action Plan for Education* containing concrete actions to be implemented in each year according to strict guidelines. These too were laudable statements but we are mindful of the policymaking processes and those operating inside and outside of government. As Hardiman (2012) put it, the dominant political discourse has tended to be favourable to globalisation, economic openness, competitiveness and, on balance, European integration (Antoniades, 2010; Schmidt, 2006; Smith and Hay, 2008). This cannot be glossed over.

Bruton's first edition *Action Plan for Education 2016–2019* (Department of Education, 2016c) contained a substantial two-page table of contents, the first half devoted to a list of statements with numbered pages, including a foreword by Bruton and a statement by Secretary General Seán Ó Foghlú. A few listed items take the eye: the political environment, the economic environment and the labour market, which suggested majority interest in Ireland's political economy with children's interests all but invisible, and 'A Programme for a Partnership Government Commitments', which indicated a sagacity about *edu-politics*. Any enthusiasm for such partnership was soon dissipated in the second half of the table of contents devoted to a tabulated list of the five goals each with numbered objectives and actions, targets and indicators:

1. Improve the learning experience and the success of learners;
2. Improve the progress of learners at risk of educational disadvantage or learners with special educational needs;
3. Help those delivering education services to continuously improve;
4. Build stronger bridges between education and wider community;
5. Improve national planning and support services.

This was presented not only as a show of concern for education but also as a form of rhetorical persuasion particularly in the way this document was graphically designed. The stated vision was striking: 'To provide the best education and training system in Europe', presumably among other EU countries striving for the same. The executive summary then elaborated this vision using the pronoun 'our' in an effort to represent the whole population and to forge a consensus:

> *Education has been central to Ireland's transformation over recent decades. It has played a very significant role in helping Ireland to successfully weather the exceptional economic crash. It will be central to our ambitions as a nation (economic, cultural, scientific and social) over the coming years. It will allow us to lead in innovation. It will help us to achieve social inclusion.*
>
> *Being the lead in Europe means an ambition to be the best at:*
>
> - *Harnessing Education to break down barriers for groups at risk of exclusion*
> - *Delivering a learning experience to highest international standards*
> - *Equipping learners of all ages and capacities to participate and succeed in a changing world*
> - *Allowing Ireland to be a leader across a broad range of fields, scientific, cultural, enterprise and public service.*

This too was a laudable vision, and while there was some acknowledgement of Ireland's economic conditions and its regional and global location, it was clearly conservative and competitive in orientation, especially when it came to the decree:

> Ireland already has a top 5 position in Europe in several important spheres (for example, post-primary literacy, third level participation, take up of STEM at third level) and a top 10 position in others (educational attainment, innovation, low dropout from school).

The Department hastened to identify 'other areas where there is significant ground to make up', again conservative and competitive in orientation but skewered towards business and enterprise: 'the achievement levels in science, take-up of gateway subjects and the availability of apprenticeships and traineeships in emerging areas of skills'.

Select item: the Inspectorate

Chief Inspector Harold Hislop's (2017) inaugural public lecture was to mark the incorporation of the Centre for Evaluation, Quality and Inspection within the Dublin City University's Institute of Education in May of that year. It was entitled, 'A Co-Professional Approach to Inspection for Accountability and Improvement: Progress and Prospects in the Irish Context'. It was a cue to develop a critical understanding of the Inspectorate, as it was alert to the government policy discourse in the actions and sub-actions on inspections in the two most recent versions of Bruton's *Action Plan for Education* available online.

Action 67 of the 2016 *Action Plan for Education*, reiterated as Action 72 in the 2017 *Action Plan for Education*, proposes to 'advance proposals for the better involvement of principals with inspection teams in primary and post-primary schools'. The involvement of principals in the evaluative process was foreshadowed by Hislop in the INTO magazine *InTouch* in June 2014:

> *We need to see an evolution in the role of the principal to a position where principals will focus a good deal more on the quality of teaching and learning rather than administrative tasks. Getting the right balance between accountability and improvement and between internal self-evaluation and external inspection will be a constant challenge.*

According to Hislop (2017), external inspection has to serve both 'accountability and improvements functions' with the greater emphasis to be placed on encouraging school improvement, although this looks to be a 'one-size-fits-all' model of decontextualized school improvement (see Thrupp, 1999, 2005; Lupton, 2006; Bibby et al, 2017 Beckett, 2014, 2016). In order to achieve these goals and to make inspection models more responsive to need, the Inspectorate developed a range of inspection models to enable them to engage with schools 'on a reasonably regular basis and for a diversity of purposes'. These included the following:

1. Frequent shorter inspections, particularly unannounced inspections or incidental inspections;
2. Medium scale inspections covering an aspect of the work of the school involving one or two school days duration;
3. Whole school type inspections of typically three-day duration including Whole School Evaluation, management, leadership and learning, and evaluation of action planning for improvement in Delivering Equality of Opportunity in Schools (DEIS);
4. 'Follow-up' or 'follow through' inspections, typically one or two in-school days.

This pre-empted the Inspectorate's focus over the next three years, which was to embed standards for educational provision through school self-evaluation; increase the effect of existing inspection models; improve ways to engage with parents and students in inspections; promote and foster excellence; begin work with a small number of schools in 'excellence and improvement visits' to advise, challenge and support school leaders and teachers in their efforts to develop innovative approaches and to improve standards; improve how to use data to support both inspections and self-evaluations; and to continue to provide the loop of learning between schools and the development of educational policy.

Clearly, there is substance here for documentary research into more rhetorical devices, but it must be noted there are good working relationships between teachers and Inspectors. This could be intertwined with a meta-evaluation of the Inspectorate, given the inexorable moves towards a regulated system that boasts external inspection and internal school evaluation (see Beveridge, Groundwater-Smith, Kemmis and Wasson, 2005). The 1998 Education Act placed inspection on a statutory basis and ever since the inspection system has undergone considerable development and reform. According to Hislop (2013), the Inspectorate's 'experience has been that, by collaborating closely with stakeholders, including teachers, school leaders and parents, (they) have managed to evolve robust yet well-accepted evaluation models'. This squared with advice from Adelman and Alexander's (1982) classic study, *The Self-Evaluating Institution*, insofar as it is be assumed that educational institutions should have procedures for subjecting their practices and ideas to open and collective appraisal, particularly if they are to be consistent with the goals they profess.

Conclusion

In 'analysing the present', it could be said Carr and Beckett (2016) fell short in their early examination of the published reform agenda of former Kenny-Gilmore Fine Gael-Labour Coalition Government Minister for Education and Skills Ruairí Quinn (2011–2014) and the OECD model for evaluation and assessment for improving school outcomes by Chief Inspector Dr Harold Hislop (2012). It needed to home in on the provenance of these ideas situated in the context of Ireland's socio-economic history, including the Celtic Tiger at the turn of the century, which preceded the 2008 GFC and Troika bailout. The point here is that these men, along with Minister Bruton, wield a great deal of power to institute vernacular forms of global neoliberalism that have become dominant.

This is all the more so given Quinn, Hislop and Bruton are apparently inspired by powerful agents and organisations such as the OECD and the National Economic and Social Council (2012) 'Smart Regulation' agenda advanced at European level under Ireland's EU presidency in 2013. This goes to show the struggles for the status of teaching allied to teachers' professionalism are not just academic; they are political. Indeed teachers and academic partners might engage efforts at reproach, but first they must broach the OECD and NESC policy influence; quality and quality assurance, and question evidence of teachers' practice; schools and social justice limited to compensatory and equal opportunity programs; and Anglo-American style school reforms, for instance. In this their struggles are political. The regulated-regulation of teaching is, as Seddon et al. (2007) intimated, a reconfiguration of education within the frames of neoliberal governance.

The INTO leaders, inclusive of current general secretary Sheila Nunan (2011–present) and Director of Education and Research Dr Deirbhle Nic Craith (2013–present), similarly wield a great deal of influence in edu-politics.[19] It is the argument of this anniversary book that this is best served by research-informed policy advocacy, ideally from research-active teachers feeding historically informed research intelligence into the teachers' trade union. But this requires some political nous of the ways the powerful edu-political machine operates, headed by government spokespersons with official sanction, Ministers, departmental officers and the Chief Inspector all taking directions from national, regional and global power blocs. They are equipped to run what might be called the Irish economic-educational complex akin to the military-industrial complex, which developed over time.[20] This harks back to teachers' organising that also developed over time in relation to the teachers' trade union movement, which could vie a state power centre in Irish governance (Hardiman, 2012).

Notes

1 We agreed on the name of the Vere Foster Trust, and then we were excited to discover a photo in the archives in PRONI of a group in the 1960s who also called themselves by the same name.
2 See https://www.lwbooks.co.uk/sites/default/files/free-book/after_neoliberalism_complete_0.pdf.
3 Different aspects of this work in Ireland are amply covered by O'Sullivan (2005), McNamara and O'Hara (2008a, 2008b, 2012), Sugrue (2009a, 2009b, 2015); Lynch, Grummel and Devine (2012); Grummel and Lynch (2012), Conway and Murphy (2013), Evers & Kneyber (2015) O'Donnell (2017); Gallagher (2017); (Wall 2017), Nic Craith (in O'Donnell, 2017). An overall synopsis, ideally by research-active teachers plugging into the INTO, is pressing in Ireland; see Poole (2015) on a synopsis of neoliberal education policies in British Columbia combined with critical discussion of the British Columbia Teachers' Federation strategies for responding to those policies.
4 At the time of finalising this anniversary book manuscript, Gunter's (2016) book on *Intellectual Histories* just came to hand following her talk at the Centre for Policy Studies in Education University of Leeds, Tuesday 13 June 2017.
5 These conference papers were delivered at the 2014 and 2015 ESAI conferences: the first was titled 'The Politics of Modernisation in Ireland: What Future for Teaching and Teacher Education?' in Athlone and the second was called 'Panel Discussion on Research for Policy Advocacy: The Case of the Junior Certificate' at Limerick.
Carr and Beckett also did a presentation titled 'Glyde Court Working Estate – A Potential for Partnership?' at the Ninth Annual Historic Houses of Ireland Conference 'Past and Future Perspectives' held at the National University of Ireland Maynooth on 8–9 June 2011.
6 The INTO took this action to ensure continuity of pay uplifts on 11 January (part payment) and 25 January 2018 (full payment) and subsequent payments to continue INTO participation in the new entrant pay process and to honour the September 2016 agreement fully restoring qualification payments to teachers who started teaching since February 2012; see www.into.ie/ROI/NewsEvents/LatestNews/Title,44415,en.php.
7 See Lingard and Ozga (2007) on what counts as policy.
8 See National Council for Curriculum and Assessment https://www.ncca.ie/en;www.juniorcycle.ie/Curriculum/Student-Voice.
9 On 22 March 2012, the Council of the OECD adopted the Recommendation of the Council on Regulatory Policy and Governance. This Recommendation was the first international instrument devised by the OECD 'to address regulatory policy, management and governance as a whole-of-government activity that was intended to be addressed by sectoral ministries, regulatory and competition agencies'. According to the OECD, the effect of the financial and fiscal crises which engulfed many states

prompted the development of new regulatory frameworks as a means of developing 'well-functioning markets and societies, protecting the environment and promoting economic growth'. The recommendations were developed to assist members and non-members in building and strengthening capacity for regulatory quality and regulatory reform. Ireland supported the conclusions of the OECD Council at the meeting in March 2012. During its presidency of the Council of Europe in 2013, the Irish government advanced the Smart Regulation agenda at European Council level. www.dfa.ie/media/dfa/alldfawebsitemedia/newspress/publications/2013-EU-Presidency-achievements-report.pdf.

10 See Department of Education and Skills, 2016a https://www.education.ie/en/Publications/Ministers-Brief-/Ministers-Brief-2016-Overview-.pdf.
11 This is the plural of Taoiseach or Prime Minister in English.
12 See Bruton's (1999) 'Quality – The Key Debate in Education', which expressed his views: 'Debate must move far beyond the UK's old-fashioned quality control approach that has typified this debate (quality improvement) in the UK. There the emphasis has been on inspection and identifying unacceptable levels of failure. Irish teachers have reacted against the crude league tables that this approach produced' (p22).
13 See The Department of Education and Skills (2012) The Forum on Patronage and Pluralism in the Primary Sector: Report of the Forum's Advisory Group. DES www.education.ie/en/Press-Events/Events/Patronage-and-Pluralism-in-the-Primary-Sector/Background-to-the-Forum-on-Patronage-and-Pluralism-in-the-Primary-Sector.html.
14 This was subject to the availability of local funds and the proviso that one-third of the cost of the school building would be borne locally. The board envisaged that the schools would be mixed schools catering for children of all denominations a view which was opposed by the various churches at the time. Despite initial reservations, however, the churches soon realised that they were in a position to provide the initial capital costs and to sustain ongoing costs and set about establishing their own denominational schools with government support. By the mid-century, the national schools had become denominational schools (Akenson, 1970).
15 Enda Kenny was elected Taoiseach and Head of Government or Prime Minister following the general election in Ireland in 2011 when the country was in the throes of a deep recession as a result of the Global Financial Crises and the collapse of the Irish economy. He is credited with leading Ireland out of recession albeit on foot of severe austerity measures and major cutbacks imposed in education, justice, welfare and health. Enda Kenny's leadership within Fine Gael came under severe pressure following the poor electoral performance by Fine Gael in the general election in 2016, and although he succeeded in forming a minority government with members of the Independent Alliance and with a confidence and supply arrangement with Fianna Fáil, a series of crises within the Irish police force considerably weakened his support within his own party. He stepped down as Taoiseach on 13 June 2017, and his successor, Leo Varadker, who, at 38 years of age, was elected as the youngest ever Irish Taoiseach the following day by 57 votes to 50 with 47 abstentions; see www.theguardian.com/world/2017/may/17/enda-kenny-announces-resignation-fine-gael-leader.
16 This is available online; see Department of Education and Skills (2016c) www.education.ie/en/Publications/Corporate-Reports/Strategy-Statement/Department-of-Education-and-Skills-Strategy-Statement-2016–2019.pdf.
17 A former leader of the Labour Party (1997–2002) Ruairí Quinn was appointed Minister for Education and Skills by Enda Kenny in the Kenny/Gilmore Fine Gael Labour Coalition government (2011–2016) in March 2011. He resigned as Minister for Education and Skills on the 11 July 2014 and was replaced by Labour

party member Jan O' Sullivan (2014–2016) following a cabinet reshuffle. Following the 2016 general election Richard Bruton (2016–present) was appointed Minister for Education in the Kenny Fine Gael Independent Alliance minority government and retained his post when Varadkar became Fine Gael leader and Taoiseach.
18 This consultation with members of the Oireachtas reflects the 'confidence and supply' arrangement between the Fine Gael and Independents Coalition Government and main opposition party Fianna Fáil. See www.oireachtas.ie/parliament/about/.
19 It is important to note that the BERA-RSA (2014) final report into the role of research into teacher education was followed up by an 'influence strategy'.
20 For example, see J. J. Lee (2008) p. 151 on the orthodox conservative authoritarian conception of the state and p. 156 on a theory of political power; presumably, this was the nineteenth century equivalent of policy advocacy (see Yeatman, 1998).

2 Introducing Vere Foster (a key figure in Ireland's struggle)

Introduction

The evidence to date shows that in Ireland, like England, alongside EU nations and others beyond, teaching and teacher education continues to experience incremental shifts towards vernacular forms of the global education reform movement or GERM (Sahlberg, 2011). These are marked by tight controls and/or constraints which brings into being new mechanisms and oversight techniques based on the principles of Responsive Regulation particularly Meta-regulation and Smart Regulation. In turn, these are designed to promote greater accountability and quality improvement in schools, which has the effect of creating for teachers a greater sense of more regulated professionalism. This is contrary to the notions of professionalism that evolved with struggles for teacher status in England and Ireland (see Whitty, 2008; Stevenson and Gilliland, 2016), not only as an expression of teachers organising in the INTO but also of the way teachers work to ensure pupil learning is secured rather than diffident.

The changing nature of professional self-determination could be a second approximation towards historicising teachers organising, mapping the pathways over time towards the regulated-regulation of teaching given what is happening to the Teaching Council in the present. Teachers' professionalism is under serious threat if teachers and the INTO are not given an opportunity to negotiate the dominant political discourse of global neoliberalism, including GERM. This predicament requires supporting and mentoring research-active teachers, building teachers' knowledge bases and constructing a flexible evidentiary standard for teachers' 'case for the defence' as a response to their disquiet with regulated professionalism. This includes revisiting professional responsibilities for regulation via the Teaching Council and finding evidenced-based and research-informed ways to engage politically and strategically with new responsive regulatory approaches. This will ensure that professional authority and occupational freedom of the teachers are not unduly eroded.

This also includes a look back to the roots of the regulation of teaching with mass education before and after the 1801 Act of Union with Great Britain. Akenson (1970) reported that a number of commissions were set up around the turn of the nineteenth century most notably in 1791, 1806 and 1824–1827 to examine education provision in Ireland, but it was the Stanley letter of 1831 that made its mark. According to Coolahan (1981), Lord Stanley did not seek to establish a new statute, thus allowing more flexibility to monitor the success or failure of the then-new system of education. The letter served as the written constitution of the primary education system up to the enactment of the 1998 Education Act. Its main features were the setting up of a board composed of men of high personal character, including individuals of exalted station in the Church, 'to exercise a complete control over all schools' which submit to its regulation; the main object 'must be to unite in one system children of different creeds'; aid to be given to schools subject to the availability of local funds; schools to be kept open for certain number of hours and days with time to be set apart for religious education 'as may be approved by the clergy of their respective persuasions'; and arrangements for the appointment of teachers to be left to the 'individuals or bodies applying for aid 'subject to certain restrictions and regulations'.[1]

This chapter continues backward mapping to Vere Foster (1819–1900), who followed his efforts on assisted emigration schemes after the Great Famine by using his own wealth to finance the improvement of nascent dilapidated national schools across the island of Ireland. Foster typified the Anglo-Irish establishment in the British-centric politics that followed the 1801 Act of Union and that marked the Victorian era with its parallel struggles for Ireland's national independence. There was much happening at the time: uprisings after the famine: the Young Irelanders' insurrection in 1848 and the Fenian uprising in 1867, but thereafter, the atmosphere in Ireland swung more towards political agitation mainly through the Home Rule movement established in 1870, with roots tracing back to Daniel O'Connell and Catholic Emancipation in the 1840s, and the boycotting of landlords during the Land War (1878–1883). Following the rejection of Gladstone's Home Rule Bill in 1873, national consciousness and community identity was awakened with the establishment of the Gaelic League on the 31 July in Dublin by Dubhghlas de hÍde or Douglas Hyde, a son of Protestant rector from Frenchpark, County Roscommon. The organisation operated under a pseudonym An Craoibhín Aoibhín, which translated as the Pleasant Little Branch, with a view to promoting the revival of the Gaelic language. Hyde was an academic, writer, linguist and scholar of the Gaelic language who was appointed professor of modern Irish in University College Dublin in 1909 – a post he held until 1932 when he retired. He was elected the first president of Ireland in 1938 a position he held until 1945.

It was amid the turbulence of mid-nineteenth century Ireland that Foster came to work more directly with national school teachers. He was well known to the Dublin Central Association, one of several teacher associations that existed across the island. He was approached by members of the Association to write one of his famous pamphlets on the appalling conditions that teachers had been enduring in national schools. Several of Foster's pamphlets had already been printed by Chamney's print shop, a Dublin firm which printed magazines and periodicals at the time. Jeremiah Henly, a prominent member of the Dublin Central Association, occasionally contributed articles to some of Chamney's publications, and thus was in a position to make contact with Foster. Henly found Foster 'most interested and anxious to help' (O'Connell, 1968), and brokered discussions between Foster and the teachers. No doubt Foster's involvement in such business enterprises and his philanthropy, a sort of social capital of the day, enabled him to draw open attention to matters like teaching conditions, school improvement, mixed schooling, teacher efficiency, equal payment, education taxes and managerial control (McCune Reid, 1956; McNeill, 1971; O'Connell, 1968; Colgan, 2001).

These were certainly bold activities, not only because of Foster's shrewdness in refurbishing national school buildings but also because of his intelligence building a professional culture for teachers and drawing together local associations. Significantly, he oriented these local associations to how power worked in edu-politics in nineteenth-century, post-famine Ireland. In 1868, he instigated beginning ways of organising teachers, probably influencing the Strabane Teachers Association motion that was instrumental in founding the INTA, the forerunner to the INTO. At the same time they no doubt benefitted from Foster shepherding the initial objects of the INTO[2]:

> *The promotion of Education in Ireland, the social and intellectual elevation of teachers, and the cultivation of a fraternal spirit and professional intercourse with different organisations in this and other countries.*

It is important not to eulogise Foster, much as he deserves heartfelt recognition given the lasting significance of his work for the public good in Ireland. As the INTO's first president, he used his social capital and respectable reputation to engage in lobbying politicians, power brokers and policymakers about Irish education, and to openly promote teachers' status. At least he is well commemorated as a key historical figure in Ireland's struggles for national schools north and south in names of buildings and memorials including a public lecture series. This will be re-launched after the publication of this anniversary book together with doubled efforts to resurrect the project for a world-class research centre at Glyde Court, or at least in what is left of the remains of the Foster family home in Tallanstown in County Louth.

What follows is another sample of the sorts of documentary research projects that could be developed using select INTO archives, which include the following:

1. 1868 letter from Vere Foster in *The Irish Teachers' Journal*;
2. 1868 Chamney's inaugural editorial in *The Irish Teachers' Journal*;
3. 1869 teachers' evidence to 'Primary Education Commission (Ireland)';
4. 1878 newspaper report of teachers' protests on performance-related pay.

Taken together, these documents show the importance of reading texts in relation to their context but also their consequences (see McCulloch, 2004; also Henry et al., 1988; Taylor et al., 1997). The peculiar edu-politics of nineteenth-century Ireland can be traced in the battles for the recognition of teacher status tied to more traditional notions of professionalism, though 'licenced autonomy' to regulate their own affairs was then in the distant future (see Whitty, 2008). This sheds light on the present, particularly the complexities of teaching and the contextual sensitivities required to critically understand teacher unions and the INTO's work, but also Ireland's sovereignty in a globalised policy setting.

1868 letter from Vere Foster in *the Irish Teachers' Journal*

The Irish Teachers' Journal was inaugurated in January 1868 by Robert M. Chamney of Dublin print-shop fame. He was noted on the front cover as the proprietor and editor. Elsewhere, he was described as a 'successful Dublin publisher, journalist and magazine proprietor whose attention to the plight of the Irish teachers had been attracted by Vere Foster's pamphlets' on various aspects of the education system in Ireland (McCune Reid, 1956). Chamney was remembered as 'an experienced and able journalist, tactful and diplomatic, whose memory deserves to be held in deepest reverence by the teachers of Ireland whom he served so well' (Doyle, 1914). Doyle went on to say,

> Occasional and spasmodic efforts were made by bold and enterprising teachers in the *Freeman's Journal, the Nation, Ulster Gazette, Westmeath Examiner, Galway Vindicator*, and *Sligo Champion*, to focus public opinion and influence members of Parliament on the galling and slavish condition of Irish teachers; but the *Irish Teachers' Journal* (originally published as a monthly organ) was 'the first great medium of communication among our scattered units, which resulted after two or three years of strenuous work in consolidating our scattered forces into one formidable and harmonious body.
> (Dublin Central Teachers' Association, 1914)

This journal is to be found in the INTO archives and as a digital version, and Foster's letter in the very first volume is a worthy documentary source because it was written at a time of rapid and no doubt threatening social change in Ireland. It is situated under the umbrella term 'correspondence', said to air viewpoints, grievances and the like. It takes the form of a 'letter to the editor':

> *Sir, I am delighted to receive your Prospectus for The Irish Teachers' Journal.*

According to McCune Reid (1956), 'This publication appeared in January, 1868, heralded by a prospectus which was distributed to every National teacher and everyone else who was in any way connected with Education'. Foster provided a ringing endorsement given this one in Ireland was to rival monthly education journals in England, such as 'The National Society's Monthly Paper', the 'Papers for the Schoolmaster', 'The Educational Times', 'The Museum', also in Canada and nearly every one of the United States. Of particular interest is the caveat that Foster put on the nature of the journal, which shows his cognisance of the necessity to negotiate the budding edu-politics of Church and State control, if only by sidestepping it:

> *I believe that such a periodical, strictly non-political and non-sectarian, devoted solely to the subject of Education, such as essays, extracts from other educational serials, popular papers on scientific subjects, correspondence etc, with a department for official notices, is much required, and may render essential service to the cause of education.*

This idea of strictly non-political and non-sectarian requires interrogation and an adumbration of the evidence. In a radio interview for Lyric F M,[3] Ferriter (2014) referred to a variety of different political and social movements that existed in Ireland at the time, with 'people agitating around land, around the cause of political nationalism and home rule, those who were working in religious organisations to pursue their particular claims and their particular interests'. He stated, 'Vere Foster stands alone outside of an awful lot of the collective of organised endeavour whether it was political or religious'. Likewise Colgan (2001), noted Foster's political views were neither 'narrowly nationalistic nor narrowly unionist: they were informed by a deep humanitarianism and so were unique in the context of the struggle over Home Rule in late nineteenth century Ireland'.[4]

Foster's letter then weighed in with an indication of his vision for teachers tied to the matter of organising but not limited to strength in numbers, given there was much to be learned across the country through the medium of this journal. It is as if Foster helped forge the common idea that professionalising teaching and building a more collaborative culture in national schools as elsewhere can profoundly shape the ways teachers approach their work:

> *It might surely be expected to find sufficient support among eight thousand national teachers besides thousands of other teachers of all grades; of public and private schools. The task which you have undertaken is a difficult one requiring the exercise of much labor and research, much judgement and discretion.*

This reference to labour, research, judgement and discretion is striking, which augured well for teaching, but in the remainder of the letter, Foster was more concerned about what was then required to secure Irish teachers' status and noted it was one of the special subjects for discussion at the then-recent meeting of the National Association for the Promotion of Social Science[5] in Belfast in 1867, which he attended:

> *The best means for improving the position of teachers, and for securing to the public sufficient guarantees of the efficacy of their teaching.*

Further investigation revealed this was Foster's paraphrase of the title of Professor D'Arcy Thompson's lecture[6] at the meeting in Belfast, which had been posed as a question: What are the best Means for Improving the Status of Teachers, and for securing for the Public sufficient Guarantees for the Efficiency of their Teaching? Foster's views were contained in his response to Thompson,[7] but in Foster's 'letter to the editor' in the *Irish Teacher's Journal*, this one quotation is pregnant with significance for the two of the main education topics at the time – namely, the suitability of the 'national' or the 'denominational' systems of education to the circumstances in Ireland[8] and finding the best means of improving the status of teachers. Significantly, this was one of the main topics at the meeting in Belfast.[9] Thompson (1867) had put it bluntly in his main address:

> *What is the reason, then, that our profession is one so seldom sought out at all; so very seldom sought out with eagerness; so often one into which, as into a pit, poverty or disappointment is pushed by an adverse fortune, or stumbles out of fear and irresolution?*

Finally, Foster's mention of the public guarantees is also highly revealing about the issue of the public interest in the teaching workforce and the debates on accountability, but it can only be he picked up the 'public guarantees' from Thompson's lecture in Belfast.[10] Nonetheless, Foster provided a valuable source of evidence about the terms and conditions of teaching, given what he believed was required to ensure the viability of 'national schools, in which at least three-fourths of the Irish school-going population receive their education'. This is a curious reference to Foster's response to Thompson's lecture in Belfast. There Foster had quoted the school tax system involving 'state tax, the country tax and the town-ship or district tax-all for the purpose of supporting schools, raised according to the means of the people and distributed according to the number of the children in each district, with modifications' as the best way forward for Ireland. As he said then, 'More than three-fourths of children of the labouring classes and the mechanics attend the National Schools in Ireland, and our teachers are miserably paid'.[11] The use of the pronoun 'our' notwithstanding, Foster's concerns with teachers' salaries, to be funded through local voluntary contributions or local taxations for educational purposes, must have been a burden on local communities in post-famine Ireland, although he made note,

> *not a tax on income but only on capital, so as properly to fall most heavily on the rich, and yet only in proportion to their means-not in place of, but in addition to Parliamentary grants.*

This is one of many references to the social class bases of education and national schooling in Ireland, which was a recurring theme, but here it is important to note that Foster declared that Irish national teachers' pay was a third of English national teachers and needed to be brought up the same level in order to retain services or attract others. He stated in Belfast,

> *They only get about one-third of the payment which is given to the schoolmasters in connexion with the State in England, which is about £95 or £96, on an*

> average, per man, while in Ireland only £32 or £33 a year is paid. Then, in England, the teachers get residences, as a general rule, while in Ireland, as a general rule, they do not. Thus the schools in Ireland stand very much in need of improvement, in so far as payment to the teachers is concerned. I believe the reason of the existing state of things to be very largely due to the great multiplicity of schools.[12]

Not surprisingly, Foster worked towards the end of his letter with critical discussion of other perennial issues such as teachers' housing, monthly rather than quarterly pay for teachers, pensions and retirement arrangements and school requisites. In closing, he returned to the journal, regarded as a medium of communication between teachers and managers but also with networks in high schools and in government. His final twin mention of the national school curriculum and the need to multiply the number of Teachers' Association was apparently a concern for teachers' organising in the interests of professional decision making, though typical of the day he urged a focus on the three Rs.

1868 Chamney's inaugural editorial

The *Irish Teachers' Journal* was evidently well received by the teaching profession,[13] given its circulation. At first, each issue of approximately 16 pages was issued weekly at 2d (pennies) per copy. It was published from 1 January 1868, until it was taken over by the *Irish School Weekly* in 1904, which consisted of 32 pages and cost one penny, so double the size and half the cost! In the first edition of the *Irish Teachers' Journal*, a table of contents came first, 'Education versus Crime and Ignorance' and 'Status of the Teacher', which happened to be the titles of Chamney's lengthy long-winded essays that provided a rationale for the journal as a venture and to introduce it as a mouthpiece for those with an interest in education. The table of contents continued: 'Correspondence' (the letter from Vere Foster), then 'Opinions of the Press',[14] another essay titled 'Education Abroad and at Home', which again points to a knowledge of the world at the time, and then 'Review, Notices, etc.' and replies to correspondents.

A few of Chamney's major points require focussed study,[15] especially as he opened his inaugural editorial with a deferential statement on ideas about education attributed to Lord Russell,[16] who had held the office of Britain's Prime Minister during the time of the Great Famine in Ireland and was a contentious figure at the time. Chamney's reference to the aristocracy should come as no surprise, given the Anglo-Irish establishment in the British-centric politics at the time, but this inaugural editorial is deftly political in character (check McCulloch b/116). Chamney cleverly used his reverent tone, perhaps to flatter and persuade, but also to enhance the prospects of education in Ireland:

> Other European nations are passing us in the educational race and the conviction increases and deepens that the status of education throughout the United Kingdom is unworthy of our wealth, industry and political power.

This reference to 'the educational race' just goes to show the long-standing concern with international competition while Chamney's very mention of Ireland, albeit as part of the United Kingdom in relation to other European nations, locates it in a broad geo-political context, paramount for those seeking national independence.[17] He then pointedly linked education, poverty, crime and ignorance in Ireland, and embarked on a discussion of the interconnections, which are no doubt open to debate given the predominantly individualist orientation but not wholly at the expense of social analyses in his argument:

> *Ignorance, power and crime are frequently if not necessarily connected. They constitute a circle of evils; they are alike cause and effect; they act and react upon each other; they produce and reproduce each other in a fatal combination of evils.*

This mention of evils is prescient of Britain's Prime Minister William Beveridge's (1942) World War II report *Social Insurance and Allied Services*, a seminal document on the establishment of the welfare state in Britain which he hoped would tackle the five 'Giant Evils' in society – namely, squalor, ignorance, want, idleness and disease.[18] Interestingly, Vere Foster had used the word evil when criticising the commissioners for establishing a multiplicity of schools in particular areas which he deemed were unnecessary and 'productive of evil rather than good' in his contribution to the National Association for the Promotion of Social Science's conference in Belfast, 1867.

Similarly, Chamney's mention of production and reproduction is suggestive of Marx and Engels' revolutionary ideologies and social theories to do with class conflict (see Berberoglu, 2005). Following a discussion of institutions designed to accommodate the poor, such as jails and reformatories, that were said to be doing good work, Chamney turned his attention to national schools and stated his political and social views, perhaps expecting to influence Ireland's education policymakers, who in turn might act back to shape the direction of the budding system:

> *We want some large national machinery for educating the poor beyond our present appliances, and we fear that to a greater or lesser extent the element of compulsion must enter our system of national education to make it what our low educational status demands . . . . For ourselves we heartily agree with the position that every child has a right to the blessings of education, and that it is the duty of the state to guard and maintain that right.*

The pronoun 'we' presumably referred to the community of teachers reading the journal, but more significantly, the idea 'for ourselves' was prescient of political slogans[19] and likely tapped a public concern in Ireland about the relationship between poverty and education. Chamney's objective was evidently mainstream change in regard to school improvement, compulsory support and the duties of the propertied classes towards the poor. While this highlighted the social order if not opposition to class privilege and prejudice, it pointed towards universal education urging equal opportunities for all children (see Simon, 1974). His concern for 'the proper management of endowed, chartered, and incorporated schools' was no doubt a bane for teachers and reflected in the following question:

> *And why should we not have a Minister for Education? Surely education demands large and liberal oversight and that official power and authority which is best represented by a department of the public service with a responsible Minister at its head.*

This provocative question provided a further source of evidence about Westminster's influence on the thinking that imbued edu-politics in Ireland at the time. Chamney's twin theme of ministerial control and 'large and liberal oversight' is an indication of both English and Irish attitudes to national schools and education for the working classes he so named. Simultaneously, Chamney's concern with 'official power and authority' portends a useful image of the teacher in the second of his lengthy long-winded essays under the 'Status of the Teacher'. Although his discussion rambles about teachers in Ireland compared with teachers who of necessity had emigrated, he made the following point:

> *The Irish schoolmaster is abroad – in Canada and the United States, teaching, trading, lumbering, [cattle] driving, or cultivating – in Australia and New Zealand gold-digging, sheep-tending, farming or trading – abroad as a sailor – abroad anywhere, doing anything that will give him the living and the hope denied at home.*

This publicity makes it easy to see dedication to Ireland, evoked in Chamney's claim, 'The progress of a nation is national education', which clearly aligns with Foster's strapline on his copybooks. But Chamney went further: 'The progress of society is the education of the world', which is here best confined not to his [now discredited] ideas about civilisation of savages but to his secular and liberal leanings to do with enlightenment, equality and the 'the wild cry of earnestness in France' named as "Liberty, Equality, Fraternity". Interestingly, this all lines up with what historian Dr Niamh Puirséil (2017) wrote about Chamney in her sesquicentenary anniversary history book of the INTO, *Kindling the Flame 150 Years of the INTO*. While he was ostensibly the editor of the *Irish Teachers' Journal*, teachers were prohibited from commenting on educational matters at the time. Yet the role of editor was fulfilled by a number of teachers with Dublin Central Teachers' Association member Jerimiah Henly, the chief leader writer, who drew attention to their plight:

> *If education is so valuable, ought not the educator to be valued? If knowledge is power, ought not the knowledge-giver to be esteemed and well treated . . . . . . for while we believe the ordinary educator is nowhere properly valued or fairly treated, we believe, at the same time that he is nowhere so badly treated as in Ireland (p. 2).*

> But the ordinary teachers – those who lay the foundation of education and erect a good deal of the building – are treated in this country in a fashion that is disgraceful to any community pretending to even 'civilization', not to speak of enlightenment.

1869 teachers' evidence to 'primary education commission' (Ireland)

Foster continued to work with teachers, enacting his vision of how an association of teachers can effect policy advocacy, and on this occasion the original primary documentary record is to be found online.[20] It is crucial to accurately capture the full title of this documentary record so as not to confuse it with the infamous 1869 Powis Report.[21]

> *Evidence of the Irish National Teachers' Association in reply to queries addressed by the commissioners to Vere Foster, Esq., and submitted by him for their consideration.*

This evidence was presented to the Powis Committee, better known as the Royal Commissioners of Primary Education in Ireland, consisting of seven Roman Catholics and seven from Protestant faiths under the chair of Lord Powis. It was established in January 1868 to 'enquire into the practical working of the system of National Education in Ireland'. The title makes it clear that Foster was transmitting the views of teachers, not his own, though Assistant Commissioner Richmond made a request of Foster to furnish information about teachers in their local communities. This could be seen as a bureaucratic effort at consultation insofar as they wanted to use Foster, probably because he held social capital and enjoyed an eminent position among Irish national teachers, as a conduit. It is interesting that Foster did not conceive of himself to be a competent direct witness, but readily acknowledged he could be a medium for obtaining much useful information for the commissioners and for Parliament in Westminster.[22] Nevertheless, this was an opportunity for teachers to operate strategically and politically during the first year of the organisation's operation, and there is a telling statement to this effect on the second page of the document:[23]

> *Eleventh Resolution of the Second Congress of Irish National Teachers, held in Dublin, on 29th December, 1868.*
> 'That Mr. Vere Foster has our sanction to publish the several replies he received from the several Associations to his circular of queries, in connexion with the Royal Commission on Primary Education in Ireland.'

This shows Foster clearly enjoyed teachers' support, but equally significantly, Foster's circular of queries suggests he gave practical expression to his views of the value of the teachers' voice underpinned by research, judgement and discretion. It is likely he used an early form of survey research to collect information

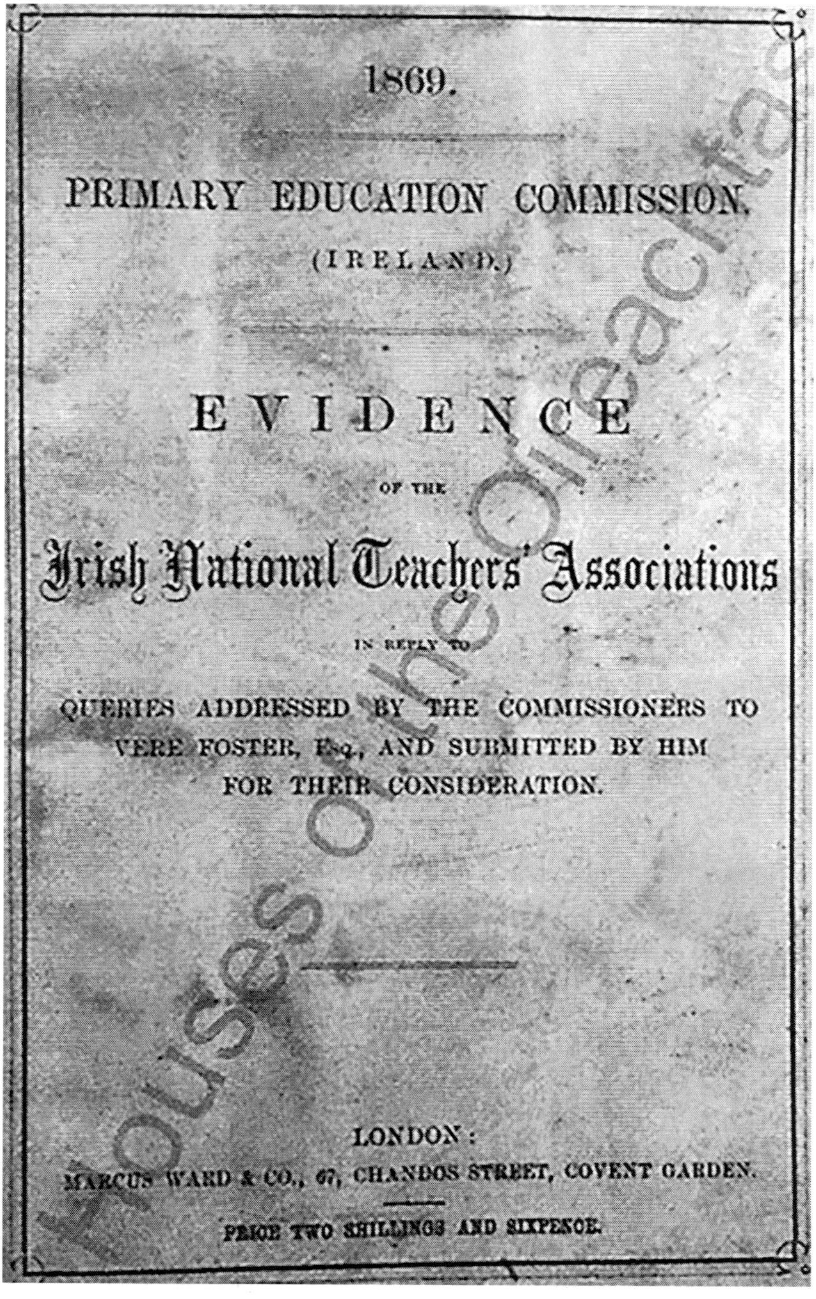

Figure 2.1 1968 Teachers' Evidence to Primary Education Commission

Source: Primary Education Commission (Ireland.) Evidence to Irish national Teachers' Associations reproduced by permission of the Oireachtas Library & Research Service.

from a large number of teachers in local communities by means of questionnaires, no doubt delivered by penny post and collected in the same way.

As noted in the document in the collation of the evidence, Foster circulated the eight queries he received from Richmond to the secretaries of the Associations of the recently formed teachers' organisation 'addressing copies of the queries also to all Teachers of rural schools containing a largely mixed attendance of Roman Catholic and Protestant pupils':

1. Are the means for the education of the poorer classes sufficient?
2. Do the poorer classes avail themselves as much as they might of the existing means of education? If not, is their neglect to do so because of

    (a) distance from the school building;
    (b) amount of school fees;
    (c) want of confidence in the teacher;
    (d) religious and conscientious scruples;
    (e) inability to forego children's wages;
    (f) or any other cause that you can assign?

3. Can you suggest any plan for inducing a better and more regular attendance by the children at the schools?
4. Is the system of educating children of different denominations together beneficial or not? And what is the popular feeling on the subject?
5. What is the general effect of the several industrial occupations on school attendance, and the period of school life? Have you any views to express concerning the operation of the factory regulations, as touching the employment of young children, whether boys or girls?
6. Is the instruction given at the schools usually gratuitous, or not? To what extent do you conceive that school fees can be advantageously imposed?
7. Have you any information or views to offer on the subject of night schools?
8. Do you consider the system of Inspection as carried out by the National Board sufficient for its purpose?

That these questions were asked in the present! Significantly, Foster added four more questions to the list:

9. What would be the best and most practicable means of improving the position of the Teachers, and at the same time increasing the efficiency of their schools?
10. Should salaries be based on the classification of the teachers only, on the proficiency of the scholars only, on numbers in attendance only or on a mixture of two or all three of these elements? If it be thought desirable to base salaries on results only – that is, on the proficiency of the scholars, should the payments be calculated separately for each scholar, and for each subject, or should they be based on the aggregate proficiency of the whole school.

11. Is the payment of school fees and other local contributions on the increase, or otherwise?
12. Are schools, not national, on the increase, or otherwise?

It is as if Foster had a commitment to practitioner inquiry, more or less confirmed in his 'Introductory Remarks' where he indicated he had adopted the following course:

> As I had been in correspondence for many years with the Teachers of nearly every National School in Ireland on the subject of School improvements, especially with reference to buildings and apparatus, and as my publications have been for some years in use in almost every such School, I thought it likely that, through the kind cooperation of the Teachers, I, therefore, reprinted the queries of the Royal Commission, with additions of my own, and addressed them to the Secretaries of the numerous Teachers' Associations which have been recently organized in nearly every county.

This respectful request for teachers' perspectives could also be read as 'history from below' as the survey was intended to ascertain, in Foster's words, 'the popular feeling in favour, or otherwise, of the present system of combined secular and separate religious instruction, and to obtain suggestions as to the best means of inducing a better and more regular attendance of scholars'. As it happened, Foster particularly targeted teachers in mixed schools in rural areas where there were largely mixed attendance of Roman Catholic and Protestant pupils. In fact, he sent the queries to the secretaries of the Associations and to teachers of mixed schools in rural areas only. In response to Foster's intended publication of the results of the survey, the Associations were initially apprehensive of the inclusion of the replies from the teachers fearing that 'a professional view of a subject is not generally a comprehensive one; and as the queries related to matters deeply effecting the teachers both in a pecuniary sense and otherwise, we thought it not unlikely that the replies would betray a narrow mindedness and show such symptoms as partisanship as to be in great measure unreliable and therefore not entitled to much consideration at the hands of the Commissioners'; however their apprehensions were 'set at rest' upon 'a perusal of the pamphlet lately issued by Mr. Foster'.[24] He reported responses from 69 Teachers' Associations and from 37 individual teachers, who were then anonymised 'for obvious reasons'. While it is striking that there was consideration of an ethics of research in mid-late nineteenth century Ireland, there was evidently concern about the contextual locations of teachers in the local parish with its church-going local communities and how these governed local ways of life.[25]

1878 newspaper report of teachers' protests on performance-related pay

Foster's letter to the editor of the newspaper *The Northern Whig* dated 18 June 1878, found in the PRONI archives,[26] is also significant given it expressed for the public record his private concerns about majority opposition to his stand on teachers' performance-related pay.[27] It was written ten years after the launch of *The Irish Teachers Journal* and the foundation of the INTA, obviously connected to his long-standing concerns that teachers' salaries be funded through local voluntary contributions or local taxations for educational purposes. This aired an edu-political issue in the popular press, said to be a reprint perhaps for distribution at teacher meetings given a major heading and subheading:

> The Irish National Teachers' Association and Payment by Results Protests of the first and second Presidents of the Organisation (Mr. Vere Foster and Mr. John Boal) against the present action of the majority

The mention of protests tells a larger story about early teacher union edu-politics in Ireland, which requires interrogation as the two INTA presidents, presumably influential at the time, responded to a backlash. This suggests widespread teacher dissent while Foster and Boal[28] were working against the odds:

> *Sir, As almost every day for the last few weeks there have been published in the Northern Whig resolutions of teachers' associations severely criticising and condemning my published opinion on the subject of payment by results . . . I request your permission to make some observations on the subject in self-defence.*

This first-hand airing of grievances suggests a proliferation of teachers' debates about their working lives, not least 'the amount and method of payment of their professional incomes' as Foster put it. While at pains to de-personalise a public issue, rising above accusations of 'meddling, unauthorised busybody', this shows he lost ground as a spokesperson for teachers even in a peripheral way. This did not dissuade him from stating his case:

> *Inasmuch as these [National] teachers are the servants of the public, and derive as a rule upward of three-fourths of their income from public taxation, to which I and the rest of the public contribute, I have felt perfectly justified in discussing a question which is not of consequence to the teachers only, but is a subject of lively interest and of the greatest importance to the public as well.*

Like Chamney, Foster is apparently highly partisan in favour of Irish teachers in a public system but he qualified it here in a statement of intent to promote in the greatest possible degree the interests of popular education. This was in reference to movements for popular education influenced by Locke and Rousseau sweeping the UK and Europe at the time, which coincided with the onset of the Industrial Revolution and continued during the Enlightenment and throughout the period of the French Revolution. Foster's view was that 'in doing so [it would act] to encourage *good* teachers'. The emphasis was in the original, and he tied it to government grants and results fees where local committees 'would make their own terms with their teachers', which gives us more insight into what was involved in structuring the teaching profession in Ireland.

Interestingly, Boal's letter is twinned with Foster's letter on the same documentary record, but three things. Towards the end of his 'letter to the editor' dated 17 June 1878, Foster introduces Boal, who succeeded Foster as INTA president along with his letter, which was said to have appeared in the previous Saturday's *Belfast Education Journal*. Reproduced in *The Northern Whig* and dated 10 June 1878, it is said to be an extract from a letter to the editor of the *Irish Educational Journal*, but the name interchanges between Belfast and Irish, suggests the journal had [then] national circulation and perhaps Foster picked up a Belfast edition. In any event, they shed light on growing organisational arrangements including meritocracy,[29] budding sets of criteria for judging teachers and up-and-coming, manager-teacher relationships. Foster argued this was universal practice in all elementary schools in England, Scotland and Wales. This not only showed where Ireland stood in relation to the United Kingdom of Great Britain, it provided important clues as to the conflictual nature of the teachers' debates, and it is worth noting that the opposition of teachers in Ireland to the payment by results system was based on professional concerns.

The INTA ran a competition in 1869 inviting teachers to air their grievances and to submit solutions. It was judged by Vere Foster. Mr P Kerlin, a teacher from Clare, won the competition with a pamphlet which became known as the 'Prize Pamphlet on the Teachers' Grievances and Remedies for their Removal'. This pamphlet cannot be located at the time of writing. However, a pamphlet by Patrick Glynn, a teacher came second and awarded a prize of £5, and his pamphlet titled 'The Irish National Teachers' Case Stated' was printed and published by Robert Chamney. In it, Glynn outlines the reasons for the teacher opposing the results system:

> *We see the impossibility of fulfilling the conditions proposed by the "Result System," without resorting to a process of mechanical drudgery quite incompatible with the true spirit and aim of education. For we are convinced that cramming, rather than mental Culture, is sure to be adopted, and the Teacher will be induced to concentrate all his energies on the instruction of those pupils who will return him "results" to perhaps the entire neglect of those who, from their irregularity of attendance, can show none. Here, then, are two evils likely to ensue from the adoption of such a system, viz. – three-fourths of the schools in rural districts will probably be closed for want of the required attendance, and an absurd system of dry mechanical instruction will be substituted for that true cultivation of the mind and moral training which it is the province of genuine education to impart.*
>
> (*The Irish National Teachers' Case Stated*, p. 10)

Foster's admitted his change of mind 'on the subject of payment by results versus fixed salaries', and acknowledged he may have been 'almost alone in advocating increase to teachers' income' in this way. In the end, Foster was exceedingly gracious, showing much wisdom in regard teachers' need to be savvy about edu-politics and structures of power in Ireland in the Victorian era:

> *If my judgement is erroneous, surely the united representations of ten thousand teachers, logically and temperately expressed without the use of personalities, will have more weight with her Majesty's Government than my single advocacy of views opposed to theirs. Magna est veritas, et praevalebit.*[30]

According to Moroney (2007), the Payment by Results System recommended in the Royal Commission of Inquiry into Primary Education (1868–1870) was implemented in Ireland in 1 September 1872. The Payment by Results system was abandoned in England and Scotland in 1895, which prompted the INTO to exert pressure on the Westminster Parliament to establish a Vice-Regal Commission to report on the education system in Ireland. The commission under Lord Belmore published its report in 1898 and recommended the introduction of a new method of computing teachers' remuneration effectively ending the Payment by Results system in Ireland.

Conclusion

There is much evidence about the histories of teachers' organising to be gleaned from these select documentary research samples that highlight the early inexpert efforts of the INTO in the years before it assumed the mantle of a registered teachers' trade union.[31] This includes signals on the Anglo-Irish establishment; the social class bases of schooling and education in Ireland; the longevity of liberal values and laissez-faire; British government structures, the Catholic Church and 'how power works' in secular and sectarian Ireland; nascent [practitioner] research efforts and teachers' democratic representation of their professional concerns about their working lives; not to forget teachers' grievances and dissent and Foster's demise!

In the end, Vere Foster resigned from working with the INTA, which became the INTO. In November 1873, in a letter to the *Irish Teachers' Journal*, he stated, 'That his resignation was necessary as his advocacy of local taxation and the necessary concomitant-schools boards might prove an embarrassment to the teachers' organisations' (McNeill, 1971 p176). Interestingly, his [policy] advocacy was at issue, not surprising given his status as Anglo-Irish in an era of burgeoning nationalism/Irish independence. Lee (2008) contrasted Anglicisation with modernisation in the years 1892–1918 in one of his chapters, which had the subtitle 'The Necessity for De-Anglicising Ireland'. This was reference to Douglas Hyde, who had delivered a lecture with the same title to the National Literary Society in November 1892. It was said to shift the focus of national discussion from politics to 'identity', similarly not surprising, as this was the Dubhghlas de hÍde who had founded the Gaelic League and went on to become the first president of Ireland from June 1938 to June 1945. Fennell (1993) suggested,

> *In Ireland in the second half of the nineteenth century, revolutionary fervour among the poorer classes took the forms of republican nationalism (mainly*

> *Fenianism), or the struggle for the land, or a combination of both. This led to arguments for land nationalisation, cooperative production, state regulation and organisation of labour and a labour party in the House of Commons.*

Ferriter (2015) called into question the effect of the Irish revolution on the transformation of Anglo-Irish relations, indicating that the impact was more nationalist and political not so much social and economic. He then maintained that even a primarily political revolution was problematic given sources on the 'history from below' suggested social and economic forces did have an impact. Further, while radical impulses may have been resisted, they had an ongoing presence while the fear of the 'rabble' and its potential to destabilise the 'political' revolution was always apparent. These contextual complexities do not diminish Vere Foster's legacy and what he did to cement the foundations of the INTO, no doubt part of the social and political reforms as a forerunner of state power structures in the present. As INTO Vice President Michael Doyle[32] (1914), who had been INTO general secretary (1910–1913), acknowledged,

> *In the early years of the National Teachers' agitation Mr. Vere Foster was the guiding spirit at the helm; and by his great exertions and sacrifices in promoting penmanship and the various branches of drawing in the schools, and his magnificent grants for their structured improvement, there is no doubt but he was eminently conducive to the progress then made. He was a powerful and consistent advocate with the Commissioners and the Government, and when he retired in 1872 from the Presidency, the Irish Teachers lost a true and zealous friend and counsellor.*

Notes

1 See the Department of Education and Skills online link for the text of Stanley's 1831 letter: http://education.ie/en/Schools-Colleges/Information/Boards-of-Management/Stanley-letter-1831-Boards-Of-Management.pdf.
2 This was reproduced in a frontispiece to O'Connell (1968), who noted the objects of the INTO were adopted in December 1868.
3 See the RTÉ feature 'Who Was Vere Foster', a radio documentary: www.rte.ie/lyricfm/the-lyric-feature/programmes/2014/0502/614976-the-lyric-feature-friday-2-may-2014/. Last accessed April 2017.
   NB. Among the contributors were Lori Beckett, John Carr, Tadhg Mac Pháidin, Diarmaid Ferriter, John Coolahan, Aggie and Sean Halpenny, Richard Barry, and Barney McGill.
4 Vere Foster had a keen interest in the main political issues of the day. For example, in 1886, concerned about the militancy within Irish Land League, he wrote to British Liberal Prime Minister William Ewart Gladstone warning him of the Ulster Protestant opposition to Home Rule expressing his fear 'that the scheme might result in a bloody Civil War between different portions of the people and between Great Britain and Ireland' (Colgan 2001 p112). McNeill (1971) reported that Foster, having long denounced British misrule in Ireland, 'felt that Ireland's best hope lay not in separation, but in a 'more perfect union' between the two countries'. Colgan (2001) added the Foster opposed Gladstone's 'Irish Land Act of 1881 and the Home Rule Bill of 1886' and that 'Vere was firmly opposed to state purchase

Introducing Vere Foster 67

of landed estates as 'the public robbery of one class . . . for the benefit of another'. Instead, he favoured the break-up of estates through the modification of the law of inheritance to divide property of deceased persons equally among the next of kin'.

5 The aims of the National Association for the Promotion of Social Science are interesting. Founded in Birmingham in 1857 by Lord Brougham, it was a social reformist group distinctly committed to 'elicit truth not to propound dogmas'. The members were devoted to social improvement and social advancement, 'without reference to class or opinion' and dedicated to 'mutual exchange of opinion, experience and information'. Their aim was 'to collect facts, to diffuse knowledge and to stimulate enquiry' by eliciting 'papers expressing and embodying experience of individuals'. The Association initially divided into five departments – namely, law amendment, education, prevention and repression of crime, health and social economy (capital, labour and production). See G. W. Hastings inaugural address Transactions of the National Association for the promotion of Social Science, 1857, p. xxvii: https://play.google.com/books/reader?id=Yj1cAAAAcAAJ&printsec=frontcover&output=reader&hl=en&pg=GBS.PA1. NB. The Association met twice in Ireland: Dublin in 1861 and Belfast in 1867. It disbanded in 1886.
6 Thompson was professor of Greek at Queens College Galway, now called National University of Ireland (Galway).
7 See the Proceedings of the Education Department of National Association for the Promotion of Social Science, Belfast Meeting 1867, on the section dealing with the Irish Education Question. https://play.google.com/books/reader?id=Yj1cAAAAcAAJ&printsec=frontcover&output=reader&hl=en&pg=GBS.PA21.
8 The issue of Denominational Education was also previously discussed at the National Association for the Promotion of Social Science's 1861 Congress which was held in Dublin, reflecting the Church-State battle for the control of education during the period in question: see the papers tabled in 1861, Education Section, which included the Education Position of the Established Church, the Present Position of Roman Catholics in relation to the State in Ireland, and on the Disadvantages of Denominational Education as applied in Ireland. https://babel.hathitrust.org/cgi/pt?id=ucl.b3008858;view=1up;seq=5.
9 Again, see the digitised version of the 1867 Proceedings of the Education Department of National Association for the Promotion of Social Science meeting held in Belfast. See: https://play.google.com/books/reader?id=Yj1cAAAAcAAJ&printsec=frontcover&output=reader&hl=en&pg=GBS.PA1.
10 Thompson linked the increased public confidence in the working of the schools with enhanced estimates in the value of the teacher and advocated that public confidence could to be achieved through external inspection procedures which included unannounced visits and annual reports. For an account of the logic of inspections, see the digitised version of the Proceedings of the Education Department of National Association for the Promotion of Social Science, Belfast Meeting 1867, notably on the section dealing with the Irish Education Question and Thompson's lecture 'What Are the Best Means for Improving the Status of Teachers, and for Securing for the Public Sufficient Guarantees for the Efficiency of Their Teaching'. See https://play.google.com/books/reader?id=Yj1cAAAAcAAJ&printsec=frontcover&output=reader&hl=en&pg=GBS.PA50.
11 ibid.,
12 See p. 148 in the digitised version of the Proceedings of the Education Department of National Association for the Promotion of Social Science, Belfast Meeting 1867, on the section dealing with the Irish Education Question. See: https://play.google.com/books/reader?id=Yj1cAAAAcAAJ&printsec=frontcover&output=reader&hl=en&pg=GBS.PA148.

13 McCune Reid (1956) speculated, 'From the first issue of the magazine it was apparent that the policy was informed by someone who had intimate knowledge of Education in Ireland, and who had a clearly defined and well thought conception of the steps that would have to be taken to redress the grievances of teachers. That this was Vere Foster there can be no doubt, though never is he openly acknowledged'.

14 The following are the sources of the extracts that appear in the first issue of the *Irish Teachers' Journal*, January 1868: *Mr. Gladstone on Education*, extract from speech, referring to National Education delivered by Mr. Gladstone at Oldham 18 December 1867; *Primary Classical Education*, extract from address by Robert Lowe, Viscount 1811–1892, Royal College of Physicians Edinburgh, to the Philosophical Institution of Edinburgh, Friday November 1867; *Compulsory Education*, Papers for the Schoolmaster December 1867; *Difficulties in the Way of compulsory Education* in Museum for December 1867; *National Education*, Illustrated London News; *Education and its influences*, Illustrated Times, 20 October 1867 and *Education at Home and Abroad Switzerland-Canton of Neufchatel* in the Museum December 1867.

15 Chamney included a critical piece 'Mr Lowe's Address' in the first issue of the *Irish Teachers' Journal* in January 1868, based on a talk entitled 'Primary and Classical Education' that Lowe gave before the Philosophical Institute in Edinburgh in November 1867. According to Sylvester (1974), Lowe was vice-president of the Committee of the Council on Education in Lord Palmerston Ministry (Palmerston was a friend of the Foster family). He held utilitarian views on education and favoured the teaching of the physical sciences as opposed to classical studies, and he promoted an examination of the three Rs as the test for the granting of public monies and insisted on payment by results. In his critical piece, Chamney developed a critical attack on Lowe's view of education: 'Mr. Lowe errs, it seems to us, in his conception of what education ought to be, and the means to be employed in producing it. He takes a low, mechanical, selfish view of what education should be. It is a thing to him not of infinite value, and fraught with immeasurable issues, but a thing very nearly confined to pounds, shillings, and pence and quite easily measured by the Revised Code. This is a radical mistake'.

16 The English historian and civil servant Spencer Walpole (1839–1907) authored the book, *The Life of John Russell*, published in 1891, which contains a chapter on Russell and education in Ireland. Russell increased Government spending on education in the 1847 Act. He published pamphlets on Ireland the third of which appeared in the form of a letter to Christopher Fortescue, his Chief Secretary in Ireland. In it, he dealt with Gladstone's Irish Church Act (which he supported if not designed) and vigorously supported the reform of the Irish Land Laws, which gave tenants security against eviction and redress in respect of land improvement. Vere Foster was a strong advocate of both issues.

17 The overthrow and collapse of autocratic political regimes across Europe, most notably the aftermath of the French Revolution, prompted a growth in nationalism ideals in Ireland. Following the collapse of Young Irelander's insurrection in 1848, some members fled to Paris, while others absconded to America and Australia, where they continued organising the overthrow British rule in Ireland resulting in a failed uprising in 1867; see https://en.wikipedia.org/wiki/History_of_Ireland_(1801–1923).

18 Professor Stephen J Ball's (2013c) paper to mark the 70th anniversary of the Beveridge Report, *Education, Justice and Democracy: The struggle over ignorance and opportunity*, considered the progress made in combating the evil of ignorance since Report *Social Insurance and Allied Services*, was published in 1942. Ball contended that 'the relationships between opportunity, achievement and social class have remained stubbornly entrenched and have been reproduced by policy.

Inequalities of class and race remain stark and indeed have been increasing since 2008[1'] (p. 4). Ball describes the prevailing system of schooling as a 'broad and fundamental failure to achieve the modest aspirations of Beveridge', a system he identifies as 'riven with divisions, inequalities, alienation, failure, despondency and bias – six evils.

19 It is interesting to search for the translations: Sinn Féin ('ourselves' or 'we ourselves') and Sinn Féin Amháin ('ourselves alone') are Irish-language phrases used as a political slogan by Irish nationalists in the late nineteenth and early twentieth century. Please see www.google.co.uk/search?q=sinn+fein+meaning&oq=sinn+fein&aqs=chrome.2.69i57j0l5.9815j0j8&sourceid=chrome&ie=UTF-8 (last accessed 28 April 2017).

20 Please see the link to Vere Foster's primary education commission evidence: opac.oireachtas.ie/Data/Library3/Library3/DCT109002.pdf.

21 This refers to the Report of the Royal Commission of Inquiry into Primary Education, better known as the Powis Report, also found online: www.dippam.ac.uk/eppi/documents/15444

22 McNeill (1971) noted Foster was initially requested by Redmond to present oral evidence before the Royal Commission but declined and instead requested that a list of 'special points on which information is desired' be forwarded to him for consideration. He indicated to the commissioners that he did not consider himself 'competent to be a *direct* witness', but preferred instead to be 'a medium of inquiry'. Despite the commissioner reiterating that it was Vere's views they were requesting, he was furnished with a list of queries which he supplemented with questions of his own and circulated them to the secretaries of the various Associations.

23 It must be noted this was published in London by Beatrix Potter's publisher: Marcus Ward & Co., 67 Chakdos Street, Covent Garden. Price Two Shillings and Sixpence.

24 Despite the fact that payments by results were strongly denounced by the teachers and that Foster gave his opinion 'strongly in favour of the mixed system' (p. 134), the Association declared its support for his document: 'On the whole the National teachers of Ireland should not be ashamed of the quota they have furnished to aid the Royal Commissioners in accomplishing their responsible task'; see *Irish Teachers' Journal*, p. 135.

25 See Garvin (2004) on moral and social conservatism: the general takeover of a large chunk of Irish civic life by the Catholic Church from 1850 accentuated the authoritarianism and intellectual conformism of the general culture; then p. 39 on British concerns focussed far more on Irish political restiveness than on the economic viability of a small, if fractious, province of the imperial kingdom.

26 *The Northern Whig*, founded by John Arnott, was first published in Belfast as a twice weekly newspaper in 1832. By 1858, it had become a daily newspaper with a liberal unionist leaning.

27 For further information, see Dolton, McIntosh and Chevalier (2003) *Teacher Pay & Performance*, published by the UCL Institute of Education in The Bedford Way series. ISBN 0854736700; also Dolton: http://siteresources.worldbank.org/INTINDIA/4371432 1194542398355/21543222/RecruitingHighQualityTeachers.pdf.

28 Similarly, Boal's letter, like Foster's letter, requires close study – a task beyond the scope of this anniversary book.

29 An interesting exploration of the social origins of meritocracy as a philosophical idea that took hold in Britain, which is significant for the work of this anniversary book scaffolding teachers' 'case for the defence'; see Nicholas (1999) http://eprints.lse.ac.uk/22385/1/wp53.pdf.

30 An online search for a translation yielded 'truth is great and will prevail': see www.google.co.uk/#q=magna+est+veritas+et+praevalebit (accessed 27 April 2017).
31 See the documentary case story on Catherine Mahon in Chapter 3, particularly note Mahon's influence on INTO General Secretary T. J. O'Connell (1916–1949) and the INTO decision/s that led to affiliation with the ITUC in 1918 in order to obtain legal status and protection provided by Trade Union Law.
32 See Doyle's treatise 'A Glance at the Past' in the Central Educational Annual published by the Dublin Central Teachers' Association, 1914.

Part 2

Theories of teachers organising: the options in edu-politics

Section essay: theories of teachers organising: the options in edu-politics

This section highlights the theories of teachers organising, which continues to speak to union-active teachers bound up with INTO struggles for teachers' status and deliberations on professional standing. It too is intended to scaffold towards teachers' 'case for the defence' in response to aspects of Bruton's *Action Plan for Education*. This theorising is crucial to teachers organising, especially since the INTO is not only confronted by teachers' disquiet over Bruton's *Action Plan for Education* but also by teachers' alienation from the Teaching Council, its own representative body, grappling with the imposition of centrally determined, top-down policies.

Sachs (2003a, 2003b) proved helpful given her concerns about a call to action for the teaching profession, which included her hesitation on the words activism and activist because of their chequered history and images of chaotic demonstrations and rabble-rousing. She made the point that in using the phrase teacher activism it was not naïve claiming of the field of dissent but rather a new and strategic energy. As she put it, 'an activist teaching profession is an educated and politically astute one'. This needed to be developed and realised, she argued, in systematic and collective ways, but this was best done to achieve socially responsible goals. She made it clear it should be about stakeholders working together to make public and to celebrate the achievements of teachers. This required 'strategies to inform those in positions of power and influence of the necessity of a strong teaching profession'. It was geared to the sort of profession that can educate our children to be socially active and responsible citizens, with an aim to frame the future agendas of schooling and education. Sachs concluded her book, *The Activist Teaching Profession*, with a plea to harness the various intellectual, social and political resources available to achieve it.

The INTO actually relies on activist teachers to engage in teacher union activities, which are best underpinned by practitioner research activities including critical policy analyses as these relate to classroom practices. As the documentary evidence shows, in the early instances of teachers organising, it was historically significant that teachers operated politically and strategically as the INTO continued to build towards becoming a state power centre in Ireland. A task in the present is for academic partners to support and mentor research-active teachers building historically informed research intelligence about struggles for teachers' status allied to their professional standing over time and then plugging into the INTO.

As the previous two chapters tried to show, teachers' work is configured by policy, which must be contextualised. Looking back into history and the Victorian era of post-famine Ireland, the dominant political ideologies were challenged by Irish insurrections but for the remainder of that century the British military forces and indeed the British civil service won out. In the present, Ireland's determination of national schooling is circumscribed by the neoliberal policies of the OECD Education Directorate, the McKinsey and Company reports (Mourshed, Chikioke, and Barber, 2010), the World Trade Organisation and the EU. These 'top-down' accounts are all a far cry from teachers' voice and student voice about national schooling, in effect 'history from below'. This synchronises with Seddon et al.'s (2007) view that this kind of critical policy scholarship can benefit education and educators because it provides a more systematic framework for analysing partnerships and their effects. They added that it also provides a basis for identifying the kinds of political interventions that make sense in today's educational landscape.

The next two chapters traverse the early to mid-twentieth century to again provide samples of documentary research on some watershed moments and to sketch some 'history from below'. This is about activist teachers' contributions to Ireland's development and modernisation albeit as it developed in different guises eventually under the auspices of revolutionary government. These samples align with Ferriter's (2016) INTO keynote on the occasion of the centenary commemorations of the 1916 Easter Uprising; they include teachers' support for nationalist causes, women's suffrage issues and what might be called Ireland's first national curriculum. These are followed by studies of teachers' struggles in regard to who might determine national schooling given a self-governing Ireland, apropos the Gaelic cultural revival and promotion of the Irish language and later still by studies of the first teachers' strike and the INTO's plan for education, not to forget the women fighting their battles to be a part of it all and the reflections on the progress made.

Chapter 3 looks back to Pádraig Pearse as principal of St Enda's school and signatory of the 1916 Irish Proclamation of Independence, Catherine Mahon as the INTO's first woman president (1912–1914), Máire Ní Chinnéide as chairman (sic) of the National Programme (curriculum) committee and the INTO Inquiry into the Irish language question. These campaigns were all led by activist teachers in regard to reform in national schools from the time of the 1916 Easter Uprising through to the era of the Provisional Government and beyond to World War II, although Ireland remained neutral. These teachers were certainly alert to the cultural, political and economic spheres of Irish society as it developed its young democracy.

Chapter 4 examines the 1946 teachers' strike, the 1947 INTO Plan for Education, the 1957 INTO presidential address by Margaret Skinnider and T. J. O'Connell's (1968) INTO centenary history book *100 Years of Progress* inspired by an early pamphlet on the INTO's *80 years of Progress*. These sample documents all help focus attention on the idea of progress as it relates to the idea of Irish nationalism not to forget women's role in forging Irish society. This is not to discount discussion of British-inspired values of conservatism and liberalism, and none of this was without deliberation, discussion, debate and dispute but feminist documentary research helps tease out the complexities.

In the course of engaging these teachers' struggles, theorising teacher activism is necessary to interrogate the conflicts and protests that were writ large. This is a crucial consideration as the task is to continue to link the past and present, especially when it comes to Ireland's democracy. Again, it is worthwhile to consider Held's (2006) point that 'while many states today maybe democratic, the history of their political institutions reveals the fragility and vulnerability of democratic arrangements'. This certainly found expression in Ireland in the early part of the twentieth century, in the aftermath of the defeat of the third Home Rule Bill, the Easter Uprising, the Treaty, civil war and then in the social and cultural upheavals that culminated in the era of World War II and its aftermath. Accordingly, these documentary research samples need to be seen in their socio-political context. To illustrate the point, we are alert to the gendered title of chairman, which signalled the thinking about women and their invisibility, but no doubt Máire Ní Chinnéide put paid to that as a notable suffragist and Irish nationalist!

3 The INTO and activist teachers

Introduction

The present generation of teachers in Ireland is fortunate to have inherited a great tradition of teacher activism from the past, especially given the work of Vere Foster (1819–1900) and colleagues including the businessman Chamney as proprietor and editor of the *Irish Teachers' Journal*. They no doubt worked to mentor and support teachers forge engagement with edu-political activities throughout the Victorian era, notably the Strabane Teachers' Association, who moved to form the INTO's forerunner, the Irish National Teachers' Association (INTA). The British-centric politics of the time was signalled by the Powis Commission, for example, but evidently, teachers' voices were marshalled and published in reports and public broadsheets.

Foster's own form of activism was effective in post-famine Ireland, controversies and conflicts notwithstanding, but when his social capital of the day[1] was exhausted, he had to succumb to a new political era. Looking back, Foster had helped shape the parameters of the debate about national schools and Irish education and he did much to characterise teacher status in Ireland when nineteenth century liberal political theory and political economy were challenged. Two points more or less summarise Foster's endowment to activist teachers in contemporary Ireland. The first was made by Irish education historian John Coolahan in the radio documentary 'Who Was Vere Foster' on Lyric FM[2] when he named Foster's interest in school democracy by shifting power and control away from the single manager:

> *If you are going to have local taxation as happened in England [and] if you are going to have local taxation in favour of the primary school system, you would also have to have managerial representation on the [school] boards. In other words the management's boards would also be represented by the tax payers not the clergy controlling the [process], and that is where it became a conflict because the Church was fighting very hard to extend the power that they had already at local level on the running of the schools and Vere Foster was absolutely committed to the idea of a local rate for education and a broader managerial perspective.*

The mention of the conflicts over the management boards are prescient of the situation in the present given the regulated – regulation of teaching. This dovetails with the second point for activist teachers, this time made by teacher and INTO historian Brendan Colgan (2001) about Foster's strong advocacy for religious equality and his ecumenical outlook. He opposed the privileged position of the Church of Ireland up to 1869, and, according to *The Irish Times* on 19 June 1865 (cited by Colgan, 2001),

> *He did not want any ascendancy at all but equality, and if they had that, there would be a great deal more union of persons of all denominations for the common good. He thought a Catholic as good as a Protestant and a Protestant as a Catholic.*

The mention of displacement of religious control is also prescient of the decline of the Catholic Church in the present, but the struggle for equality remains. This is particularly significant following the rise and fall of the Celtic Tiger and the GFC, Brexit and threats to national and regional stability. It is also significant in the face of concerns about any potential for England's Ofsted-type 'failing' schools that could then herald Anglo-American corporate system reforms into Ireland's national schools.

Foster's ultimate retirement to Belfast was tied to a major victory for so-called native values over English-inspired liberalism, given burgeoning Irish nationalism with the goal of independence. The irony is that he had recognised that the Irish national school system had both economic and social functions for generations of the poor of Ireland, which holds in this era of global free-market capitalism. But as Hall, Massey and Rustin (2015) warned, it is more about generating vast profits for multi-nationals, investment institutions and venture capitalists and huge accumulations of wealth for the global super-rich, while grossly increasing the gap between rich and poor and deepening inequalities. Yet the immortal words on the front cover of Foster's copybooks holds just as much now as it did then:

A nation's greatness depends on the education of its people.

Bruton made a similar statement in his foreword to the original *Action Plan for Education 2016–2019*: 'Few areas are more pivotal than education to our ambitions as a nation', and in the updated version, 'Education is at the heart of all of our ambitions as a nation'. The pronoun 'our' notwithstanding, these appeals to consensus given the Celtic Tiger, GFC, Brexit and other threats act as signals on 'the state of the nation'. Significantly, if the INTO is to engage policy debates about national schools harnessed to the future of Ireland, and if teachers' professional self-regulation is to hold, it requires focussed attention. The INTO needs to be buttressed by research-active teachers and academic partners plugging historically informed research intelligence on policy and practice into the teachers' union. This is not necessarily 'extra' to teaching practice in the present, given Gary Granville's (2012) *Dublin in 1913: Lockout & Legacy*, which supports Irish teachers to spark students' historical-sociological imagination about the early twentieth century. This presents as a learning opportunity to canvass both teachers' and students' beliefs about Ireland; its socio-political complexities including the social divide along socio-economic, racial, ethnic and gendered lines; the emigration of young people; the realities of poverty and its effects; and fighting for the rights of working people (see Wrigley, Thompson, and Lingard, 2012; Sachs, 2003).

In this chapter, the aim is to draw out the characterisations of teacher status tied to different notions of professionalism in different guises throughout the early part of the twentieth century, which was marked by power struggles. What follows are further samples of documentary research that could be developed to inform INTO policy debates about national schools harnessed to the future of Ireland. This sample sheds light on some watershed moments, captured in the following:

- 1916 Padraic Pearse's (1916) pamphlet titled *The Murder Machine*
- 1916 Catherine Mahon and women's struggles
- 1922 National Programme of Primary Instruction
- 1941 INTO inquiry into the Irish language question

These samples align with Ferriter's (2016a) INTO keynote on the occasion of the centenary commemorations of the 1916 Easter Uprising, when he markedly posed the provocative question about the republican promises of 100 years ago:

> *But what was going to be involved in fulfilling these revolutionary promises of 100 years ago. What was the reality of what children were experiencing or what teachers were experiencing 100 years ago?*

In a cursory reply, Ferriter cited the bitterness and difficulties of the civil war (1922–1923), but he also talked about the difficulties of trying to put some kind of meaning on the promises in relation to children, in relation to social improvement, in relation to equality and in relation of course to education. This sits well with a critical- interpretive reading, but as McCulloch (2004) advised, it is necessary once again to understand documents in relation to their milieu and to find out as much as possible about the document from the internal evidence of the text itself. No less important is the need to discover how and why it was produced, and how it was received. These explanatory points are crucial when it comes to an examination of documents as social and historical constructs and none more so when it comes to the documents selected here to tease out the sufferings and injustices of Ireland's past, as noted by Ferriter (2016a).

1916 The murder machine

This curiously named pamphlet on education foreshadowed 'A Plan for Education' (INTO 1947). It was collated in Pearse's collected works[3] in the volume titled *Political Writings and Speeches*, which at once signals Pearse's personal and professional background: barrister, teacher, educator, writer and a poet with the financial capital to publish; the enterprising school head of St Enda's School or Scoil Éanna in Gaelic that he set up in 1908 as a secondary school for boys in Ranelagh, Dublin[4]; and part of a generation of Irish nationalists who seriously challenged the British empire. Pearse was a Gaelic revivalist[5] and commander-in-chief during the 1916 Easter Uprising of the rebels who took up arms in its cause; he was the principal author and one of the seven signatories of the Irish Proclamation of Independence, who actually read it out to a small gathering of passers-by in front of the GPO Dublin. At the risk of understatement, Pearse was a revered public intellectual who agitated for Ireland's independence and for education in the new Irish nation.[6]

In the preface, Pearse indicated this pamphlet was the third if not fourth version dated 1 January 1916, presciently written on New Year's Day in what was to become a year that transformed Ireland and reverberated down the rest of the century. It was probably first printed in 1916 as a penny pamphlet, given the cost stamped on the copy held by the National Museum in Collins' Barracks Dublin. It was a lengthy essay of 20 pages and a rough count suggests over 10,000 words, but strictly speaking it could not be considered Pearse's recollections of occupational life because it was written in anticipation of developments, marked by the wisdom of foresight! It was not an impartial account and contained much personal bias, but it is striking reading, poignantly telling the story of this aspect of Pearse's working life only months before his execution.[7] It was reprinted in the collected works published almost a decade later, a lasting (auto) biographical tribute.

Its purpose is readily distilled in three major themes that are relevant to our concerns with characterisations of teacher status marked by deliberations on democratic professionalism, especially given Pearse's evident intentions to provoke conflict and controversy about education. Not surprisingly, there is vehement rejection of the so-called English system of education in Ireland, which explained the curious title to do with 'the hideous wrong to be righted' (Ferriter, 2015). According to Pearse, the promise of education was fiercely denied in Ireland:

[The English] have planned and established an education system which more wickedly does violence to the elementary human rights of Irish children than would an edict for the general castration of Irish males.

The reference to violence not only helped explain the curious title of Pearse's pamphlet but it was repeated in relation to England's colonial power and its machinery of governance through strict factory-like schooling with its multiple boards of education, inspectors, and compulsory programmes of teaching: 'The education system here was designed by our masters in order to make us willing or at least manageable slaves' and further 'the schools and colleges and universities may be looked upon as the symbol of Ireland's penal servitude'. Pearse contended 'education in Ireland is founded on a denial of the Irish nation' and expounded a detestation of 'a sound modern education' tied to the probable effect of Home Rule[8] synonymous with devolution but controlled by Westminster (see Ferriter, 2015; Foster, 2012).

This was borne out in an Radio & Television Ireland (RTÉ) Radio 1 broadcast when teacher Frank Flanagan (1994), who coincidentally worked in the same school campus with co-author John Carr, delivered a paper on Pearse that contributed to Programme 8 of the Great Educators. Some points are noteworthy: Pearse had written extensively on educational issues in *An Claidheamh Soluis*, a weekly bilingual paper published by the Gaelic League in which he 'stressed the importance of educational reform in securing the intellectual and political independence of Ireland'. Although supportive of the aims of the Gaelic League, Pearse relished 'the prospect of the children of Sandy Row'[9] being taught to curse the pope in Irish. He rejected a mono-lingual Ireland realising 'that Ireland could have the best of both worlds (economically and culturally) by pursuing a policy of *bilingualism*' similar to the Belgian model. It is perhaps regrettable that Saorstát Éireann or the new Free State of Ireland did not take up Pearse's bilingual concept instead of imposing a Gaelic revival programme on schools and using children in the quest for the restoration of the Irish language. He did, however, stress the principle of Tír gan teanga, tír gan anam (A country without a language is a country without a soul). This meant a language is evolved by a nation for the purpose of expressing its thought. Thus a nation's speech is, in a real sense, the creation of that nation.

A second key theme identified by Pearse in *The Murder Machine* was the preferred substance of Irish education in the cause of the nation, which called into play 'the work of the first Minister of Education in a free Ireland' and an ideal of education in the words of the old Irish: 'The teacher was *aite* (fosterer), the pupil was *dalta* (foster-child), and the system was *aiteachas* (fosterage)'. Pearse's narrative on the whole captured his vision of the complex nature of Irish education overlapping with social histories looking back to the old Gael, pagan and Christian, but also to Europe in the Middle Ages, through to English colonisation, the Great Famine and Gaelic resistances to the injustices suffered by a great majority of people who lived in wretched conditions. That the experience of extreme poverty carried into the early twentieth century and into Dublin, well known for the real squalor in 'Strumpet City'[10] (see Hegarty and O'Toole, 2006), coupled with the suppression of the Gaelic language,[11] was not lost on Pearse.

A third theme had to do with charting the structure of a so-called native Irish education system, said to be possessed pre-eminently of two characteristics he named freedom and inspiration. This was classic Pearse the idealist but it was a heartfelt plea for Irish education to stand in contradistinction to the 'grim jest' imposed by the English. Pearse anchored his social vision in principles because it 'was not the education system of an aristocracy, but the education system of a people. It was more democratic than any education in the world'. The teacher was central and 'so it was all through Irish history', which signalled an embrace of teacher's professional responsibilities[12] with the intention to 'transfer the centre of gravity of the system from the education office to the teachers; the teachers in fact would be the system. Teachers, and not the clerks, would henceforth conduct the education of the country'. The details are worthy of close study.

This pamphlet was a product of its time, albeit conceptualised towards activist ends, which prompts critical consideration of Ferriter's (2016a) claim in his INTO keynote that these pronouncements were really about the republican search for purity in the revolutionary documents 100 years ago. Interestingly,

Ferriter's (2015) book *The Irish Revolution* alerted readers to the inevitable selections if not silences of the accounts of the revolutionary period, relevant to how this era is taught in schools.[13] This is a crucial matter, tied to 'how we came to know what we know about the period, who told us and why; its impact, legacy and how it has been remembered' (Ferriter, 2015, p. 13) – a reflection of Brady's (1994) *Historikerstreit* for Ireland. It raises a question about teachers' professional knowledge bases not only to do with the politics of curriculum (see Coolahan, 1981; Ó Buachalla, 1988; Sugrue, 1997; Kelly, 2002; Gleeson, 2010; O'Donoghue and Harford, 2012; Walsh, 2012; Looney, 2014) but also Irish governance and edu-politics. Ferriter (2016a) went on,

> The INTO was certainly aware at that stage of the gulf between rhetoric and reality of the challenge that would be involved in delivering a new educational system, the education system that was promised.

1916 Catherine Mahon and women's struggles

It is crucial to come back to Ferriter's (2016a) purpose in bringing this history to teachers, not only to tease out the markers of Irish historical writing but also to explore Irish education-society links alert to women fighting a battle to be a part of public life and to be a part of public discourse.[14] He named Catherine Mahon, not only the first woman president of the INTO (1912–1913) but also whose service to the organisation (1906–1920) spanned a critical period in Ireland's history.[15] This gave expression to Ferriter's (2015) concern about those who would not have been mentioned or considered to the same extent in earlier decades, particularly how the revolution affected the people of the era, combatants and non-combatants, male and female, in effect 'history from below'.

Teacher activism contributes much to teacher unions in terms of tactical strategy. An INTO publication on Catherine Mahon,[16] prepared and written by Síle Chuinneagáin (1997, 1998), who adapted her M.Ed. research thesis 'Women Teachers and INTO Policy 1905–1916' was exemplary. This is significant work and the teachers' union is fortunate to be in receipt of a publication by a research-active teacher, who clearly had the support of local INTO branches and 1996 INTO Annual Congress, INTO Treasurer Michael Moroney (1968–1995), General Secretary Senator Joe O'Toole (1990–2001) and the INTO policy team led by INTO Research Officer Dr Deirbhile Nic Craith, who is now INTO Director of Education and Research (2013–present).

Chuinneagáin (1998) provided good directions to primary sources, research-informed commentary and reporting and an insightful acknowledgement of committed women with political nous in the INTO. As she put it,

> Women teachers, individually and collectively, have been instrumental in shaping the policy and direction of the INTO. Their contributions to the development of the Organisation have, as yet, received little attention. Where there has been historical investigation it has emphasised the INTO's work for women rather than the benefits to the INTO of women's membership.

McCulloch's (2004) advice, citing Purvis (1985), is pertinent here. Documentary research that is cognisant of feminist perspectives is useful to a critical-interpretive reading. For one thing, it is not always easy to find texts that have survived often because they were not worth preserving, which relates to male definitions of knowledge. This relates to *Historikerstreit* in Ireland (see Brady, 1994). Purvis (1985, cited by McCulloch, 2004) advised that the feminist documentary researcher needs to embark on an analysis of the situation of women and the hidden or obscured power relations between the sexes, as well as to promote awareness of the experience of women in the past and in the present.

Chuinneagáin (1998) recognised this obscurity:

> *In One Hundred Years of Progress; The Story of the INTO 1868–1968, T. J. O'Connell observed a marked "awakening of a new and more healthy spirit" among the rank and file of the INTO during the first twenty years of the century. O'Connell did not, however, acknowledge the role of women teachers in this development. He fleetingly mentioned Catherine Mahon's "brilliant" leadership in 1913 but he did not assess her achievements although he described, in some detail, Mahon's disagreement with INTO policy in 1920.*

This lines up with Irish feminist historian Rosemary Cullen Owens' (2005) concern with INTO General Secretary T. J. O'Connell (1916–1949), which prompts a pause on his idea of progress, given his reorganisation of the INTO between 1917–1919. According to Owens, this was allied to the INTO affiliation with the Irish Trades Union Congress (ITUC) in 1918, but it saw women's influence diminished.[17] She cited the discontinuation of the two places reserved for them on the INTO's CEC and the lack of women on delegations to the ITUC. Owens reminded readers in the course of her book that this requires tracing the injustices but also the campaigns fought to right them [and] locating these struggles in the wider social context in which they took place:

> *Through the work of campaigning activists, equal educational and political rights were eventually attained. From the early 1900s there was some expansion in female employment . . . The civil service – a major employer in an economy that was generally un-dynamic and stagnant – operated a bar on married women for much of the period.*

Owens (2005) devoted a chapter to 'Developments in Female Education' in Ireland along with numerous other page entries to the INTO: its conference that led to the 'First National Programme' on the school curriculum; the INTO's admittance of women, given its status as a trade union, twice mentioned; T. J. O'Connell's input into the edu-politics of the time, including his support for the marriage bar although women teachers were ultimately exempted; and the INTO that enabled women to hone their political skills of organisation and lobbying. Owen's findings are essentially complimentary to Chuinneagáin's (1998) analyses of Catherine Mahon, described as 'a spirited public speaker, an effective, energetic lobbyist . . . a keen nationalist and a lifelong supporter of the Irish

82 *Theories of teachers organising*

language. . . [with a] passionate concern for a wide range of issues'. These details too are worthy of close study to add gender-sensitivity to a critical understanding of teacher status tied to notions of professionalism.

Thankfully, Catherine Mahon is not lost to the INTO in the face of Ferriter's (2015) alert on the inevitable selections if not silences of the accounts of the revolutionary period. As General Secretary Senator Joe O'Toole said in his introduction to Chuinneagáin's (1998) book:

> *Of the many women during the period who were committed activists Catherine was the most outstanding. Not only did she fight for equality issues such as equal pay and representation for women on the INTO Central Executive Committee, but she set the INTO on a course of expansion with her recruitment drive, and led the INTO to affirm its position as an independent, representative body. Her remarkable and courageous leadership during these years contributed enormously to the development and strength of the INTO.*

O'Toole was prescient in his call, 'To this day we remain in her debt'. In so many ways it is possible to imagine what drove Catherine Mahon, given the role and status of women, their lifestyle options and the wider socio-political struggles of the period. She probably took to heart the 1916 Proclamation, which declared 'The Republic guarantees religious and civil liberty, equal rights and equal opportunities to all its citizens', which presumably resonated in the INTO.[18] But a conundrum now is that women teachers evidently received so little attention at the time, and in looking back, it is necessary to be 'a better detective' when it comes to feminist documentary research. Not surprisingly, much remains to be done even by Chuinneagáin's (1998) own admission, which includes interrogating Mahon's influence on O'Connell and the INTO decision/s that led to affiliation with the ITUC in 1918 in order to obtain legal status and protection provided by Trade Union Law.[19]

1922 national programme of primary instruction

This pamphlet of 32 pages, significantly signed on the eve of the transfer of powers to the Provisional Government of Ireland,[20] is a national official record of a broader coalition of interests working cooperatively and collaboratively to give concrete expression to what Ferriter (2016a) called 'the revolutionary promises':

> *[Tied to] the challenges then of State-building in the 1920s, again coming back to the idea how to build a new education system . . . [this relates] to what the difficulties would be in a supposedly free and Gaelic Ireland.*

Ferriter then posed the question, 'What exactly would this mean for education?' and named the proclamation, religion, the Irish language crusade, the 1920s conferences and the Gaelic League. This 1922 document is an artefact from one of these conferences. However its title prompts a double-take given the

Figure 3.1 National programme of Instruction issued by The National Programme Conference 1922

Source: Reproduced courtesy of the Department of Education and Skills.

word programme, which at first signals a national curriculum. A cursory glance at the text shows this was registered as 'subjects of instruction' in the parlance of the time. The title also suggests a conference agenda given the pamphlet was said to be issued by The National Programme Conference. Although no date and place for a conference was provided on the front cover, the text inside shows mention of a first meeting held on 6 January 1921. The timing, exactly five years and five days after Pearse wrote his tract, is indicative of his influence if not another New Year resolution.

Yet this programme was published a year after that meeting, and prior to the transfer of powers to the Provisional Government, perhaps for the purposes of consultation and/or to shed light on deliberations about teaching in national schools as an exemplary instance of transformative edu-politics. In any event it proves to be a valuable source of information about concerns in regard to Ireland's nation-state building at the time: the Irish Revolution, including suffrage, was in full swing leading up to the Anglo-Irish Treaty and partition. The inside front cover provided clues about who was involved in this venture:

> *The National Conference was composed of Representatives from the following bodies: Aireacht an Oideachais, the General Council of County Councils, the National Labour Executive, the Gaelic League, the INTO, and the Association of Secondary Teachers (Ireland).*

This was a formidable group of stakeholders, including the Ministry of Education, said to be representative of public opinion on Ireland's new education system. Their resolve was spelled out in the unsigned introduction although towards the back of the pamphlet it was marked 'Signed', as if electronically, by a committee with Máire Ní Chinnéide[21] as chairman. The very term signified the very real barriers that confronted women and girls to be recognised, but pointedly a suffragist and Irish nationalist was in the chair. The other ten committee members, all men and all but one with Gaelic names, were listed with their representative affiliation to match the inside front cover. Interestingly five of these ten represented the INTO, including Tomas Ó Conaill also named as Honorary Secretary. This was INTO General Secretary T. J. O'Connell (1916–1949).

The INTO was evidently a politically astute group, which confirms Owen's (2005) point about their political skills of organisation and lobbying. The introduction began with note of public criticism and complaint about the unsuitability of [extant] 'Programmes of Instruction' said to fall under two headings in numerical order: (1) too many obligatory subjects with practically no freedom for teachers' choice of subjects and (2) the Irish language had been placed in a subordinate position contrary to the wishes of the vast majority of Irish people. Curiously, or perhaps cautiously given the political economic context, the committee noted in narrative form not numbered sequence:

> *In addition the programme, generally speaking, was felt to be out of harmony with national ideals and requirements.*

These were not elaborated in the text, but it was likely so-called native values, principles and strategies were vigorously discussed by the committee chaired by Máire Ní Chinnéide[22] in the first meeting and in the conference proper. The introduction continued in narrative form to outline the difficult task for teachers to give practical effect to the (extant) programme given defects and to decry their protestations had been in vain, which is a crucial point. Then came the statement that by 1920 conditions had changed.[23] Reflecting the edu-political atmosphere at the time, the INTO CEC succeeded in having a resolution adopted the 1920 INTO Annual Congress directing the CEC to take steps to convene a representative conference in order:

To frame a programme, or series of programmes, in accordance with Irish ideals and conditions – due regard being given to local needs and views.

It was further noted that invitations were issued to a range of interested people and bodies, including stakeholders already named plus an extensive list of delegates.[24] The details of this edu-political venture are ripe for close study, especially given the sectional interests, but for the purposes of this anniversary book, it is noteworthy to mention that teacher status tied to notions of traditional professionalism (see Whitty, 1998) was seemingly taken as read:

Teachers are at liberty to draw up and submit for approval of the Education Authority special programmes to suit the circumstances of their individual schools taking into account the number and attainment of staff, the local needs, etc., but all such programmes must be framed along the lines of the National Programme.

While this hints at the educational administration if not managerialism, it was no doubt a welcome statement denoting trust in teachers who were not only credited with intellectual and moral vision but with a knowledge of their local school communities. The rest of the 1922 pamphlet was devoted to a sketch of this proposed Irish (national curriculum) programme, including mention of the universities' role in the so-called training of teachers, but this was all preceded by 'Some Notes on the Subjects of Instruction', more or less a rationale for curriculum decision making. Two items stand out. Fatefully, English was to be relegated in relation to the works of other European authors given Irish pupils were to be exposed to European thought and culture. This should come as no surprise because at the time the revolutionary guard wanted to locate Ireland in Europe clearly beyond the boundaries of the United Kingdom (see Pearse, 1916). Just as expressively, the teaching of history was to develop national character and inculcate national pride and self-respect, an acknowledgement that 'the Irish nation has amply justified its existence'.

This 1922 pamphlet is striking reading, and is worthy of attention particularly to draw together history and sociology of curriculum: on the one hand, of the ways these Irish school subjects were historically constructed and why, what happened and then how and what changed, which is part of the social histories of curriculum (see Goodson and Ball, 1984; Goodson, 1985; McCulloch and Richardson, 2000). On the other, of the possibilities and problems of transforming the nature of educational activity, part of the politics of school knowledge (see Whitty and Young, 1976; Young and Whitty, 1977; Young, 1971, 1998; Whitty, 1985).

This aligns with Ferriter's (2015) critical discussion of the politics of the history curriculum to do with the suppression of knowledge about the divisive Irish revolution and Ferriter's (2016a) INTO keynote where he named the 1920s conferences. The Second Programme Conference in 1926 was convened under the auspices of Cumann na nGaedheal[25] party leader W. T. Cosgrave (1923–1927), who had formed government in Saorstát Éireann or the Free State of Ireland.[26] Minister for Education Eoin Mc Neill (1925–1926) was responding to representations by the INTO who argued that the necessary conditions to implement the 1922 programme had not been put in place and there were detrimental effects on young children as a result of the language (see O'Connell, 1968).

In the report and programme presented by the National Programme Conference to the Minister for Education, the INTO had endorsed the 1922 programme, but the INTO entered a reservation that it sought a reduction in the number of compulsory subjects. It recognised the 'unique burden imposed on the schools by the effort to restore Irish as a vernacular, involving as it did the concurrent teaching of two languages in the primary school, the necessity for concentration on essentials was all the more clearly established'.[27] This foreshadowed a major cultural conflict. Indeed Ferriter (2016a) named the Irish language crusade in his INTO keynote:

The idea of Irish having to be the language of the medium of instruction; that it had to permeate everything and that children had to be the foot soldiers, tiny foot soldiers in the linguistic revolution that we have come to characterise the new Free State. It was quickly forgotten of course that the Proclamation of 1916 was written in English. That the proclamation of 1916 was signed by Patrick Pearse using the English version of his name.

1941 INTO inquiry into the Irish language question

This 76 page A5 size booklet was headed Cumann na Múinteoirí Náisiúnta (INTO) on its front cover with the lengthy title: 'Report of the Committee of Inquiry into the Use of Irish Language as a Teaching Medium to Children Whose Home Language Is English'. The notation below the title indicated it was 'issued by order of the Central Executive Committee', and it was priced one shilling. The table of contents was telling. The first three chapters were named 'Historical Introduction', 'The Terms of Reference of the Inquiry' and 'The Medium of Instruction in Infants' Schools'. The next five chapters were named 'The Use of Irish as a Medium of Instruction in the Teaching of Mathematics' and then 'History', 'Geography', 'Music' and 'Needlework', all indicative of what could be called an idiosyncratic social constructivist approach to the 'knowledge question' in the fledgling Saorstát Éireann or the Free State of Ireland[28] (again see Coolahan, 1981; Ó Buachalla, 1988; Sugrue, 1997; Kelly, 2002; Gleeson, 2010; O'Donoghue and Harford, 2012; Walsh, 2012; Looney, 2014). This was tempered by the last four chapters named 'Religious Programme', 'Irish as the Medium of Instruction in Individual Subjects', 'Miscellaneous' and 'Conclusion'. The table of contents also listed an appendix, which was the questionnaire sent out to teachers and which was to be regarded as strictly confidential.

This request for teachers' perspectives could also be read as a research effort to glean some 'history from below' as the stated intention was to inform the INTO's investigation and obtain evidence to enable the organisation to arrive at well considered conclusions. Once again, it is striking an ethics of research was in operation, this time in the early to mid-twentieth-century Ireland, but there was evidently concern that 'only teachers who themselves have taught through Irish should answer the Questionnaire'. This was borne out in the foreword written by INTO General Secretary T. J. O'Connell, who declared,

> *The investigation was undertaken because of the growing doubts among the teaching body as to whether the use of Irish as a medium of instruction in English-speaking districts was hindering rather than helping the cause of the language revival.*

Such growing doubts were a long time in the making, given the backstory. A revised Programme of Primary Instruction had been issued in 1934 by the newly elected de Valera Fianna Fáil Government (1933–1937) Minister for Education Thomas Derrig, apparently arising from the party's impatience with the progress of the promotion of Irish language and culture in schools. This had been clearly conveyed to the INTO by the then chief inspector Mr Franklin at a meeting in the Department of Education in June, 1934. The programme was designed to 'foster a patriotic and Gaelic outlook' (Coolahan, 1981, p. 42) with English no longer to be taught in infant classes and English to become optional in first class. According to O'Connell (1968), in a bulletin issued by the INTO CEC to branches and County Committees in January 1936, teachers expressed concern that the policy on Irish was 'not alone detrimental to the educational development of the children, but was a hindrance to the progress of the language'. In fact it was the dissatisfaction with the Government's Irish language policy that led the INTO to establish its Inquiry.

In the foreword, T. J. O'Connell indicated the Committee, consisting of representative national teachers were five men supported by INTO General Treasurer Michael Linehan, who was also secretary to this committee. O'Connell noted an interim report dealing with the issue was submitted to, and adopted by, the INTO CEC on 25 March 1939, and that a copy was forwarded to the Minister the following May. While there is no indication of a response, it can only be presumed that this final report with the five men as signatories, which was presented to the INTO CEC on 25 March 1941, and ordered to be printed, was also forwarded to the Minister. O'Connell's closing statement in the foreword is particularly significant to activist teachers working in the INTO, now as then:

> *It is hoped that this report, based as it is on first-hand evidence, will serve as a useful contribution towards the settlement of a question which has given rise to much discussion in recent years.*

This speaks directly to the then-extant edu-political settlement evidently laid out in the report, which is addressed to the president and members of the CEC of the INTO:

> *A Chairde (literally translated means Dear Friends or simply just Friends)*
> *At your meeting held on 2 May, 1936, you appointed us the Committee of Inquiry mentioned in the following resolution, passed at the previous Killarney Congress of the Organisation, and referred the resolution to us as our terms of reference:*

> 'That it seems a widely accepted opinion that the use as a teaching medium of a language other than the home language of the child in the Primary Schools of Saorstát Éireann is educationally unsound, we instruct the C.E.C. to select a committee of teachers, representative of different types of schools in each electoral area, to make a full examination of the whole question and to issue a detailed report of the results in their deliberations.'

The teachers' opinion was then substantiated by what can only be described as an extensive practitioner research effort, effectively five years in the making, given it began with 'the preparation and distribution among serving teachers of a questionnaire covering the various aspects of the matter under consideration'. It first had to be submitted to the full INTO executive meeting on 13 June 1936, and with approval distributed to over 9,000 teachers in the following September. Replies were requested by 1 November but an extension was granted to 1 December, and there were 1,347 respondents. This would have provided an extensive amount of data, identified in relation to the Department of Education Report for the school year ended in June 1937 that showed 288 schools in English-speaking districts[29] used Irish as a sole medium of instruction while 2,032 schools Irish was the medium of instruction in certain classes and standards.

The report proceeded to register the decisions in regard collation and summaries, including the need to preface it with an historical introduction. That not only set out the various developments that brought about the predicament for teachers but also shows the significance of Ireland's social and political histories to education and national schooling. The representative Committee's work, albeit male dominated, was certainly extensive and well considered. The whole Report is worthy of close study but it is the eight-plus-page conclusion that drives home these national teachers' political nous undergirded by a capacity for critical thinking, given they declared whole-hearted support for the movement for the revival of Irish and the many powerful influences outside the school against that revival:

> *They desire that the language revival in all its aspects gets a fair trial, and are ready and willing to work to the utmost, any method that will yield compensating results. They believe that no stereotyped plan or method will suit every school, every teacher every class. They plead, therefore, for greater freedom for every teacher to devise his (sic) own methods and his (sic) own plan and for greater sympathy and co-operation between those directing the system and the individual teacher.*

Their conclusions added much to teachers organising for professional autonomy, notably in curriculum decision-making conscious of its complex relations to the cultural, political and economic spheres of Irish society including its young democracy. Needless to say the report received a cool reception from Education Minister Derrig who had been presented with a copy for his observations before publication. In a written reply to INTO General Secretary T. J. O'Connell, the Minister stated 'the representatives of your Organisation are fully aware of the views of the Department, and the Minister does not find it necessary to add anything by way of formal observations' (O'Connell, 1968). This did not auger well for good industrial relations, given the inevitable conflicts that followed, but of significance to a critical-interpretive reading was the INTO's involvement in the 'knowledge question'.

The teaching of Irish was controversial from the inception of Saorstát Éireann or the Free State of Ireland and on that occasion it was de Valera's Fianna Fáil Government (1938–1943) exercising authority over teachers, ignoring their views to the detriment of Ireland's development and modernisation. Ferriter (2016a) explained this in his INTO keynote when he said the teacher union had made it absolutely clear that using a language other than the home language as the medium of instruction was doing great damage. Moreover, it was retarding progress in so many different areas, and what the INTO had done in that 1941 report was dared to dispel the illusions that had been fostered by a pious government. With similar reservations, Garvin (2004) indicated the idea that Ireland's future lay with the Irish language revival was an elite conviction after the 1922 strike for independence essentially derived from the Gaelic League. He posited it was never an authentic or widely held popular belief that came to be a cultural and intellectual trap.[30] Likewise, Fennell (1983) identified the consequences in the politics of decolonisation from Britain, which reached their peak in Ireland during the 1940s, when questions began to emerge regarding the State's ability to 'achieve what two centuries of nationalism had predicted it would – namely, economic prosperity and cultural revolution'.

Conclusion

This chapter has done much to explore different conceptualisations of teacher status tied to deliberations on different forms of professionalism, including teacher activism in some watershed moments of early twentieth-century Ireland. This was a time when Anglo-Irish power relations were ever more fraught and complex as decolonisation became the lived reality, coupled with the complexities of nationalist causes including women's struggles, an Irish curriculum and the Irish language question.

These were all marked by tricky backlashes, but the teachers were stalwarts. A story makes the point about their engagement in the edu-politics during the critical if not dangerous times of Saorstát Éireann or the Free State of Ireland. It happened the entire clerical and administrative work in connection with the 1922 conference was carried out by the INTO, as was the entire cost of printing, publishing and circulating the final Report. All meetings, except one, were held in the INTO Head Office. O'Connell (1968) pointed out the difficult circumstances under which the group were operating: 'At one critical period when a meeting became necessary, it was felt that the Gresham (Hotel) afforded more safety for men "on the run" than No.9 Gardiner Place' (INTO Head Office).

Notes

1 Again, Judith Sachs' (2003b) BERA keynote titled *Teacher Activism: Mobilising the Profession* is pertinent given she cites Robert Putnam's (2000) reference to a decline in social capital and civic engagement in more recent times to an erosion of trust in teachers, which has an effect on the teaching profession, whose reputation is tarnished. This adds to a critical understanding of what happened to Foster in mid-nineteenth century Ireland, given the decline of the Anglo-Irish, and what could happen to teachers in twenty-first-century Ireland if/when Anglo-American style corporate school reforms comes into play. The competitiveness can be soul destroying: witness the two school heads who resigned in protest in England, as reported by Education correspondent Sally Weale (2017) in the article 'Married Head and Deputy Condemn Education Policy in Resignation Letter', *The Guardian*, Saturday 29 April.
2 See the RTÉ feature on Lyric FM: www.rte.ie/lyricfm/the-lyric-feature/ . . . / 614976-the-lyric-feature-friday-2-may-2014/ (Last accessed April 2017).
3 We each purchased the volume containing *The Murder Machine* from Antiquarian and second-hand booksellers in Dublin, sadly, as a single book, but there are other volumes: *Collected Works of Padraic H. Pearse, Plays, Stories, Poem*; *Collected Works of Padraic H. Pearse, Political Writings and Speeches*; *Collected Works of Padraic H. Pearse*; *Songs of the Irish Rebel and Specimens from Irish Anthology*, *Collected Works of Padraic H. Pearse*; *The Singer and Other Plays*.
4 See the Office of Public Works Museum: http://pearsemuseum.ie/.
5 This arose from a lecture delivered by Douglas de hÍde in 1892 to the National Literary Society entitled 'The Necessity for De-Anglicising Ireland' in which he advocated the revival of the Irish language. Conradh na Gaeilge (the Gaelic League) was established in 1893 by Eoin Mac Neill and other Gaelic language enthusiasts with a view to encouraging the greater use of the Irish language in everyday life. The Gaelic League published its own paper 'An Claidheamh Soluis', of which Padraic Pearse was one of its most famous editors. It campaigned to have Irish included in the curriculum and eventually developed its own programme for Irish which was promoted locally with evangelical enthusiasm by Gaelic language enthusiasts, which became a factor in the INTO calling for the establishment of the National Programme Conference in 1922 (see O'Connell 1968).

6 Ferriter (2015) described Pearse as a militant educationalist and language activist, someone these days we might call a teacher-soldier (see Spencer, 2001).
7 The ringleaders of the 1916 Uprising were secretly tried at the British Richmond Army Barracks in Dublin by court martial. Denied legal representation, they were all found guilty and led to their execution in the Stonebreakers Yard in Kilmainham Jail. On the morning of the 3 May 1916, three of the four signatories of the 1916 Proclamation, Padraig Pearse, Thomas Clarke and Thomas Mc Donagh, were shot by firing squad; they were followed on 4 May by another three, Joseph Plunkett, Willie Pearse and Sean Mac Diarmada; the seventh member, James Connolly, faced the firing squad on the 12 May 1916 sitting in a chair, because he was unable to stand up from injuries he sustained during the fighting at Easter.
8 The Home Rule movement started under Isaac Butt who founded the Home Government Association in 1870. This was followed by the Home Rule League in 1873. Home Rule was pursued by the Irish Parliamentary Party in the Westminster Parliament from 1882 particularly by Charles Stewart Parnell, who was instrumental in having the First Home Rule Bill introduced by British Prime Minister Gladstone in 1886. This was only defeated by a split in the Liberal Party. A Second Home Rule Bill was introduced by Gladstone in 1893 and while it succeeded in the House of Commons it was defeated in the House of Lords. A Third Home Rule Bill was enacted in 1912 but suspended again following the outbreak of the WW1. Support for Home Rule dissipated after the war in favour of independence and the 1916 Uprising; the Irish Parliamentary Party was heavily defeated thereby ending the Home Rule movement's activities.
9 Sandy Row is one of the oldest streets situated in south Belfast. A predominately working class area its inhabitants are staunchly loyalist and fervent supporters of the Orange Order, which on the eve of the 12 July each year, sees the erection of the largest bonfire in Northern Ireland to commemorate the defeat of Catholic King James 11 by the Protestant William of Orange of the Netherlands at the 1690 Battle of the Boyne. This was on the banks of the River Boyne near Slane and Drogheda in County Louth.
10 This is a reference to the 1980 television series produced by the public broadcaster, Raidió Teilifís Éireann or RTÉ. Based on the popular novels by James Plunkett, it is advertised as a panoramic saga of Dublin life during one of its most turbulent eras.
11 The Irish language arrived with the Celts in Ireland around 500 BC. It thrived in various forms, both written and spoken until its demise was accelerated during the period of mass emigration arising from the Great Famine and the introduction of National School Education in 1831. Although it still taught in all schools except schools for children with certain special needs, it remains vibrant as a spoken and written language in All Irish Schools, Irish Departments of Universities and Irish speaking areas along the south and west of Ireland, albeit the language is currently under threat from modernisation in these areas too. Attempts at the revival of the Irish language were made towards the end of the nineteenth century and following independence. Several attempts were made by successive governments to implement programmes designed to strengthen the national fibre by having the Irish language, culture and music taught in schools. This often attracted criticism from parents and teachers that the language policy was having a detrimental effect on pupils' development (O'Connell, 1968, p. 336). The policy towards the language in schools changed after the introduction of the 1971 Curriculum given the emphasis on child-centred philosophies. While the Irish Language is still part of the national curriculum there is an emerging view that standards in the Irish language are on the decline in many schools due mainly to a lack of support among the general public for survival of the language.

12 One cannot help but be struck by Pearse, who seemingly foreshadowed an idea about teachers' democratic professionalism: again see Whitty's (2008) prototype models of teachers' professionalism, which includes traditional, collaborative, managerial and democratic, also Gilliland and Stevenson (2016), who developed the idea of democratic professionalism for Irish teachers.

13 See Ferriter's chapter, 'Closing Young Minds?' which raises multiple concerns about the politics of curriculum prescription to do with stakeholders' vested interests. In regards the 1916 Easter Uprising it had to do with the ways Irish nationalist history was 'relegated behind world and British history' and conversely the way the unionist contribution was ignored.

14 The centenary of the 1916 Easter Uprising brought a plethora of publications to mark the commemorations, and women figured prominently; see, for example, Gillis (2016) *Women of the Irish Revolution*. Yet ten years earlier, women were absent in the roll-call of the forces that fought in Easter week; see Hegarty and O'Toole (2006), who named Countess Markievicz on pp. 32–33. Conspicuous by their absence was Cumann na mBan, Gaelic for 'League of Women', formed in 1914 as an auxiliary corps to complement the Irish Volunteer Force (IVF); see www.bbc.co.uk/history/british/easterrising/profiles/po13.shtml also McCarthy (2007) *Cumann na mBan and the Irish Revolution*.

15 Catherine Mahon was the first woman to be elected vice-president of the INTO in 1911 and was elected president in 1912. She became the only president to have served a second term in 1913 since the rules governing the election of presidents were changed in the early 1900s. Of the many women who were involved in the INTO at the early 1990s Catherine Mahon was the most formidable. Not alone did she campaign for equal pay and representation on the Central Executive Committee, but she also recruited many women into the organisation. She was described by Joe O' Toole in the foreword to Chuinneagain's book on Catherine Mahon as a remarkable and courageous leader who contributed enormously to the development and strength of the INTO.

16 This INTO publication is available for sale as a book from the INTO: www.into.ie/ROI/Publications/PublicationsPre2000/Title,17311,en.php and it is also digitised: www.into.ie/ROI/Publications/PublicationsPre2000/CatherineMahon1998.pdf.

17 See Henry Pelling's (1963) *A History of British Trade Unionism*. A small Pelican book, it noted on p. 254/255 that 'Unionism made little progress among the white-collar workers, whose numbers were increasing comparatively rapidly; and a few of the large unions in this field, several – notably the Local Government Officers and the NUT – were not affiliated to the TUC'. That trade unions were a male bastion of blue collared workers is no doubt part of the story, anchored in history.

18 An interesting idea to resonate in the INTO today is what might a new Proclamation of Independence for Ireland look like if it had to be written in the present, which stems from O'Neill (2002) *2016. A New Proclamation for a New Generation*. This is pertinent to our anniversary book project, given concerns about the ways research-active teachers working with the INTO might exert some influence on education policies in Ireland's national interest. It is noteworthy that O'Neill is an economist and chairman of Amárach Research, which is an independent market research agency and which could prove useful to the INTO and other like-minded organisations interested in the project to reclaim and refurbish Glyde Court as a world-class research facility; see www.amarach.com/.

19 In order to have INTO rules and objects approved by the Register of Friendly Societies, the Register at the time refused to accept 'the promotion of education in Ireland' as a suitable object for a trade union and refused to grant a registration certificate unless it was omitted (O'Connell, 1968). The executive of the INTO 'believing that its omission could not affect the furtherance of this desirable

object, reluctantly agreed'. In later years, this object was re-introduced and in 1967 after almost 100 years it read, 'To promote the interest of education and to strive for the raising of educational standards' (Connell 1968). At the time of writing this anniversary book, 150 years later, the object reads, 'To promote the interests of education and to support the concept of equal access to full education for all children, and to strive for the raising of educational standards'.

20 The Provisional Government of Ireland or *Rialtas Sealadach na hÉireann* in Gaelic operated throughout 1922 as a transitional administration between the ratifying of the Anglo-Irish Treaty and the establishment of the Irish Free State.

21 Máire Ní Chinnéide (1878–1967) was a teacher in St Mary's High School in Donnybrook in Dublin and an active member of Craobh an Chéitinnigh (lit. The Keating Branch) of Conradh na Gaeilge (the Gaelic League) She became vice-president of the Gaelic League in 1920. It is interesting to speculate how she became chairperson of the conference in view of the fact that prior to the convening of the conference, teachers were coming under immense pressure to implement an Irish language programme drawn up by the Gaelic League, without prior consultation with the INTO. Patriotic fervour for the revival of the Irish language resulted in visits to schools by local Sinn Féin and Gaelic League enthusiasts demanding the immediate implementation of the Gaelic League programme. Calls for the dismissal of teachers who did not have proficiency in the language or who were non-compliant provoked talks of strikes among members of the INTO. The INTO approached Sinn Féin as represented by Aireacht an Oideachais and the Gaelic League, the two groups that could effectively curtail the activities of their members at local level, and an agreement was reached to convene this 1922 National Conference as proposed by the INTO (O'Connell, 1968, p. 342–343).

22 Even a short foray to explore (her) biographical details including associates like suffragette and Irish nationalist Hanna Sheehy Skeffington (1877–1946) suggests Máire Ní Chinnéide had impeccable credentials when it came to this project. There remains a question as to whether she was appointed by the INTO to chair this National Conference Programme, or if she was elected by the committee. In any event, it is a fascinating insight into the edu-politics of the time, and would make for an ideal study by a research-active teacher for a Masters or doctorate then INTO publication.

23 As Coolahan (1981) pointed out 'the years leading up to 1922, particularly after the Sinn Féin victory of 1918, formed a heightened patriotic fervour and idealism, and it was an accepted element of nationalist belief that in laying the foundations for a new state, the schools would be geared to promote the revival and extension of the Irish Language and Gaelic culture'. Teachers were very active in the various branches of the Gaelic League and were, according to O'Connell (1968), largely responsible for the inclusion of Irish as an extra subject in the national school curriculum. O'Connell went further: 'They joined in the public outcry against the removal of Irish from the school programme in 1905 and were prominent in the agitation which succeeded in having it restored in 1906'. In 1907, four Irish speaking organisations were appointed to the National Board of Education and the teaching of Irish as a subject was becoming more common in schools in Gaeltacht (Irish speaking) areas and among schools were teachers were competent to teach the Irish language. O'Connell (1968) also made the point that during the 'closing years of the British regime' it was becoming 'increasingly evident that a radical change in the Government of the country was on its way and that whatever form the new regime would eventually take, education would most certainly come under the control of its elected representatives'(O'Connell, 1968, p. 341)

24 This original invitation from the INTO included Professors of Education in Dublin and Queen's University and in the University Colleges of Dublin (UCD), Cork and Galway, Aireacht na Gaeilge, the General Council of Co. Councils; the National Labour Executive; the Gaelic League; three School Managers'

Associations, the Association of Secondary Teachers; the Catholic Headmasters' Association; the Christian Brothers and the School Masters' Association. The Schools Managers" Association declined to ask its members to 'attend a conference for such a purpose at this season of the year, and in the present condition of the county'. The Revd. T Corcoran, S. J., D.Litt., professor of education in UCD, while refraining from joining as a member of the conference intimated his willingness to offer the benefit of his advice and experience (Connell, 1968, p. 344).

25 Cumann na nGaedheal held office from 1923–1932, but in 1933 it merged with others to form Fine Gael (see Knirck, 2013; Farrell, Knirck and Meehan, 2015).

26 It should be noted that continuous references to 'the State' in Ireland are a shorthand for the Free State of Ireland called Saorstát Éireann in Gaelic, but as noted earlier, the official reference was changed towards the mid-twentieth century given the 1937 Constitution of Ireland or Bunreacht na hÉireann followed by The Republic of *Ireland* Act *1948* (No. 22 of *1948*) as an Act of the Oireachtas which declared that *Ireland* may be officially described as the Republic of *Ireland*.

27 The 1941 INTO *Report of Committee of Inquiry into the Use Of Irish As A Teaching Medium to children Whose Home Language is English* deserves further sample documentary study to yield additional insights into where and how Ireland's edu-politics was played out in the early life of the republic.

28 The Free State of Ireland called Saorstát Éireann in Gaelic was in existence from 1922–1937 until the Constitution of Ireland or Bunreacht na hÉireann came into being, which was followed by the Republic of Ireland Act 1948 (No. 22 of 1948) as an Act of the Oireachtas which declared that Ireland may be officially described as the Republic of Ireland. www.irishstatutebook.ie/eli/1922/act/1/enacted/en/html.

29 For a more in-depth understanding of the areas see www.udaras.ie/en/an-ghaeilge-an-ghaeltacht/an-ghaeltacht/.

30 These insights may well prove useful to the public debates in Northern Ireland in the present given republicans have demanded a stand-alone Irish Language Act, which at the time of writing has stalled the re-establishment of a power-sharing government; see McDonald's article, 'Row on status of Irish language still blocking Stormont deal', in the *Guardian*, Monday 3 July 2017, and BBC online www.bbc.co.uk/news/uk-northern-ireland-38601181

4 Irish national schools

Introduction

The legacies of teacher activism continued to be forged long after Pearse, Catherine Mahon, Máire Ní Chinnéide and the INTO campaign on the Irish language question. The mid-late twentieth century was also marked by instances of teachers' organising that required much thinking and theorising as the INTO came to negotiate the burgeoning nationalist state power structures. Another story from O'Connell (1968) drives home the point. In 1941, when the country was faced with grave risks, financial and otherwise arising from World War II, the INTO made an interest-free loan of £10,000 to the de Valera Fianna Fáil Government (1938–1943) Minister for Finance Sean T. O'Kelly. This amount was no doubt gratefully received given waves of credit and debt crises that plagued government, but it was repaid a year or two later.

These legacies were more or less noted by INTO General Secretary Senator Joe O'Toole (1990–2001), who is worth quoting from the opening part of his foreword to the INTO publication (McCormick, 1996) on the 1946 teachers' strike:

> *The strength and influence which the INTO enjoys has been built by generations of teachers who over the last 128 years regularly stood against injustice, rallied in support of victimised colleagues and sacrificed as required to improve the professional status of teachers.*
>
> *Today's INTO is an inheritance from our former colleagues rather than any tribute to those of us privileged to be the current leadership.*
>
> *We owe a debt of gratitude to those past generations and none more so than the Primary teachers of 1946.*

At the time of writing this anniversary book, another 20 odd years can be added to the INTO's record, but on that occasion, O'Toole's reference was to Irish teachers' first foray into industrial action just after World War II. The year of the strike was a significant year because it marked the expiry of arrangements in place during the war, which has a backstory given Fianna Fáil Taoiseach de Valera's stand in regard to Ireland's neutrality. De Valera was a teacher and proponent of the Irish language revival,[1] and described as 'the man who was Ireland' (see Coogan, 1993b; Lee, 1989; Fanning, 2016). This was for his role in the Easter Uprising and 1922–1923 civil war together with his anti-treaty bias in favour of Saorstát Éireann or the new Free State of Ireland. In 1937, de Valera authored the new constitution with the Gaelic name Bunreacht na hÉireann, which asserted Irish sovereignty as a Western democracy, though not yet a republic,[2] and served several terms as a prominent head of government and head of state. In response to the outbreak of World War II, which conferred widespread powers on government in terms of applying media and postal censorship, an Emergency Powers Act was enacted in 1939 to enforce internment and control economic activity. This effectively suspended democracy until the state of emergency finally expired in September 1946 (Girvin, 2006; Coogan 1996, 2015; Fanning, 2016).

This chapter continues to draw out the characterisations of the INTO's ongoing struggles for teacher status and their professional standing and remains focussed on activist teachers' support for national schools in relation to Irish nationalism and republicanism. These were not without considerable deliberations, discussion and debate as well as dispute in the INTO, but this time the emphases was on the idea of progress. Lukacs (2005) provided a forearming perspective in his discussion of British-inspired conservatism and liberalism: 'Conservatives were more attached to religion, monarchy, classes, traditions and land' with 'liberals to reason, parliamentarianism (if not republicanism), free speech, commerce and trade, industry' signalled by 'progress'. The differences if not the alignments of these two camps can be identified in yet another sample of documentary research projects that could be developed to inform INTO policy debates about national schools in the present harnessed to the future of Ireland. This sample sheds light on some watershed moments, captured in the following:

- 1946 teachers' strike
- 1947 INTO Plan for Education
- 1957 INTO presidential address by Margaret Skinnider
- 1968 INTO centenary history book *100 Years of Progress*

These samples of documentary research projects also align with Ferriter's (2016a) INTO keynote on the occasion of the centenary commemorations of the 1916 Easter Uprising. As he said, with the teachers' strike, the INTO needed to keep a focus on teachers organising and to make the link between education and society. It was about the status of teaching as a profession, although Peadar O'Donnell,[3] the veteran socialist republican, had maintained that the teaching profession was clearly not considered of very much importance by the State at that time. This too sits well with a critical-interpretive reading. To compound matters in 1941, in tones reminiscent of the 'Payment by Results' era, de Valera announced his intention of introducing a primary certificate examination based on the 'need for accountability in teaching to justify public expenditure and the desirability of concentrating on the three Rs' (Coolahan, 1981). Responding to teacher objections, de Valera replied in Parliament, 'I am less interested in the teacher's methods of teaching than I am in the results he (sic) achieves and the test I would apply would be the test of an examination' (Dáil Éireann Proceedings vol. 83, col. 1097, 27 May 1941, cited by Coolahan, 1981). This formed part of the backdrop to the decade or so following, where relations between the next de Valera Fianna Fáil Government (1944–1948) and teachers deteriorated to a low level.

1946 teachers' strike

This A5-size booklet of 58 pages is another INTO publication, prepared and written during the period of office of INTO General Secretary Senator Joe O'Toole (1990–2001). In the foreword, he paid tribute to author Eugene McCormick (1996), and once again, the archives boast a publication providing 'history from below' by a research-active teacher, who clearly had the support of INTO senior leaders. He also had grassroots support, given O'Toole's acknowledgement of colleagues in the preparation of this booklet. This included Dónal O' Loingsigh, CEC representative for District 9, who initiated and helped get the project off the ground. Coincidentally, as part of the 125th anniversary celebrations of the INTO, he organised a photographic exhibition in the Teachers' Club which included images of the 1946 strike. A number of former members who were involved in the strike attended the exhibition and related their stories, which prompted O' Loingsigh's proposal that the INTO should commemorate the 50th anniversary of the 1946 strike. Since McCormick had already completed his MA thesis on the subject, he was commissioned by the INTO to adapt his research thesis, 'The INTO and the 1946 Teachers' Strike', for the purpose.

The booklet contains a prologue and eight chapters that provide an historical sketch of the dispute relevant to teachers' politicisation (Bascia, 1994, 2015; Ghale and Beckett, 2013). It also contains an image of a poster headed 'Dublin Trades Council Central Council of Parents Association' that advertises a 'Demonstration of Parents' who were instructed to assemble for an evening meeting 'to demand re-opening of schools and justice for teachers'. As well, there are ten photographs inclusive of two on the front and back cover, which are equally worthy of documentary study. In the prologue, McCormick (1996) declared that the teachers strike in Dublin that went from March to October 1946 was a surprise event:

> *The national teacher had been closely identified with the heart of Irish society for the previous one hundred and fifteen years. The position and deference of respect which teachers enjoyed within the community made them unlikely members of the vanguard of militant trade unionism. All this changed in 1946 and for over seven months teachers organised by the INTO threw down the gauntlet to the Government over its treatment of teachers.*

This reference to the centenary and more goes back to 1831 and the establishment of the National School system based on Lord Stanley's letter, while the mention of militancy hints at the struggles of the working people of Ireland over

Figure 4.1 The INTO & the 1946 Teachers' strike

Source: https://www.into.ie/ROI/Publications/PublicationsPre2000/Title,16295,en.php. Reproduced by permission of INTO.

Irish national schools 99

Figure 4.2 Teachers' strike

such a long period of time. In many ways this was continuous with teachers' experiences during post-famine Ireland and into the revolutionary era of the early twentieth century, but the teachers' strike was at the close of World War II when peace was paramount. Of particular interest here is McCormick's discussion about the unpopularity of the de Valera[4] Fianna Fáil Government (1944–1988); the note of Dublin, given the strike, was confined to city-based teachers; their experiences of impoverishment in that time; and their decision 'to resort to militant action at a time of financial stringency in the nation's economy'. McCormick credits the teachers as the first professional group in Ireland to use 'the strike weapon'[5] who were followed by other professional groups, to an extent a signifier of teachers' status and social standing.

This was evident in the photographs of teachers' industrial action[6] and in the parents' poster, which can be vital in illuminating the collaborations between parents and teachers with shared values but also public support for activist teachers. For example, the photographs show striking teachers ostensibly doing outreach, standing on stages at microphones addressing open-air audiences; marching in lines outside the Department of Education in Marlborough Street, Dublin, with uniform placards bearing the signage 'INTO strike' in Gaelic and English; and walking in queues on the perimeter of the playing pitch in front of a capacity crowd at Croke Park.[7] But in broaching these visual sources, McCulloch's

(2004) advice, citing Tosh (2002), is sage about the analyses of these documents, because they require much careful appraisal. Interestingly, Marlborough Street is named after the Duke of Marlborough known for his success at the 1704 Battle of Blenheim, while Tyrone House is named after the 1st Earl of Tyrone, Sir Marcus Bereford (1694–1763), who was an Irish peer and politician. This now houses the Department of Education and Skills, the site of many INTO street protests.

McCormick (1996) usefully noted his purpose to examine the development of events and assess their effect on Irish society together with the short-term and long-term implications for those most closely involved. At issue were the teachers' part in the Irish language revival, widespread dissatisfaction with the direction of education policy and with the teachers' treatment at the hands of the educational administration, a deterioration of relationships between the INTO and the Fianna Fáil political party, de Valera's reneging on a salaries promise and Minister for Education Thomas Derrig's insistence on outmoded teaching methods.[8] As if that was not enough, this all resulted in a head-on confrontation with disastrous results for de Valera's government while the Catholic Church weighed in with recognition that 'the INTO was a force to be reckoned with'.

When it came to those most closely involved in the 1946 teachers' strike, de Valera really needs no introduction. He was a significant figure in Ireland's political history who founded Fianna Fáil in 1926 along with other opponents of the 1921 Treaty that divided the country into north and south.[9] According to Tim Pat Coogan's (1993b) magisterial study, de Valera campaigned more or less for his whole political career on the treaty. More to the point, according to Coogan (1993b), the 1946 teachers' strike was de Valera's undoing, 'an electoral runaway rolled out in front of a new party waiting to take office'. As it happened, this was Clann na Poblachta[10] (clan or family of Republicans) that stood in opposition to Fianna Fáil but which also advocated social reform, clearly attractive to teachers. As Coogan put it,

> *Either then or now, it would be difficult to imagine two other groups in Ireland which could match the commitment and energy of a combination of the Republicans and the teachers. Disillusioned with Fianna Fáil, a significant proportion of the membership of the teachers' trade union . . . swung over to the new party.*

McCormick (1996) teased out these details across the eight chapters, which are equally worthy of close study given they link past and present. A few items stand out: 'a reign of terror [that] existed among teachers', the instruments of which were the board's inspectors, which presages Ball's (2003) concerns about the terrors of performativity, and 'the language problem' which had become a cause of 'unexceptionable nationalist authenticity' (Brown, 1981) with inordinate effects on teacher-State relations during the first two decades of independence.[11] Then McCormick devoted a chapter to 'the salary question', which harked back to the 1923 salary cut of 10% on the 1920 pay settlement imposed by de Valera's

Fianna Fáil Government Minister for Finance Ernest Blyth, over which teachers 'regarded as an unwarranted breach of faith on the part of Government'; the deep resentment and growing discontent among teachers arising from the temporary cuts imposed in 1933 by de Valera's Fianna Fáil Government, exacerbated by a modification of the cuts for Civil Servants; the Government's refusal to enter discussions with the INTO on teacher salaries on the basis of the operation of Emergency Order Number 83, better known as the Standstill Order which gave power to the Government to freeze wages and salaries during the war Emergency. The next Minister for Finance Frank Aiken stated in a memorandum[12] dated December 1944 that 'to give in on the demand for a basic increase would give rise to corresponding demands from other public service sectors' and infringe the whole spirit of the National Wages Standstill Policy.

As Ferriter (2016a) advised in his INTO keynote,

> *Enough was enough by 1946 and the teachers went on strike [which] it seemed was not successful, [yet] it certainly created an impact because it affected 49,000 children and because it was the first use of the strike weapon by a professional group. This was a new era for teacher activism.*

Ferriter (2016a) further advised that 'the INTO learned from this experience and it learned from the experience of 1946 in a much more effective way than other trade unions were to do after their strikes at a later stage'. Then Minister for Education Derrig had accused the teachers of holding the State to ransom and of allowing themselves to become a play thing in the hands of irresponsible groups. That this was not the case was one of the key messages from the strike, but this is not to ignore what 1945 INTO President Kathleen Clarke said in her presidential address to the 1946 INTO Annual Congress in Dublin about a smouldering resentment that had built up in relation to bureaucracy, in relation to the treatment of women, in relation to the system of inspectorate and the ratings of teachers. Ferriter then referred to the events of the following year when the INTO turned its attention to its monumental study, *A Plan for Education*, also a landmark, acknowledging once again the failure of Irish as a medium of instruction and insisting that no educational opportunity exists as long as the education for the majority ended at primary certificate level, which meant raising the school-leaving age as it was identified by the INTO in 1947. The concern for Ferriter was that by that stage the revolutionary promises seemed so stale.

1947 INTO A Plan for Education

This 123 page A5 size booklet was issued by the INTO at a price of one shilling and sixpence, which curiously did not boast a Gaelic translation of its title.[13] By way of introduction, McCormick (1996) is worth quoting, as he had much to say about *A Plan for Education* at the end of his study on the 1946 teachers' strike: 'The pervading educational atmosphere was hardly an ideal launching pad' for the initiative. He then paraphrased INTO General Secretary T. J. O'Connell, who authored the foreword and declared,

> *In September, 1943, the INTO Executive, recognising the necessity for a well-planned integrated system of National Education, if this country were not to be left helplessly behind in the post-war world, appointed a Committee to prepare a Plan for Education suitable to the needs and aspirations of our people and which would at the same time set forth in a general way the educational ideals of our Organization.*

It should be noted that, at that time, World War II was still underway, which says much about the INTO engaged in edu-politics. It showed concern for education, the needs and aspirations of the general public, the educational ideals of the teaching community and the authority of the INTO speaking on professional issues. Just in passing, O'Connell's reference to the INTO executive was in fact the INTO CEC, which remains an integral part of the INTO governance structure. O'Connell then hinted at the complexities given the realisation that 'the work of preparing such a Plan would involve much more consideration, discussion, and research' than first anticipated by the INTO CEC, who met at infrequent intervals. The task of preparing a plan in 1943 was delegated to one of its own members, INTO President Dave Kelleher, who was also teaching in St Patricks National School attached to St Patricks Training College. In turn, he was authorised to call on the assistance of INTO members, mainly residents in Dublin, latterly named by O'Connell as the Select Committee.

Significantly, it was the Dublin Branch of the INTO that proposed a motion of no confidence in the CEC at a branch meeting on 22 February 1944, held in the Teachers' Club at 36 Parnell Square, Dublin. According to a report in the *Irish School Weekly*[14] (Vol XLV, No. 41/42, October 1943, cited in McCormick, 1996), this was because of the mounting discontent among INTO members about lack of progress on a previous motion put at their meeting on 2 October 1943. This had demanded 'an immediate increase in the remuneration of teachers commensurate with the great rise in the cost of living'. Although the 'no confidence' motion was defeated by a large majority, it was symptomatic of the increasing discontent within the INTO in relation to a multiplicity of factors coming together including criticism of the inspection system, the position of women teachers and the teaching of the Irish language (McCormick, 1996). A subsequent report in the *Irish School Weekly* dated 6 May 1944 commented on the despondent atmosphere at the 1944 INTO Annual Congress in Killarney:

> *The pity is that the tradition of bad school buildings, underpaid teachers and rigid bureaucratic control is as strong as ever it was and the public have come to regard education, not as something productive and basic, but as a big debt in the National Accounts.*

This was surely not surprising in the latter stages of World War II, but it does go to show the long roots of contemporary teachers' disquiet, resistances, protests and challenges!

A Plan for Education was a seminal document and four years in the making, also not surprising, given it was a critical time for Ireland, which had adopted a policy of neutrality and non-alignment during the war, attracting considerable anger in Britain while preparing for a possible invasion. Restrictions and food rationing, particularly in relation to tea, sugar, flour and butter remained in place after the war had ended and fear of hunger had united Ireland. Although the nation-state was geographically isolated from the rest of Europe, a deeper sense of community and self-reliance was encouraged which consolidated statehood and contributed towards a greater sense of Irish identity.

The INTO publication was a credit to the work of INTO President Dave Kelleher and the Select Committee of research-active teachers in Dublin, who were acquainted with the national and international educational issues of the day. Despite opposition from the incumbent de Valera Fianna Fáil Government (1944–1948) apropos the teachers' strike, they were evidently not deterred from addressing the pertinent issues effecting teachers and children. These were spelled out in the short preface, which opened with the caveat that the plan was put forward 'not as a blue-print for acceptance, but as a draft for discussion'. Kelleher with editorial assistance from *Irish School Weekly* editor John Sheridan stated they expected criticism but they were obviously pragmatic: 'it is only through discussion and consultation that we can finally plan a new and better education system'. No doubt the pronoun 'we' referred to the authors of a *Plan for Education* but also its audience of readers inclusive of teachers, parents and other stakeholders:

> *We think that our basic principles will be endorsed by everyone who believes that the child has a right to the fullest education we can provide for him (sic), and that this right is conditioned only by his (sic) ability to profit by that education.*

From the vantage point of the early twenty-first century, it is easy to identify the gendered language and the language of meritocracy, which reflects and influenced those educators' thinking and theorising. It is also easy to name the principles of fairness, equity and justice necessarily required to create a system that meets the complex needs of boys and girls, and different groups of boys and girls, given more recent recognition that they are marked by the intersectionality of gender, race, ethnicity, social class, disabilities and sexualities. Such complexities go past their own individual hard work, talents and capacities to make a success of national schooling, which relies on an acknowledgement of social and educational inequalities and the shortcomings of meritocracy (Littler, 2017; Beckett, 2018). This was in effect at the heart of *A Plan for Education*, but couched in relation to the pressing issues of the day. For example, the concern then was with raising the then-statutory, school-leaving age, recommending new curriculum subjects and new treatments of existing subjects, and calling for a longer period of compulsory schooling. Indeed, the preface broached the terminology of what could be nowadays called equity policies when it foreshadowed the need for primary schooling to be part of an integrated system of education:

> *We believe, too, that most of the faults of the present system can be traced to the failure to regard it as a single integrated system, and that the view that certain kinds of education are suited to certain grades of society rather than to certain aptitudes and abilities goes directly counter to the ideal of equality of opportunity.*

These well considered beliefs were clearly articulated to herald an integration of primary, secondary, adult and vocational education but also to be the basis of the INTO CEC, Kelleher and the Select Committee's intention to 'stir the public conscience and intensify the growing demand for better schools and better schooling'. It was made clear the planning of the Irish education system then could not be left to the bureaucrats nor to any one section of the community, which echoed an inclusive engagement with education reform:

> *The Church and the parents, the State and the teachers will have to play their parts in the shaping of a composite plan which will represent the best efforts of our wisest heads, and that will be in accord not only with the needs of our children and of the country they live in but also with the enduring principles of Christian philosophy.*

This opening statement, albeit with an Irish cultural accent, in effect traversed some major themes in regard to child-centred education, nationalism and religion though not necessarily sectarianism, presumably coupled with a form of western capitalism and preferably with a social conscience. This was borne out in the table of contents that included chapters devoted to an articulation of defects in the present system; the call for a Council of Education; notations on the recruitment and training of teachers, inspection and the curriculum up to 16 years of age; and chapters on specifics of music, arts and crafts, modern teaching aids, school libraries, secondary and vocational education and examinations. The last five chapters were devoted to examinations, school buildings; health of the school child; adult education; and language revival.

This sample document demands close study to tease out the details of the 'state of the nation' as this is described by social commentators (see Fennell, 1983, 1984; Hardiman, 2012; Munck, 1985) but also some 'history from below' given the role of the INTO, teachers and national schooling in nation-state building. Three relevant matters in *A Plan for Education* stand out. Firstly, the introduction opened with an intention to trace the development of Ireland's education system, which pointedly hinted at its chequered history given British influence but also Pearse's (1916) *The Murder Machine*: 'Revolutionary changes are needed if we are to keep pace with rapidly changing conditions and to build up a system in closer accord with the philosophy and the ideals of a genuinely democratic people'. This was a recurring theme, but Kelleher and the Select Committee then demonstrated a certain level of political maturity by acknowledging an understanding of the historical circumstances influencing educational policy.

> *We feel that the Government should show more courage and vision in its approach to education, and that progress has been hindered by considerations of false economy, though in apportioning blame we must not ignore the influence of certain historical factors on the mind and thought of our people in the early days of our restored political independence.*

This brings to mind the revolutionary promises identified by Ferriter (2016a) in his INTO keynote, which interconnects with the second relevant matter logged in the section entitled 'Defects in the Present System – Suggestions for Reform', under the subheading 'Need for Research', among others. This declared 'our education system is defective in its almost complete absence of provision for educational research', and then citing Pearse (1916), its failure 'to keep the teachers in touch with educational thought in other lands'. This concern with practitioner research intelligence dovetailed with the third related matter in *A Plan for Education*: the call for the establishment of a Council of Education. This had been INTO policy since 1926 when it urged the Cosgrave Cumann na nGaedheal Government of *Saorstát Éireann* or the Free State of Ireland (1923–1927) to set up a Council for Education following a resolution which was passed at the 1926 INTO Annual Congress in Cork. This was then reiterated in 1947 in *A Plan for Education*:

> *Representatives of parents, whose interests are preponderant, and of all bodies directly concerned in the various branches of education, religious and secular, viz., the Churches, universities, headmasters and teachers. It would act as an Advisory body to the Minister and be without executive or administrative powers. It should conduct a continuous review of the educational system, and consider and report to the Government on all important proposals before a decision is made.*

It was envisaged that the proposed Council for Education would review annually the educational activities of the Department and publish an annual report outlining defects in the system and offering solutions. In 1945, when it was proposed in the Dáil Éireann or Irish parliament that a Council of Education was to be established, Education Minister Derrig objected on the grounds that such a council 'would lead to a clash between the principle that the Minister should be responsible to the Dáil and the idea that the proposed Council should have administrative, executive or financial authority'. This was perhaps a calculated misreading of the 1926 INTO Annual Congress resolution, but de Valera was more emphatic in his condemnation. For him, the notion of a council was 'simply and solely a vote of censure on the Government' and the motion, if adopted, would mean 'turning the whole organization of legislation in Parliament topsy-turvy'.[15] This was evidently a deliberate attempt to prevent any potential challenge to the political influence that de Valera's Government (1944–1948) exercised over education policy and its implementation.

This resonated with McCormick (1996) on the reception of *A Plan for Education* in its entirety. Apparently, Derrig was of the view that criticism of the education system was a result of misrepresentation, and he questioned the basic understanding of teachers of the education system and its working. He also opposed the call for a Council of Education to investigate dissatisfaction with the system because he had not seen such evidence. Again from the vantage point of the twenty-first century, it must be said it is heartening to learn Derrig operated on the strength of evidence, but he left himself open to charges of his own critical misunderstanding of edu-politics given what followed.

1957 INTO Presidential Address by Margaret Skinnider

Skinnider, who used her Gaelic name Mairéad Ní Scineadóra, was infamously called a 'suffragette, sniper and school-teacher'[16] given she was a member of Cumann Na mBan (see McCarthy, 2007) and rebel in the 1916 Easter Uprising in Dublin. Significantly, Pearse gave her military command of a small band of men at St Stephen's Green since she was adept in the use of weapons and had smuggled bomb detonators in her hat, with the heroic distinction of being the only woman wounded in action. Having written her memoir entitled *Doing My Bit for Ireland* (Skinnider, 1917), published by the Century Company in North America, it was republished by Aengus Ó Snodaigh[17] after his research into the women rebels.

In a biographical statement in *Women of the Irish Revolution*, Gillis (2016) noted Skinnider trained to be a teacher, but luckily she had not been arrested after the 1916 Easter Uprising. Following a lecture tour of North America, she returned to Ireland and again linked up with Cumann Na mBan, joined the anti-treaty side and was arrested in 1922 for the possession of a firearm. When released, she resumed her work as a teacher and joined the INTO, where her long and distinguished career was marked by militancy. Not surprisingly, Rooney (2016) noted that at the beginning of the teachers' strike, Minister for Education Derrig noted in the Dáil Éireann or the lower house of 'agitators and malcontents in the teaching body who were bent on stirring up mischief'. Skinnider was probably to be counted among them as a founding member of Clann na Poblachta, the party that stood in opposition to Fianna Fáil and that won support from teachers given its platform for radical social change.[18] Further, Rooney (2016) noted Derrig criticised teachers for challenging the authority of the State and threatening the government, convinced the strike was the result of 'the activities of a small but active minority among the teaching body who had agitated among the women teachers'. This hinted at his critical misunderstanding, given teachers' concerns about pay equality.

Skinnider was obviously a formidable woman and certainly not one to be underestimated as an activist teacher, INTO member and then INTO president-elect in 1956. Ferriter (2016a) made reference to Skinnider after Catherine

Mahon in his discussion of the 'women fighting a battle to be a part of public life and to be a part of public discourse'. This continued in the process to secure a military pension, awarded to those who had served time during the revolution period. Skinnider applied based on her 1916 service, which precipitated a 13-year battle before her service was recognised having been told by the Department of Defence in 1924 that the pensions legislation referred to soldiers as understood in the masculine sense. Skinnider continued fighting a battle as INTO president for equal pay and equal status given the matter of common incremental scales for women and single men during that era. As Ferriter put it, 'There are always those battles to be fought, at 1916 and well after 1916'.

A search for a verbatim copy of Skinnider's (1957) INTO presidential address at the 1957 INTO Annual Congress held in Killarney proved frustrating, but a newspaper report on it in the *Irish Examiner* on 23 April 1957 is reproduced as an appendix in Rooney's (2016) book. This copy of 500-odd words is sufficient to outline a sample documentary study for the purposes of this anniversary book, which needed to recover activist women in INTO histories. The newspaper report serves the purpose, as McCulloch (2004) citing Tosh (2002) noted, the press constitutes an important type of public source material. As it happened, it recorded Skinnider's influential political and social views, provided a day-to-day record of the event and offered a thorough inquiry into the issue of teachers' worth that merited public concern. It quoted her as saying,

> *We today must not be unmindful of the glorious heritage handed down to us, and we must prove ourselves worthy successors of the great saints, scholars and teachers of the past.*

Such was the platform for Skinnider's disquiet, useful to Irish historians and social researchers, about the forces at work against the whole Christian way of life that target the youth of any country ripe for conversion to so-called pagan philosophy. The forces were not named as such but this accords with the Irish cultural accent on religion, though not necessarily sectarianism, expressed in *A Plan for Education*. However, Skinnider went past it to reflect on what would have likely been perceived as real imminent threats in the Cold War period. As she put it, 'The greatest bulwark against this attack on the minds of our children is the teaching body and especially the national teachers'. Step-by-step, she came to the matter of teacher status and their professional standing, and regaled against lowering the practice of the profession, lessening the influence for good on pupils and the local community and the recruitment of teachers with conditions that had the effect 'to depress them socially and spiritually by low wages, over-crowded classrooms and veiled threats of dismissal'. She went further and posed a challenge in the tradition of INTO support for research-active teachers that would possibly have made Derrig and his successors smart:

> *But if teachers do belong to a profession they must not be controlled by tyrannical pressure. They are entitled to their academic freedom, to responsible participation*

in scholastic efforts, to respect in the community and to remuneration to enable them to maintain standards proper to their position as professional men and women.

This recognition, inclusive of gender equality, was a salutary reminder of the shared responsibilities between the INTO and government about building a professional culture in schools: 'The members of that profession have the right to speak frankly on their professional problems and to demand favourable conditions that will not paralyse their efforts to deal with these problems'. Her astute concerns from the outset were that there was an absence of provincialism in Irish education and learning through the ages. 'The curriculum was based on national and European sources, well-balanced both as to subjects of instruction and as to languages of instruction'. She ended on a note about the good school but not as a palatial building, as if echoing those who had gone before. 'What it does mean are thoroughly competent and properly trained teachers with every moral and intellectual qualification for the all-important task of forming citizens for the nation, and citizens for heaven'.

The emphasis on religion notwithstanding, Skinnider forecast a continuity of professional concerns about teaching and teacher education across Europe in the present. As Jones and O'Brien (2014) described it, while policies on professional development and professional learning are changing across Europe, there remains a need to examine how these policies change even with continued diversity of the education systems of the countries involved, despite moves towards economic and social integration. Following suit, this really should be a critical understanding of the importance of professional learning and development. This is best seen as a bulwark nowadays against likely threats to inequalities from the dominance of Anglo-American school reforms with a penchant for standardisation and corporatisation. Ideas certainly matter!

1968 centenary book *100 Years of Progress*

T. J. O'Connell (1968) suggested in his authoritative centenary book on the INTO that it might be regarded as a corollary to the social and political history of Ireland. He explained that this was not just because national teachers have always been prominent in the movements for national resurgence and national revival but because of the importance of primary education for national self-respect. As he put it,

For the story of the INTO is not just the story of the national schools: it is the story of the nation-builders who taught, or learned their first lessons, in them and dreamed of making them what they should be.

These are stirring words from the man who held the office of INTO general secretary for 30 odd years (1916–1949), which is not to forget his efforts in regard the INTO affiliation with the Irish Trades Union Congress (ITUC) in

1918 and the subsequent lack of women on delegations. A question to be asked is whether O'Connell actually worked with women who were seemingly made invisible if his claim about the INTO is anything to go by:

It was founded by resolute men in days when any attempt by the teachers to organise in their own defence was regarded as little short of treason, and that throughout the years almost every demand for educational reform met with bitter and determined opposition.

This declaration at once summarises so many complexities to do with teachers organising in tandem with addressing social and educational disadvantages, including gender and how it signals the reinforcement of power or domination over women teachers. Ferriter (2016a) offered this advice in his INTO keynote about INTO General Secretary T. J. O'Connell, in 1916:

T.J. O'Connell, Central Secretary of the INTO in 1916. Very active in the Labour Party and a Labour Party TD in the 1920s. Have a look at the vision . . . [and] . . . the objectives outlined by TJ O'Connell and his colleagues in 1926, 10 years after the Easter Rising.

This suggests O'Connell was a significant parliamentary figure who operated with a support group, no doubt replete with men trade unionists and cognisant of how power worked in regard to the multiple major parties and ongoing power struggles (see Lee, 1989; Coogan, 1993a, 1993b; Fanning, 2015). This included nationalist parties but also a Labour Party that was dedicated to a workers' republic (see O'Riordan, 1977). The objectives outlined by O'Connell and his colleagues embraced the need for a comprehensive education programme posited on the principle that socio-economic disadvantage should never be an obstruction to proper educational opportunity: the need to raise the school-leaving age to at least 15, to reduce the pupil teacher ratios, to modernise teacher training and to repair school buildings.

These laudable objectives were recalled in O'Connell's centenary book of nearly 500 pages, which was something of a memoir about 'history from below' and which could be described as the work of a research-active teacher. In the foreword, he acknowledged his long personal association with the INTO dating from his first appointment as a paid monitor under the National Board[19] in 1895. O'Connell also admitted this was not an impartial and objective history, but an effort to showcase the INTO position when it came to controversies throughout its first one hundred years. He declared it was derived from reports and statements published in the *Irish School Weekly*, official files of daily newspapers, and reports to the Annual Congress. He also acknowledged the documentary source material was supplemented by his own memories.

These recollections and memory work would have mediated O'Connell's account (see Rosen, 1998, cited by McCulloch, 2004), but be that as it may, he was very much a public figure with extensive involvement in the edu-political arena. As McCormick's (1996) citation of his views on the 1946 teachers' strike showed,

> Dr T.J. O'Connell laid responsibility for the strike and the ensuing bitterness with Mr de Valera. He wrote that efforts at settlement failed because of the intransigence of a Taoiseach 'who despised appeals from the public, the press and from Parliament itself [which] could not be moved from a position he had taken at the very beginning. One word from Mr de Valera could have prevented the strike. One word would have sent the teachers back after it had begun. It was to be unconditional surrender as far as he was concerned and none of his ministerial colleagues were free to say otherwise'.

O'Connell's absorbing evidence over 12 chapters demands close study to tease out the details about the relationships between different governments and the teachers' union. These were titled 'The INTO', 'The Managerial System', 'Security of Tenure', 'Remuneration', 'Women Teachers', 'The MacPherson Education Bill', 'The Curriculum – Irish Language', 'Compulsory School Attendance', '[Teacher] Training', 'School Buildings' and 'Miscellaneous Activities'. Of particular interest is the chapter titled 'The Managerial System', which is a crucial backdrop to understanding managerialism as the mode of governance used by Kenny-Varadkar Fine Gael minority-led coalition government in the present to promote neoliberal economic and social policies (see Grummell and Lynch, 2016).

This select chapter provided great insight into the role of Protestant and Roman Catholic clergy, not least because of the full-page photograph of Archbishop John Charles McQuaid of Dublin, also Catholic primate of Ireland (1940–1972) and renowned for his extensive influence on successive governments. Lee (1989) described McQuaid as a key figure with an exalted sense of the dignity of the professions to the point where in 1946 he had expressed 'full sympathy' for striking teachers as representing a profession. This was reference to his letter that asked Dublin teachers to consider the advisability of returning to work 'in consideration of the welfare of children who are under my pastoral care, more especially in view of their spiritual and moral interests which as time passes, are being seriously endangered' (McCormick, 1996). This was not without controversy. Sean Brosnahan, chairman of the INTO Dublin City Branch and an active member of the Strike Administration Committee, opposed the termination of the dispute and successfully stood for election as INTO president at the 1947 Annual Congress in Cork.

McQuaid's intervention, however, was entirely in keeping with O'Connell's rendition of the clerics' functional roles as managers of schools. He articulated the notion of school patronage as the person or body who first applied to establish a school in any given area and traced its historical development from the Stanley letter of 1831 through to the then latest edition of the Rules for national schools issued in 1965 by the Department of Education.

> The patron has the right to appoint or remove the manager or act as the manager himself (themselves). The Minister [of Education] has power (as

the Board had) to withdraw recognition of a manager for failure to observe the rules or if the educational interests of the district require it.

The gendered language to one side, these interests were not specified but an economic bent can be gleaned from O'Connell's subsequent critical discussion: about the logistics of teacher appointments, payment of salaries, building maintenance, improvement in conditions for health and comfort of children and teachers, including sanitation. O'Connell named the Catholic Clerical Managers Association, established in 1903, and the Association of Protestant Managers for the Church of Ireland, Methodists and Presbyterians, which presumably dated from the same time. There was curious discussion about the personal interests of teachers, given their claims for increased remuneration and better conditions of service, where 'the managers collectively and individually were always most helpful and cooperative':

> *The support given by the ecclesiastical authorities to the salary campaigns launched by the [INTO] from time to time under the British and Irish governments helped materially to create public opinion in favour of the teachers and was much appreciated by the Organisation.*

Taking McCulloch's (2004) advice, there may well be inconsistencies and contradictions in O'Connell's narrative, where the whole may be self-serving if not self-deceiving. This was to all appearances in his discussion of two further matters: firstly, teachers' fight for civil rights, which were not specified although they were named in a previous INTO pamphlet entitled *Eighty Years of Progress*[20] to do with teachers' full rights as citizens, with an oblique reference to universal franchise granted in 1919, and eligibility to stand for Parliament and local administrative bodies. O'Connell truncated civil rights to the matter of managers' opposition to teachers as elected members of the Oireachtas coupled with the 'character query', which had to be testified by the manager four times in every year, but added nothing in terms of analysis much less objections.

Secondly, O'Connell named the 'the fight made by the [INTO] against *the disabilities* inflicted by the Department on women teachers through Rule 92(j), the marriage ban, and enforced retirement at 60' (emphasis added). He included the proviso that these matters got no support from the ecclesiastical authorities, but added nothing of his own view on women forced to resign on marriage. This was perhaps indicative of disquiet and resentment among politicians and male trade unionists at the rising number of women in industry (see Owens, 2005). Despite O'Connell's boasts about his work of special interest to historians and students of history, these two select items exemplify the way Irish national schools at the time were fashioned in accord with a political economy managed by clerics who placed constrictions on the practising teacher and the learning of children. This is not to forget the complexities of edu-politics that confronted if not confounded the INTO, which is continuous with the present given the waning of the Catholic Church's influence.

Conclusion

This chapter has also done much to explore different theorisations of teacher status marked by deliberations on forms of professionalism, including alternatives to regulated professionalism. It showcased teacher activism in some watershed moments of mid-twentieth-century Ireland: the 1946 teachers' strike, which attracted such vitriol from conservative politicians who in turn created such a negative atmosphere that provoked the Dublin teachers' return to work. That teachers acted decisively on McQuaid's advice in the interests of children and local communities and collectively on their occupational concerns was prescient of Whitty's (2008) collaborative professionalism. There was also the 1944 vote of no confidence in the INTO CEC, which had such a damaging effect on morale of teachers, yet in 1947, *A Plan for Education* was launched very much in the national interest. That teachers acted democratically in the wake of World War II and in middle of adversity foreshadowed what McCormick (1996) said:

> *It did, however, mark the emergence of a force of increasing power in the field of education in the 1950's and since.*

Skinnider was such a spirited egalitarian, along with other names from that era, but as Rooney (2016) intimated, the challenge is to ascertain what made them so. It is instructive to revisit the idea of progress, especially as it featured in the title of the INTO's (1948) publication on *80 Years of Progress* and then O'Connell's (1968) *100 Years of Progress*. This points to theorising teachers organising in relation to [gendered] power relations and interactions with the nationalist causes promulgated by the State, by then officially described as the Republic of Ireland given the 1948 *Republic of Ireland Act*. Yet Lukacs (2005) drew attention to the democratic and liberal idea of 'progress' in Europe and what happened in the second half of the twentieth century when the authority of and respect for the State, a creation of the modern age, began declining. The contributing factors were the obvious limitations of the territorial sovereignty of states in an age of air and space travel, the increase in international commerce and trade, the increasing movement of goods and people and the existence of international, or more precisely, inter-state and super-state institutions. Then there was the often evident dissatisfactions of the masses of people with the cumbrous and sometimes stultifying bureaucratic nature and uniformitarian institutions of modern states. It must be asked if this holds for Irish national schools as they moved into the second half of the twentieth century, particularly in view of Lee's (1989) note that emigration would reach unprecedented levels. It happened that in the period 1945–1960 Ireland would boast the highest rate of female emigration of any European country.

Notes

1 See www.bbc.co.uk/history/historic_figures/de_valera_eamon.shtml.
2 As noted in the last chapter, 'the State' was shorthand, but the official reference was changed after the 1937 Constitution of Ireland or Bunreacht na hÉireann with

the Republic of Ireland Act 1948 (No. 22 of 1948) as an Act of the Oireachtas, which declared that Ireland may be officially described as the Republic of Ireland.

3 Co-author John Carr shared his recollections of Peadar O Donnell, a national teacher from Donegal, a trade unionist, novelist, journalist and socialist republican who was active in the Black and Tans (former soldiers recruited by the British government to assist the Royal Irish constabulary) during the war of independence in Ireland and opposed to the Treaty in 1921. He was a radical socialist who strived for a workers socialist republic in the tradition of James Connolly. The student teacher cohort in St Patrick's Training College during 1965–1967 had a standing invitation to meet Peadar O Donnell on Sunday at noon in the Gresham Hotel, where he would enthral with stories from his past, no doubt to radicalise these student teachers towards socialist ideals.

4 It is interesting to read Ronan Fanning's (2015) article 'Why Is Éamon de Valera so Unpopular on Both Sides of the Irish Sea?' in *The Irish Times* dated 24 November 2015. www.irishtimes.com/culture/books/ronan-fanning-why-is-%C3%A9amon-de-valera-so-unpopular-on-both-sides-of-the-irish-sea-1.2441872; also see Fanning's (2015) book, *Éamon de Valera: A Will to Power*. Faber and Faber.

5 An interesting note on the origins of the word 'to strike' is to be found in Pelling (1963) p. 19 who noted that in the sense of 'stoppage of work' it was apparently an innovation of the early nineteenth century. However, the phrase 'strike to work' was used in the eighteenth century presumably as an analogy of a ship striking sail.

6 It is noticeable that in all these photographs, teachers were dressed in professional garb: the men in suits and ties and the women in frocks with hat and gloves. Wow, so fashionable, but what does this say?

7 Gaelic games have been played in Croke Park since the establishment of the Gaelic Athletic Association (GAA) in 1884. Although originally a racecourse and sports ground it was purchased by the GAA in 1908 and incrementally developed over time into one of the finest stadiums in the world, a major feat for an amateur organisation which promotes Gaelic and Hurling Games. This stadium was the site of the 1920 massacre known as Bloody Sunday, best captured in the heading 'Bloody Sunday 1920 in Croke Park – 90 seconds of shooting that changed Irish-British History'. This was for an online book review of Michael Foley's (2014) *The Bloodied Field*. The O'Brien Press. See www.the42.ie/bloody-sunday-1920-1767626-Nov2014/.

8 This seems extraordinary given Derrig trained as a teacher: see J. J. Lee (1989) p. 134.

9 It is immensely interesting to read the home page of the Fianna Fáil party, which is a showcase of its history and party structures like the Women's network but also contemporary policy concerns in a list of items said to be of concern to the voting public, including Brexit and education: see www.fiannafail.ie/

10 It is likewise immensely interesting to read an online article dated 16 July 2016, 'Clann na Poblachta – Founded 70 Years Ago This Week' by Shane MacThomáis, who provides a potted history of this party that lasted only 19 years in mainstream politics accompanied by a pictorial representation of an INTO flyer titled 'Political Parties and the Teachers' from 1946; see www.anphoblacht.com/contents/26209.

11 As noted in the previous chapter, this resulted in the INTO calling for two conferences in 1922 and 1926, not to forget the agitation between INTO and de Valera's Fianna Fáil Government in regard to role of the inspectorate in implementing teacher efficiency ratings system especially linking of efficiency ratings of teachers with proficiency in Irish. There was also the promulgation of a Revised

Programme of Primary Instruction in 1934 to 'make for more rapid progress and more effective work in the teaching of Irish and in the development of teaching through Irish', and the establishment of the INTO 'Committee of Inquiry into the Use of Irish as a Teaching Medium to Children whose Home Language is English' in 1941, which lends itself to a sample documentary study.

12 See Memoranda from Minister for Finance on Derrig's offer, S.P.O 18 Dec. 1944, S10236.
13 This was likely a reflection of the thorny question of the restoration of the Irish language which had dominated edu-political relations between the INTO and governments over the previous 25 years and which was deemed 'perhaps the most controversial of all our educational questions'. The title in English is *A Plan for Education*; notwithstanding, it devoted 20 pages to the Irish language question.
14 This was the official journal of the INTO after the *Irish Teachers' Journal* ceased publication in 1904.
15 These views expressed by de Valera were tracked to Minister Derrig in the course of a resumed Dail Debate on Wednesday 18 April 1945 on a private Deputies Business (2048) motion on the establishment of a Council for Education (Dáil Éireann Debate Vol 96, No. 20 p. 25): http://oireachtasdebates.oireachtas.ie/debates%20authoring/debateswebpack.nsf/takes/dail1945041800025?opendocument.
16 See the poster headed Fáilte go Corr na gCoillte or Welcome to Cornagilta, the ancestral homeland of the Easter Week 1916 heroine Margaret Skinnider; see http://tydavnet.com/tag/margaret-skinnider-appreciation-society/.
17 Ó Snodaigh is a TD or Teachta Dála akin to 'Member of Parliament' or 'Member of Congress' elsewhere, one of two Sinn Féin candidates in the Dublin South Central constituency which was twice re-elected to the Dáil following his first election in 2002. According to the Sinn Féin party website, he is spokesperson on social protection and party whip, recently successful in getting all-party support for his report opposing the downgrading of social welfare payments into a single lowest common denominator payment. He has been central to drafting and presenting Sinn Féin's alternative, anti-austerity budgets, as well as publishing major policies on disability rights and opposing JobBridge. Ó Snodaigh also introduced several Dáil motions to reverse government social welfare cuts effecting the elderly, disabled, lone parents and children in particular, and the first Gender Recognition Bill, which successfully led to full gender recognition by the Irish state; see www.sinnfein.ie/aengus-o-snodaigh.
18 Rooney (2016) posited that the majority of the executive of Clann na Poblachta had been in the post-Treaty Irish republican Army.
19 O'Connell' (1968) prologue is devoted to sketching the history of the National Board of Education.
20 This pamphlet, less that A5 size and 20 pages long, was published by the INTO in 1948, with a cover note: 'A Brief Account of the INTO and of the Benefits Derived from Membership'. Even though the author is not named, it too is another sample source ripe for documentary research especially given the curious continuity of its title with O'Connell's (1968) book.

Part 3

The practical politics of teachers' organising

Section essay: the practical politics of teachers' organising

This section highlights the practicalities of teachers organising given edu-politics in the present but not before a foray into its forerunners in the mid-late twentieth to early twenty-first centuries, which are all within living memory. It continues to speak to union-active teachers bound up with INTO struggles for teachers' status and professional standing, notably around salary claims. This is crucial given they are confronted by arguments from Minister for Finance Paschal O'Donohoe in the Kenny-Varadkar Fine Gael-led minority coalition government (2016–present) in talks on the 2017 pay agreement 'Public Service Stability Agreement'. At the same time, the concern is to pinpoint conflictual matters in Bruton's *Action Plan for Education* but also for the Teaching Council given efforts that threaten these arrangements. This is best helped by a look back to the roots of the extant edu-political settlement that was so hard won given efforts to establish the 2001 Teaching Council Act for *An Chomhairle Mhúinteoireachta*.

Ghale and Beckett (2013) provided something of a template for teachers' politicisation. This could be considered a strategy to mentor and support practitioners to stand up for teaching as an intellectual activity and participate in edu-politics at the micro- and macro-levels where power struggles are being played out. They too demonstrated the work of a practising teacher cum teacher unionist with an academic partner, albeit in England as it happened. There a radical-conservative neoliberal experiment was then spearheaded by the Cameron-Clegg Conservative-Liberal Democrat Coalition Government (2010–2015). Ghale and Beckett could see merit in building collective intelligence to insist on what was then required to deliver quality teaching to ensure equitable academic and social learning outcomes for all students whatever their family and social background. Plus, they took the opportunity to articulate the interconnections between research, theory, policy and practice in teaching and teacher education, whether located in schools and/or the university. They should have added teacher unions.

The INTO is reliant on teachers' critical understanding of how power works in twenty-first century Irish edu-politics. Teachers' politicisation is crucial, given the tasks at hand to confront the root cause of teachers' disquiet, resistances, protests and challenges to myriad 'top-down' accounts coupled with imposed policies. It would be beneficial if teachers and academic partners working with allegiance to the INTO could engage with ideas about the best ways to respond politically and strategically – for example, to pressing matters like teachers' alienation from the Teachers' Council, its own representative body, and delays in the development of strategies and policies that should have been realised by a well-functioning Teachers' Council. This is best done when research-active teachers are supported and sponsored to articulate their professional concerns, especially when they have edu-political significance, and they are research-informed.

As the earlier two chapters showed, activist teachers in the early to mid-twentieth century worked in a policy climate framed by a considered sense of national schooling inextricably intertwined with Irish history but also Ireland's sovereignty in the face of regional and global pressures. The social circumstances of teaching married to the complexities of history in Ireland a century ago were remarkable given strikes for independence, civil war, the treaty and partition into north and south. The uncertainty of nationalist government followed into the mid-twentieth century, which came to a peak with civil rights and citizenship once the Republic of Ireland was secured after World War II, as the INTO *80 Years of Progress* document intimated. Ferriter's (2016a) reminder in his INTO keynote is something to carry forward:

> *You are members of a towering trade union that has achieved so much in striking a balance between looking after the interests of its members and serving a progressive approach to education.*

In the next two chapters, which traverse the last 50 years, the focus is on the immediate past that is in the present and on some more 'history from below' scaffolding towards teachers' 'case for the defence'. This third section is intended to practically inform teachers' participation in policy debates about past, present and potential futures. This means negotiating what could be called the contemporary economic-educational complex akin to the military-industrial complex. Raworth (2017) provided some inspiration with the question: 'What if we started economics not with its long-established theories, but with humanity's long-term gaols, and then thought out the long-term economic thinking that would enable us to achieve them?'[1] So it is with economic-educational thinking in Ireland, and it is worth recalling what McCormick (1996) said about 'life in Dublin [which] was not easy in 1946 and no group was more aware of the deprivation which existed than teachers who were dealing with the economic realities on a daily basis'. The same holds in the present about teachers' knowledge of the lived realities of Ireland's political economy in local school communities.

Chapter 5 continues to draw on co-author John Carr's recollections as memory work supplemented by personal records as a teacher (1967–1989) with a particular focus on his designated work as INTO branch officer and member of the INTO CEC. This includes his professional diaries and journals which inform these samples of documentary research, including the 1969 INTO submissions to the Tribunal on teachers' salaries, 1970 INTO Comments on the HEA Report on Teacher Education, 1971 curriculum and 1988 INTO position paper on curriculum prescription. There are lines of continuity in this chapter on teachers' salaries across generations, which has relevance to teachers organising in the present.

Chapter 6 goes further with co-author John Carr's recollections as memory work and his collections of documentary source material as trade union official in the INTO (1989–2010) with a particular focus on his designated work towards *Comhairle Múinteoireachta. A Teaching Council*. This provides much insight into Ireland's edu-political machine, given he was instrumental to negotiations on social partnerships and the conceptualisation and rationale for the Teaching Council: the 1990 INTO letter on the Teaching Council and the 1994 proposal. This foreshadows another critical look at Bruton's *Action Plan for Education*, but this time the select items are school self-evaluation, *Droichead* or induction and *Cosán*, the first national framework for teachers' learning.

These two chapters exemplify the necessity for teachers' research-informed knowledge about contemporary Ireland's edu-politics as the INTO responds to GERM and Brexit and the possibility of a new settlement given reflections on the predicament for teachers and democracy in Ireland. Northern Ireland's Democratic Unionist Party made an agreement with the May Conservative Government (2017–present) after the UK-wide election in June, 2017, to maintain a Westminster majority among other developments to support its neoliberal agenda. Such professional knowledge should stand research-active teachers, academic partners and the INTO in good stead, especially in the face of threats to democracy. It remains to be seen if Held's (2006) claim a decade ago would still hold in the foreseeable future in regard to the locus of power:

> *In the mid-1970s, over two thirds of all states could reasonably be called authoritarian. This percentage has fallen dramatically; less than a third of all states are now authoritarian, and the number of democracies has grown. Democracy has become the leading standard of political legitimacy in the modern era.*
>
> (Held 2006, p. x)

Note

1 This question was put in a review of Raworth's (2017) book, *Doughnut Economics: Seven Ways to Think Like a 21st Century Economist*, by Richard Toye in *The Guardian Review*, Saturday 10 June 2017.

5 Ireland in the global neoliberal policy regime

Introduction

INTO General Secretary T. J. O'Connell (1968) was of the view that the centenary years were years of unremitting effort, and the INTO's reputation hard won and long in coming. As he put it, 'Slowly but surely it has improved conditions in the teaching service, and it now had a voice in the planning and shaping of education'. This was no doubt also a credit to the resolute women who worked side-by-side with the men, where the focus on collective teachers' voice is crucial in any critical discussion of ongoing power struggles. However, if the work of teacher unions was simply a matter of giving voice to teachers, their need for organising would have been met long ago.

Teachers' voice can be a seductive notion without due regard to the details of the way the Irish state is structured to relate to the main organised interests in Irish society (see Hardiman, 2012). This connects with co-author John Carr's critical reflections on the slow but unwitting embrace of vernacular forms of global neoliberalism in a process described by Ball (2013a) as 'other to myself'. This was a way to describe what it means to be a teacher in the twenty-first century, which is a reminder of what might be involved in politicising teachers cognisant of the complex power relations in Irish governance and edu-politics. It fills in the blank spaces of policy learning in education, more often than not conjoined with the cycles of boom and bust.

It happened in the mid-twentieth century that economic activity of unprecedented proportions occurred as Ireland transformed into a more industrialised nation.[1] Education was destined to play a greater role in this economic regeneration as evidenced by the Lemass Fianna Fáil Government's 1958 *Programme for Economic Expansion*, which emphasised 'education as an economic investment rather than taking the traditional view of education as a consumer service' (Coolahan, 1981). The 1963 *Second Programme for Economic Expansion* was more explicit: 'Since our wealth lies ultimately in our people, the aim of educational policy must be to enable all individuals to realize their full potential as human persons'. It went on to see education more in economic investment terms: 'Even the economic returns from investment in education and training are likely to be as high in the long-run as those from investment in physical capital' (O'Sullivan, 2005, p. 13).

This chapter sketches some of that policy discourse in the forerunners to the present, where there are lines of continuity with the past. For example teachers' salaries featured in the 1946 teachers' strike and subsequently as a mechanism for settling points of contention between the INTO and government. What follows is yet another sample of documentary research that sheds light on some groundbreaking work by the INTO on teacher status tied to notions of professionalism that was years in the making:

- 1969 INTO Submissions to the Tribunal on Teachers' Salaries
- 1970 INTO Comments on HEA Report on Teacher Education
- 1971 curriculum
- 1988 INTO position paper on curriculum prescription.

These are the evidentiary bases for research-informed policy advocacy which could be developed to inform current INTO policy debates about national schools harnessed to the future of Ireland. But this is not the half of it given international agencies also influence educational thinking in Ireland. In particular there was the United Nations Organization for Education, Science and Culture, the OECD and, nearer home, the National Industrial and Economic Council. For example, the OECD (1965) report, *Investment in Education*, highlighted deficiencies and inequalities in the Irish education system, which prompted a plethora of political responses by the Lynch Fianna Fáil Government (1965–1969): the abolition of the primary certificate examination, the introduction of free post-primary education, the provision of free transport as an equality of opportunity measure and the redesign of new school buildings, among other major initiatives.

1969 INTO submissions to the Tribunal on Teachers' Salaries

Co-author John Carr had much to say about the matter of teachers' salaries. As one of a group of newly qualified activist teachers (1967–1989), he was acutely aware of the INTO leadership at the time dealing with a string of salary disputes, which ultimately led to his election as INTO branch officer. Although the 1946 teachers' strike ended in defeat, for the INTO, it had a profound effect on the subsequent activities of the organisation. According to O'Buachalla (1988, p. 95) 'The internal cohesion generated by the strike and the depth of public support which it attracted gave a new strength to the INTO'. The spirit of the strike had been kept alive by the new generation of INTO leaders which emerged after the strike, most notably General Secretaries Dave Kelleher (1949–1967) and Seán Brosnahan (1967–1978) and General Treasurer Matt Griffin (1966–1978).

Under their leadership, INTO pay policy was directed at restoring relativities with civil servants and with pursuing 'status' claims to eliminate the disparity in salaries between primary and post-primary teachers. Again, according to O'Buachalla (1988, p. 96), primary teachers 'resented deeply the differential status and the public esteem which was implied in the salary differentials which existed between themselves, vocational and secondary teachers'. This was stark given the Association of Secondary Teachers (ASTI) persistently argued, 'The greater length of their pre-service training, the fact that secondary teacher qualifications were university awards and the academic level of their work entitled them to more favourable salary arrangements than the national or vocational teachers' (Coolahan, 1984, p. 244).

It happened that the report of the Burnham Committee in England, which granted pay parity to primary and post-primary teachers in 1947, gave added impetus to the INTO's demands for pay parity. However, primary teachers' hopes were quickly dashed when the recommendations of a Committee on National Teachers' Salaries, set up under Judge Roe in early 1949 by Costello/Norton Fine Gael, Labour et al Coalition Government (1948–1951) Minister for Education General Richard Mulcahy, were rejected by the government. INTO's expectations on pay parity were further eroded when Mulcahy informed the INTO in December 1954 that he could not accept the principle of pay parity for all teachers (Moroney, 2007, p. 158). Reacting angrily to this rebuke to the status of primary teachers, the INTO embarked upon a major salary 'status' campaign resulting in a series of 'leapfrogging' pay settlements which continued well into the next decade.

It also happened that two unsuccessful 'status' claims were submitted by the INTO to the National Teachers Arbitration Board in 1955 and 1957. In 1958, a Teachers' Salary Committee failed to resolve the salary differentials and although the INTO succeeded in narrowing the pay gap to 89.4% of a secondary teachers' salary; in November 1961, this was negated by the subsequent granting of salary awards to post-primary teachers in March 1962. In response, the INTO lodged another unsuccessful 'Status Salary Claim' on 28 September 1962. In November 1963, the INTO succeeded in narrowing the relativity of scale salaries between primary and post-primary teachers to 94% of a secondary teachers' salary.

The INTO settled another 'status' claim in February 1964, according to the INTO CEC Report 1963–1964, only to discover soon afterwards that secondary teachers had negotiated a secret salary deal with the Catholic Headmasters Association (CHA) which materially altered the relativities in the salaries paid to primary and post-primary teachers. This prompted the INTO to lodge a second claim in December 1964, but it rejected the salary offer that emerged in February 1965. This convinced the Lemass led Fianna Fáil Government (1965–1969) to offer a common scheme of Conciliation and Arbitration for all teachers. This offer too was rejected by the INTO in January 1967 pending the resolution of the primary teachers' parity claim.

In order to resolve the ongoing fraught teacher industrial relations atmosphere arising from continuous salary 'status' settlements the Lynch Fianna Fáil Government (1966–1969) Minister for Education Donagh O'Malley appointed an ad hoc salary tribunal on 15 December 1967. This was chaired by Louden Ryan,[2] Professor of Political Economy at Trinity College Dublin, to recommend a common basic scale of salary for teachers in national, secondary and vocational schools and to recommend what appropriate additions might be made to the basic scale in respect of qualifications, length of training, nature of duties etc. Interestingly, the Association of Secondary Teachers of Ireland (ASTI) was reluctant to participate in the Tribunal initially because the terms of reference implied acceptance of the principle of the common basic scale for all teachers (Coolahan, 1984, pp. 248–249).

The INTO presented evidence to the Tribunal on two occasions: 17 January 1968 and 24 February 1968, which were subsequently published in the 1967–1968 CEC's report to the 1968 INTO Annual Congress in Killarney. This provides the archival source material for this sample documentary case story, which indicates teachers' persistent demands to unite the teaching profession through the elimination of salary differentials. This also sheds light on the edu-politics and matters negotiated at the time to help politicise Irish teachers engaged in salary disputes in the present.

INTO first submission: 17 January 1968

In its first submission, which was reproduced in the CEC Report, 1967–68 to the 1968 Congress in Killarney, the INTO welcomed the establishment of the Tribunal as the first opportunity 'for a realistic rationalisation of the teachers' salaries situation' and a 'unique chance of bringing about some measure of unity and harmony in the profession'. 'Such a process is long overdue' the INTO contended in order to eliminate what Dr McQuaid, Archbishop of Dublin, described as 'the insensate rivalry between the various categories engaged in teaching' and alleged that 'The rivalry and disharmony which [have] existed between the various groups of teachers in the past [has] not helped to improve the prestige of the profession'. Stressing the concern of the educational service with the 'complete development of the human being' the INTO highlighted the fundamental importance of the teaching service as 'a key factor in the quality of education':

> No system of education can rise above the level of the teachers.

The significance of attracting and retaining the best calibre of teachers was emphasised along with the importance of equating teacher status with the provision of 'a rewarding future by way of remuneration' and warned that 'to offer salaries which compare unfavourably with those paid to others in the community, [is] to exclude the best and attract the second-rate'. Referring to ample evidence of resentment with the prevailing differential between the salaries of primary and post-primary teachers and the low official status accorded to the work of primary teachers' the INTO contended that

> there has always been considerable volume of discontent among teachers because of the inadequacy of their salaries and the denial of status commensurate with the importance of their work . . . The time [is] now opportune to eradicate this discontent.

INTO repeatedly referred in its submission to the denial of status accorded to primary teachers:

> *In order, therefore, that a proper spirit of enthusiasm should animate the teaching service under the new system it is of vital importance to remove any sense of grievance and frustration which arise from inadequacy of and a denial of status.*

The INTO went on to develop the arguments in favour of the need for a single profession of teaching claiming that education was a gradual process and each stage of a child's education was interdependent and of equal importance and added 'It is logical, therefore to think in terms of a **profession of teaching** with due regard to specialisation' (emphasis in the original).

INTO second submission: 24 February 1968

In the second submission the INTO outlined a wide range of professional issues that members were pursuing including upskilling and knowledge acquisition, engaging in continuous curriculum development, supporting the development of art and craft activities, engagement in supporting the introduction of decimal coinage and the metric system, approval of the principle of amalgamation, examining the impending curriculum, supporting the establishment of the Department of Psychology in University College Dublin (UCD), assisting children with special needs, applying group teaching, adapting to new teaching methodologies and changing modes of assessing pupils.

In anticipation of any arguments that might be presented to the Tribunal that the level of teaching at primary level was less arduous and therefore perceived lower in consideration, rank and importance, the INTO argued against differential salaries for teachers:

> *As teaching presents different challenges at different levels, it is impossible to say that one level more arduous than another. Therefore, there is little justification in a salary scale based upon the school in which the teaching is done, or on the age level taught.*

The INTO also challenged the length of training arguments asserting that 'other factors have to be taken into account in assessing the qualification of a national teacher vis-à-vis that of a post-primary teacher' including what it called in a subheading entitled the 'Calibre of the Trainee':

> *The calibre of a student entering the training college is much better than that of most students entering a university.*

This second INTO submission then presented its conception of a common basic scale 'which would be common to teachers possessing the minimum qualifications required to serve in any of the three categories-primary, secondary or vocational'. It outlined the minimum qualifications required for recognition in the various categories of schools and taking into account the arguments based on the following factors:

1. Importance of work;
2. Responsibility;
3. Difficulty of work;
4. Skills required.

Its conclusion was telling: 'There is no justification for discrimination'.

Once completed, the Tribunal's Report was presented to the Lemass/Lynch-led Fianna Fáil Government (1965–1968) Minister for Education Brian Lenihan on 23 April 1968. The Tribunal's key recommendations included a common basic scale for all teachers, a points rating system for determining promoted positions in schools, a common contributory superannuation scheme for all teachers and a common conciliation scheme. While the report of the Tribunal was meant to unify the teaching profession, it sparked off a four year period of industrial conflict and unrest including strike actions. It took until 1973 for the ASTI to accept the implementation of the common basic salary scale, and a new common system of Conciliation and Arbitration became operative on 9 October 1973. The INTO's long-fought demand for pay parity had, at last, been settled.

1970 INTO commentary on HEA report on teacher education

In addition to the elimination of pay differentials with post-primary teachers, another major battle for the INTO on teachers' status tied to notions of professionalism was its long-standing demand that primary teachers should be able to aspire towards full degree status. This too was a long-fought campaign then dating back decades because it was during the passing of the 1908 University Act,[3] for example, that the INTO made repeated efforts to get a clause inserted providing for the affiliation of the Training Colleges to the Universities. Yet according to INTO President Catherine Mahon (1914),

> *Their efforts were fruitless, mainly no doubt, owing to financial considerations, but also in some measure to public apathy and to the secret opposition of the class of 'patriots' who hold up their hands in the pious horror at the idea of 'the unwashed, unkempt child' of the bog and the glen wasting his time on self-culture.*

Mahon was also critical of Teacher Training Colleges at the time which she claimed were 'mainly grinding institutions for the passing of a Certificate Examination, with just a modicum of what is called practice thrown in, and no attempt to specialise in educational methods'. She did, however, temper her judgement claiming,

> *It would be unfair to hold the Training Colleges entirely or to any large extent responsible for this. They must cater for the National Board's requirements, and if they get students with a low minimum of attainments, and have to make them up in a score of subjects in two years, they can afford no time for general culture of particular specialisation.*

Little progress was made before the INTO convened a conference in February, 1923, involving the INTO and representatives from University College Dublin (UCD), University College Cork (UCC) and University College Galway (UCG) to discuss the question of university training for teachers. It was agreed between the parties at the conference that

> *on or after a date to be determined, a professional degree [shall] be a necessary qualification for first recognition of a national teacher and that the duration of the course [shall] be four years.*

Confident of success, the INTO CEC informed the 1924 INTO Annual Congress in Dublin 'that the Senate of NUI had at last agreed on the broad lines of a scheme which if put into operation would secure for future teachers . . . the benefits of University education and training' (INTO Commentary on HEA Report). It only remained then for the Cosgrave Cumann na nGaedheal minority government (1923–1929) to put the scheme into operation, and apparently there had been every reason to hope that no difficulty would be encountered here for Minister for Education Professor Eoin McNeill had already said 'let the teachers and the University authorities agree on a scheme and then bring it to Government' (INTO Commentary on HEA Report)

Despite such an assurance, McNeill failed to address the matter, and it happened that for the next 40 years, repeated attempts by the INTO to pursue the 1923 Conference agreement on the degree status for national teachers were unsuccessful (O'Connell, 1968, p. 400). This was not surprising because, according to Coolahan (2017, p. 150), higher education did not feature prominently in public consciousness during the first four decades after independence. From 1960 onwards, however, it was accepted that 'the whole question of higher education, which would form a crucial element in the planned socio-economic development of the state, needed to be examined' (Coolahan, 2017, p. 150).

It happened that in 1960, the Lemass Fianna Fáil Government (1959–1961) Minister for Education Patrick Hillary established a Commission on Higher Education to undertake a comprehensive survey of higher education in Ireland, the first such commission to be established since Irish independence. The Commission concluded its report in 1967 and while it recommended that the period of training for national teachers should be extended to three years, it proposed that the Training Colleges should be associated with 'new colleges' to be established in Dublin and in Limerick. This was rejected by the INTO based on its policy that teacher training should be linked to the universities.

Then in 1968, the Lynch Fianna Fáil Government (1966–1969) established the Higher Education Authority (HEA)[4] to inquire into and make recommendations in relation to university, professional, technological and higher education generally. The INTO was to be afforded the opportunity to contribute to the HEA's final report, but it was never consulted. Despite this major snub, the INTO decided to issue a commentary on the findings of the HEA's 1970 Report on Teacher Education, a summary of which was published in the INTO CEC Report to the 1971 INTO Annual Congress in Tramore. The INTO's summary commentary provides the source material for this sample documentary research case story because it was an astute edu-political move by the INTO designed to influence wider public discussions on the future direction of talks on the degree status for primary teachers.

It also happened the INTO was sympathetic to the complexity of the task faced by the HEA's constitutive members,[5] who had been charged with 'encompassing a variety of interests, a variety of institutions, each having developed 'its own traditions and, dare one say, its own prejudices', each one jealous of its 'traditional autonomy and reluctance to accept new disciplines'. Taking into account the prevailing 'haphazard systems for providing teachers' and the problems facing the HEA, the INTO regarded their report as a document 'of vital importance to the future welfare' of Ireland' and therefore worthy of constructive criticism.

In its opening commentary the INTO reiterated its strongly held view that there was 'a distinct relationship between educational standards and the calibre of those who serve the system' and added,

No system of education can rise above the competence and enthusiasm of its teachers and no nation with any regard for its future can neglect teacher education. A nation which does not recruit persons of the highest quality, and give the best possible education for teaching, can never rise above mediocrity.

Two areas were highlighted as important to the INTO to ensure continuation of the highest standards:

a) Parity of financial treatment for student teachers with university students;
b) A challenging and worthwhile course leading to an acceptable professional qualification.

The INTO commentary reported that a proposal by the HEA to establish *An Foras Oideachais* or the Education Foundation[6] was greeted 'with widespread approval among members of the INTO'. The INTO fully supported the proposed duties assigned to *An Foras Oideachais* especially how best to educate teachers; to supervise their training; to foster, encourage and promote the educational and professional interests of teachers; and to 'advise the Minister for Education and other competent authorities on all these matters'. While the INTO was favourably disposed to the majority of the proposed functions assigned to *An Foras Oideachais*, paragraphs 11, 12 and 17 of the HEA Report (on pages 13, 14, 15 and 17) raised 'fundamental issues for the INTO regarding the institutional arrangements for teacher education and the nature of the qualification to teach'.

Acknowledging that there was 'only one art of teaching which can be varied according to the particular age group taught', the INTO argued that there should therefore 'be only one basic training and qualification in teaching and that qualification should have its origin in the university'. In support of its argument, the INTO cited a prevailing belief among educationalists 'that the linking of Training Colleges with Universities would be beneficial to teachers and education at all levels'. Also in support of its case the INTO outlined the vital role of the teacher in a changing society where, in the past, 'education was mainly the affair of the family and standards were patterned on the moral order of the community'. In order to fulfil that important role 'the teacher of the future must be, not alone a person highly skilled in the art of teaching, but [he] must also be a person of broad vision, and deep appreciation of [his] status and [his] function (sic)'. The gendered language to one side, this was the nub of the 'inferior' status which national teachers perceived to be due to the nature of their qualifications:

> *That teachers generally do not have that complete feeling of confidence in the prestige of their own qualifications is illustrated by the fact that year after year the Annual Congress of the I.N.T.O. has called for university training for teachers.*

The INTO acknowledged the following statement contained in the HEA's Report regarding the award of degree status to primary teachers:

> *A degree is the qualification for most professions and the view is held and more widely that primary teachers, who form the very base of the educational system, should by way of their training course, be enabled to attain to this qualification.*

The INTO, however, expressed surprise in its summary commentary that the 1970 HEA Report did not recommend that the degree for primary teachers should be awarded by one of the existing universities. It proposed instead that the conferring authority should be a proposed Council for National Awards (CNA) in consultation with *An Foras Oideachais*. It was likely clear to the INTO that, whereas the 1970 HEA Report was advocating that the place for teacher education was within the university structure, it was also suggesting an alternative mode of graduation. This prompted the INTO to warn,

> *It would be disastrous if the finger of suspicion could be pointed at either the nature of the qualification or the status of the conferring authority or, if society at large, and the whole teaching profession in particular, were not absolutely convinced of the high merit of the qualification and of the unquestionable academic prestige of the conferring authority.*

In the concluding remarks of its summary commentary, the INTO restated its belief that 'the ultimate goal should be the placing of teacher education within the University structure regardless of what interim steps may be immediately decided upon to improve the current situation'. As an addendum to this documentary case story it is worthwhile noting that following the 1971 INTO Annual Congress in Tramore, Co Waterford discussions continued between the INTO and representatives of individual Training Colleges, (renamed Colleges of Education) culminating in a meeting with all the colleges on 4 April 1972. Achieving agreement on the establishment of degree status for primary teachers was not possible because of the divergence of views that emerged between the different colleges on issues such as the duration, structure and the nature of the terminal qualification.

Further, it happened that the Cosgrave-Corish Fine Gael-Labour Coalition Government (1973–1977) Minister for Education Richard Burke promised in his address to the 1973 INTO Annual Congress in Wexford to introduce a three-year course, leading to a university degree. This evidently followed agreement with the universities according to the INTO Central Executive Committee Report to 1974 INTO Annual Congress in Kilkenny. Likewise, according to the INTO Central Executive Committee Report to the 1976 INTO Annual Congress in Killarney, the Senate of the National University of Ireland (NUI) at its meeting on 17 April 1975, decided that St Patrick's College, Our Lady of Mercy College and Mary Immaculate College of Education would be accepted as Recognised Colleges of the NUI. The Colleges of Education were authorised to provide degree courses for students to be validated by the NUI and conferred by the recognised Colleges. Finally, the INTO Central Executive Committee concluded with the remark,

> *Since 1908 a campaign for the inclusion of Colleges of Education within the Universities, has been carried on, and it is with very great pleasure that we now record the success of that campaign.*

1971 Curriculum

Co-author John Carr again had much to say about the 1971 curriculum, which became known as the 'New Curriculum', having replaced the 1922 National Programme of Instruction, revised in 1926 and 1934. As such it was in operation in Ireland's national schools for almost 50 years. The INTO responded positively to the development and implementation of the 'New Curriculum' given a shared commitment to a view of the child as learner and, crucially, of the teacher charged with mediating its underlying principles and philosophies. This was considered important as it enabled the INTO to comprehend the effects of the changing economic, social and cultural environment on curriculum policy, which simultaneously contained a perspective on the level of freedom available to teachers to exercise their professional judgements and discretions. The INTO was certainly alert to any emerging attitudes or trends towards the recognition of the status of teachers tied to the professionalisation processes.

This preliminary narrative proved useful to this sample documentary research into an unpublished paper by Inspectorate staff member Seamus de Buitléir (1985), *Towards a General Theory of Curriculum and Evaluation*. This foolscap-size, bound, 135-page, typed document is more a personal archive of de Buitléir's work, as noted in the preface:

> On various steering committees of the primary inspectorate that formulated the rationale of the new curriculum in 1967; which prepared the working document that was circulated by the Department in 1968; and which assumed responsibility for the two volume [Primary Curriculum] teacher's handbooks [Part 1 & 2] associated with the formal introduction of the curriculum in 1971.

De Buitléir (1985) presented his paper to INTO General Secretary Gerry Quigley (1978–1990) on 15 November 1990 with a handwritten inscription in Gaelic on the front cover: 'in fond memory of the days we got to know each other at Barretstown Castle'.[7] This referred to meetings of the Primary Education Review Body, which was established by the government in 1987 to examine all aspects of primary education and reported to the Taoiseach and Minister for Education in 1990. This was in response to INTO demands that a major review be undertaken to examine all aspects of primary education.[8]

De Buitléir's (1985) preface went on the say, 'In these matters I can now be regarded with a certain justification as being an Oisín i ndiaidh na Féinne', which is a proverbial expression that means all the old comrades are long gone. The paper is not easy reading with its flowery language. For example,

> *far from demanding a revolutionary approach to the future servicing of educational provision involving unconditional commitment to an ever-increasing financial investment, the paper takes the line that the task facing us is essentially attitudinal, the proper response to which, in the first instance, lies in a process of careful pruning, grafting and nurturing of what already exists in order to revivify the best of what is native to our own climate and soil.*

This was no doubt a verbose claim that Ireland needed a national curriculum but mindful of international influences and an appeal to consensus, the pronoun 'us' notwithstanding. In the remainder of the preface, de Buitléir recounted his documentary sources as 'a number of histories, records and reports'. Although these were not named at the outset, a cursory reading of the text indicates that this report was soundly research-based with well documented references synchronised with critical reviews of literature. In closing the preface, he was true to form:

> *Always with the aim in mind to create sufficient room for reflection in regard decisions to be made in the near future. To enhance the quality of reflection, extensive quotation is engaged in from certain philosophical writings because of a firm conviction that it is only by being borne aloft on the wings of eagles that*

> *each one of us, wren-like, make the final hop towards the vantage point where he (sic) can have a panoramic view of his (sic) own particular landscape.*

The report contained 16 chapters inclusive of an introduction and conclusion with chapter headings devoted to a wide range of curricular areas: 'Models of Human Behaviour', 'Generative Principles in Irish Education', 'Assessment and Certification: Preliminary Considerations', 'Examination of Curricular Models', 'The Primary School Curriculum', 'The Compulsory School Continuum; Evaluation: Some General Considerations', 'The Question of Public Accountability', 'Strategic Evaluation', 'Responsibility and Decision Making', 'Support Systems in Irish Education', 'The Question of Cost', 'Evaluation at School Level' and 'Assessment and Certification: The Question of Relationship and Balance'.

De Buitléir did not always achieve his desired aim, choosing instead to engage in a series of ramblings and musings albeit from an extremely knowledgeable and informed point of view. His account of the preparations for the 1971 curriculum was enlightening, keenly perceptive and offered vital clues, hitherto unknown but to a few, in regard to the prevailing political and social norms that guided the underlying principles of the then 'New Curriculum'. This included the abandonment of the politically oriented and nationalistic-driven curriculum of the previous 40 years. Interestingly, he borrowed one of the key principles of Catholic Church thought known as 'subsidiarity' to explain:

> *The validity, within limits, of the original political-cultural principle which dominated government policy heretofore (in theory if not in practice since 1948) was fully acknowledged by the Inspectorate, but was regarded by them as subordinate to what they considered to be the over-riding generative educational principle, namely, that each person is of infinite worth.*

This was clearly key to the Catholic Church dominated edu-politics of the era, but licentiously continuing with the religious metaphor, de Buitléir expanded on the point by making a distinction between worth and achievement:

> *It compels us to separate the question of worth from the question of achievement in that it holds each person to be infinite worth not because what he or she does, no matter how impressive or otherwise that my appear to be, but more simply and gratuitously, because he or she is. It follows if this conclusion is taken as a point of departure, that all principles which guide action must seek universal justification.*

It is important to note the inclusive language, but then de Buitléir again referred to the spiritual dimension of the curriculum given he claimed that such experiences influenced the central significant principle in a draft working document which was submitted to the various vested interests:

> *Each human being is created in God's image. He (sic) has a life to lead and a soul to save. Education is, therefore, concerned not only with life but with the*

purpose of life. Since all men (sic) are equal in the eyes of God, each is entitled to an equal chance towards optimum personal fulfilment.

With the inclusive language abandoned, de Buitléir turned his attention to curriculum design and again the primacy of the generative principle of subsidiarity was seen 'to be abundantly rich in its consequential inferences'. He went on in half-a-dozen pages to elaborate on the consequences of adopting a subsidiarity stance in developing the curriculum:

1. It posits 'not merely a child-centred curriculum but a person-to-person living interrelationship based on boundless respect between teacher and child, between teacher and teacher, between child and child and between all humanity';
2. 'It provided the grounds for an integrated curriculum so structured as to take into account of the ways in which communication and learning are made meaningful and enriching and may be adapted to be made continuously more so at the different stages of personal development *for all concerned* in the education process';
3. 'The relationship between first language (a basic tool in personal development, whether used as a means of concept formation, of social communication or of expression) and target language (with its particular dependence on readiness, on motivation and on transfer of learning skills developed in the first language) could now be made explicit';
4. 'In the wider vocational perspective, teaching, like the other established professions, could be clearly identified in this stronger light as an occupation that exists to address complex problems in areas of human *uncertainties* and to have its own set of principles and methodologies'.

As if to give credence to the research bases, de Buitléir cited the early twentieth-century political philosopher Mary Follet's (1868–1933) scientific view of professionalism in support of his argument. As well, he cited the first director of Ireland's Institute of Public Administration Tom Barrington (1980) on 'the urge to professionalism' as one of the 'key systemising forces currently operating in the world'. De Buitléir went on to explain, again quoting Barrington, 'this urge can be stimulated by external pressure; but at heart it comes from internal promptings, from self-consciousness, from the concern for order, rationality, efficacy and style'. Interestingly, de Buitléir also added an addendum:

The urge to professionalism expresses itself characteristically in an ethical code of conduct which, can be identified as an outward manifestation of what might be termed the collegiate professional conscience.

This was all prescient of the INTO's subscription to social partnerships. However, according to de Buitléir, this had a particular bent in that by accepting the concept of subsidiarity it illustrated the divesting of authority to the school and by implication to the teachers, albeit with the caveat of teachers behaving responsibly:

> *Hence, if one accepts the principle of subsidiarity, it follows that the school as the basic organisational unit staffed by responsible professionals, must be the obvious context in which particular curricular and organisational problems affecting the stage of compulsory education will henceforth seek both their specific definition and, when at all possible, their happy resolution.*
>
> (Ibid, p. 6)

Applying the concept of subsidiarity, however, did not entail delegating complete autonomy to the schools. As de Buitléir put it,

> *It hardly needs saying, however, that the principle of subsidiarity here described must relate back to the source from which the implied delegation of authority derives both its validation and its limitation.*

When seen in the light of this documentary evidence, the 'New Curriculum' represented the settlement of two major issues: the question of the Irish language and the status of the teacher who was now seen by Government in a new professional light. This was substantiated in the fact that de Buitléir's views were incorporated into the teacher's handbooks that accompanied the introduction of the 1971 curriculum, particularly those referring to the role of the teacher, who was expected to act in a professional capacity:

> *He [sic] will be expected to know each child as well as he [sic] can, and keep detailed records of his [sic] all-round progress. His [sic] preparation will involve over-all planning of work as well as adequate provision for each stage of learning.*

Even if the Inspectorate and the Department of Education were not then alert to the developing areas of scholarship to do with gender reform and feminist policy priorities and practices, the teacher was expected to keep abreast of educational study and research and to develop expertise to inform his or her practice:

> *His (sic) awareness of the varied needs and interests of his (sic) pupils, and his (sic) appraisal of the environment for the opportunities it provides together with his (sic) general reading and attendance at in-service courses study circles, teachers' centres, and lectures will all help to ensure that the work in each area of the curriculum is planned along suitable lines.*

Although there was much conceptual work to be done in regard gender issues and other inequalities, the 1971 curriculum envisaged a more fully professional role for the teacher unlike the situation that prevailed during the previous 50 years:

> *The added responsibility arising from the changing role of the teacher, will bring its own rewards-a deeper professional consciousness and a greater opportunity for personal fulfilment.*

Any wonder de Buitléir shared his unpublished paper with INTO General Secretary Gerry Quigley (1978–1990). At that point, the backstory on the INTO's call for teacher professionalism stretching back a century was significant[9]: following the enactment of the 1914 Intermediate Education (Ireland) Act, a Registration Council for teachers in Ireland was established in 1918. According to co-author John Carr's research for *Comhairle Múinteoireachta. A Teaching Council*, the INTO demanded that national teachers be represented on the Board of the Registration Council but their demands were rejected.[10] This prompted the INTO to raise the question in the *Irish School Weekly* dated 20 June, 1914, of whether

> the time (has) not arrived when the National Teachers of Ireland should inaugurate a movement for regulating the entrance to their profession? Why should they not, like the medical profession, hold their own examinations and take care that only the qualified pass through the entrance gate to the profession?

Evidently, Irish teachers had long been prepared to engage the discussions and debates to regulate their profession.[11]

1988 INTO position paper on curriculum prescription

The economic activity of unprecedented proportions that had occurred during the mid-twentieth century as Ireland transformed into a more industrialised nation came to a halt with the severe economic crises during the 1980s. This was mainly because of unsustainable expansionary policies which were pursued by successive Irish governments in the previous decade, financed largely from major deficit borrowings (Honohan, 2009; Whelan, 2013). This, in turn, generated fiscal adjustments during the 1980s. The austerity measures which followed, particularly relating to the primary education sector, spread discontent among teachers culminating in labour unrest and sporadic industrial action.[12] This ultimately extended to primary curriculum matters, but again the backstory is crucial.

The INTO was already on alert to any potential threats to primary teachers, who had enjoyed considerable professional and pedagogical freedom subsequent to the introduction of the 1971 curriculum. Then came the 1985 Primary Curriculum discussion document issued by the Curriculum and Examination Board, which contained a proposal that 'sequenced objectives should be formulated for a development programme in certain aspects of the Curriculum'. This fuelled INTO suspicions regarding the type of objectives envisaged, that is, behavioural or expressive objectives, and the potential narrowing of aspects of the curriculum. It should be noted that at the time the Curriculum and Examination Board was dominated by post-primary representatives, who surprisingly chose as their first action to review the Primary Curriculum.

It happened the INTO issued a strongly worded written response to the proposals on national objectives in the 1985 Primary Curriculum discussion document, which was reported in the INTO CEC Report to the 1986 INTO Annual Congress in Tralee. The INTO expressed total opposition 'to the prescription by

Figure 5.1 1988 INTO position paper on curriculum prescription

Source: Primary Curriculum and Related Matters: Report of Conference (https://www.into.ie/ROI/Publications/PublicationsPre2000/PrimaryCurriculum88.pdf). Reproduced by permission of the INTO.

a central body of objectives for a developmental programme for different aspects of the curriculum'. Instead, the INTO supported

> *the maintenance of broad curricular guidelines which allow the teacher to select content appropriate to the skills, aptitudes, interests and stages of the development of the pupils and that schools should be free to select from prescribed curricular guidelines, the appropriate sequential developmental objectives for the children in each class in their schools.*

The INTO added that it was 'not possible to determine such objectives nationally and also take into account the needs of individual children and their homes and school backgrounds'.

Then INTO suspicions about the potential narrow 'back to basics' focus which could gain momentum as a result of the Curriculum and Examination Board's 1985 Primary Curriculum discussion document were confirmed by the decision made in October 1987 by the Haughey Fianna Fáil minority government (1987–1989) Minister for Education Mary O'Rourke to establish a Review Body on the Primary Curriculum. It apparently had a narrow remit to embark on an analysis of the aims and objectives of the 1971 curriculum with particular reference to Irish, English and Mathematics. It was also to examine the structures that could be adopted to ensure that the objectives were being achieved and students' progress evaluated (see 1990 Report of the Review Body on the Primary Curriculum).

Throughout this time too, the validity of the 1971 curriculum principles were the subject of sustained criticism led by two academics, Dr Daniel Murphy (Trinity College Dublin) and Dr Patrick Wall (Our Lady of Mercy College, Dublin), who were apparently overseen by Dr Pádraig Hogan (Maynooth College). Murphy's (1984) first critique entitled 'The Dilemmas of Primary Curriculum Reform' appeared in the 1984 spring issue of *Studies in Education* of which he was joint editor. Dr Murphy expressed grave reservations as to the validity of the principles underlying the 1971 curriculum on the grounds of their philosophical, psychological and pedagogic inadequacy. Hogan (1985) rebutted the claims made by Murphy in the 1985 spring issue of *Studies in Education* and, in the same issue, Murphy wrote a rejoinder to Hogan's article. This was followed by Wall (1986), who made his criticisms in a review of the Curriculum and Examination Board's 1985 Primary Curriculum discussion document, which was published in the 1986 spring issue of the journal *Studies in Education.*

Of particular concern to the INTO was the Department of Education decision to publish both Murphy's and Hogan's articles in *Oideas* 29, 1986, its academic journal designed to disseminate information and ideas about educational issues in Ireland. In preparation for the professional implications arising from any future prescribed curriculum and in order to circumvent threats to teacher autonomy arising from the criticisms of the principles underlying the 1971 curriculum, the INTO directed its Education Committee in May 1985 to generate research evidence on teachers' attitudes to the primary curriculum and its operation in primary schools. A curriculum survey was conducted by the INTO Education

Committee in October 1986, the results of which were presented at the INTO 1987 Education Conference in Bundoran.

The INTO had invited Hogan to give a keynote address to enlighten delegates on ways of confronting the prevailing debate on the 1971 curriculum. Hogan's paper entitled 'They Are Never Idle' – Current Concerns about the 1971 Curriculum' was published by the INTO in a collection edited by INTO Education Officer Charlie Lennon (1982–1988) entitled *Primary Curriculum and Related Matters*, which was coupled with a report of the conference in Bundoran.[13] In his introduction, Lennon declared,

> *The atmosphere in the education service had become one of retrenchment and regression rather than one of development.*

It is Hogan's paper, amounting to 5,710 words, that is the target of this sample documentary research case story: not only because he waded into the 'battle of ideas' on the strength of his apparent belief in primary teachers' capacity for curriculum theorising but also his criticisms of politicians' efforts to overturn the edu-political settlement on primary curriculum and embed a new curriculum orthodoxy. A close study is required, but it can be said this seemingly coincided with the introduction of vernacular forms of global neoliberal reforms and the GERM, which was becoming apparent in other nations (see Beckett, 1996). Hogan alluded to the 'New Educational Virtuousness' engulfing certain elements of the traditionalist movement's thinking in Ireland which could, he warned, 'readily recommend itself as educational probity in the uncertain and straitened circumstances in which our schools [are] placed at [present]'. He was unrestrained in his criticism of the new educational piety:

> *To put it frankly, the new educational virtuousness is that of crass efficiency rather than that of the energetic and disciplined imagination.*

Hogan identified three areas of concern relating to the 1971 curriculum:

1. Criticisms inspired by ideological considerations;
2. The political imperatives of current economic realities;
3. Parental and public anxieties.

Each of the three areas had, according to Hogan, an urgent significance for the INTO because of what he perceived as 'the most determined attempts being undertaken [by government] to identify where further savings to the Exchequer might be made' (p. 7). 'Regrettably', Hogan asserted, 'informed and disciplined *educational* debate has invariably been the first casualty whenever, as the phrase puts it, 'the debate got politicized'. Hogan advised teachers to establish more 'firm links' with parents regarding the 'educational interests of their children and in an energetic, enduring way', more, he exhorted, as a 'professional necessity than as a political necessity'.

Hogan proceeded to indicate he was rather 'perplexed' when he read Wall's review in the 1986 spring issue of the journal *Studies in Education*. Hogan quoted it at some length and added that he was 'taken aback not merely by the unwarranted note of certainty in the idiom' but more particularly by the stark inaccuracy of 'the sweeping misrepresentations of scholars like Dewey and Piaget, and by regrettable instances of rhetorical innuendo which was directed without any attempt at substantiation, at the primary curriculum'.

Turning to Murphy's denunciations of the 1971 curriculum in the 1984 spring issue of *Studies in Education* and in the 1985 spring issue of *Studies in Education*, Hogan scrutinised the validity of two of Murphy's assumptions: that the primary curriculum was based on the discredited principles of 'progressivism' and that the philosopher John Dewey was the main author of the 1971 curriculum's 'syllabus of errors'. Firstly, Hogan asserted that the publication of the Department of Education 1951 document entitled *An Naí-Scoil the Infant School*[14] substantially anticipated the child-centred principles contained in the 1971 curriculum. Secondly, Hogan, quoting Richard Peters (1969), who argued that Plowden's (1967) recommendations for primary schools in England would, if carried out, lead to a marked improvement in primary school education'. Thirdly, Hogan stated that 'progressivism' must be sharply distinguished from the more mature, distinctive and enduring philosophy of John Dewey as 'concisely and incisively' expressed in Dewey's (1938) book *Experience and Education*. Finally Hogan stated that Murphy was 'wide of the mark' to suggest that 'progressivism' was the main inspiration of the 1971 curriculum.

Curiously, Hogan agreed with Murphy description of the main features of 'progressivism':

1. The downgrading of the teacher's importance by a 'child-centred' approach;
2. The threat to traditional disciplines of study arising from a so-called integrated curriculum;
3. A neglect of the authority of tradition.

But Hogan went on to argue that Dewey was not guilty of any of these charges, and he quoted extensively from Dewey's (1938) *Experience and Education*. On the contrary, Dewey asserted, 'A more sophisticated and more professional conception of the business of educator'; that Dewey was not attempting to dismantle 'the accepted division of human knowledge in its various disciplines of thought' but persistently maintained that the background and interests of pupils as embodied in the quality and range of their present experiences were the first importance in deciding how to organise and present material for study. Hogan contended that Dewey envisages anything but the displacement of the teacher foreseeing 'more, not less guidance by others' in the child's education. He was opposed to pressing a 'cultural heritage into service for any kind of propaganda or sectional proposes'.

In conclusion, Hogan warned teachers of the dangers of the new educational virtuousness which he observed was 'dazzled by the prospect of results to the singular neglect of consequences' and warned against the ominous prospects of this virtuousness – namely,

1. Centralising of decisions about curricular policy and priorities, with more power being concentrated in the hands of the Department of Education and less in the hands of schools and teachers;
2. Disimprovement in the working conditions of teachers and this in the name of greater efficiency;
3. Downgrading of the professional nature of the teacher's work in a way that is reminiscent of the class distinctions of a former era;
4. Restriction of the range of imaginative experience available to pupils, coupled with a bleaker outlook for the disadvantaged;
5. Restoration of an insistent utilitarian ideology, inspired by a spurious concept of efficiency.

Hogan then suggested ways for teachers and the INTO to forestall these 'looming dangers' and to adopt them as measures for professional self-empowerment, self-criticism and self-enrichment:

1. The development of the 'Plean Scoile' (School Plan) idea to include systematic self-evaluation by the school;
2. A sharing of perspectives, difficulties and ideas on teaching;
3. An open, responsive, personal approach towards parents with built-in safeguards to protect teachers from irrational demands;
4. The promotion of participatory in-service courses by teachers, (including a role for the inspectorate) on issues such as 'shared area', history and geography trails, drama, mixed ability groupings, the principal's role, etc.

Finally, Hogan reiterated earlier advice that co-operation with parents was a political and professional necessity for teachers in Ireland:

> *Co-operation with parents is wrongly viewed as a political necessity however. It is, much more appropriately, an **enduring professional necessity**. The opportunity to make progress towards this end is present now to an unprecedented degree. The mutual trust which can thus be built up will distinguish teaching as a profession in Ireland from the downgraded occupation it has become in those countries to the east and the west of us.*

Conclusion

This chapter also has done much to demonstrate teachers' politicisation marked by the practical politics of campaigning that of necessity had to be responsive to transformations in Ireland's political economy. This continues to characterise the 'battle of ideas' about young teachers' demands for pay parity in the present characterised by consecutive neoliberal governments' programs of austerity. It is a prime example of the ways professionals are directed and constrained by budget cuts and the shrinking of public funding giving rise to gross inequalities.

It would be so beneficial if knowledge of teachers' campaigns that featured in the 1946 INTO Teachers' Strike through to the 1969 INTO submissions to the Ryan Tribunal on Teachers' Salaries could plug into the INTO as it responds to contemporary teachers' demands. These were articulated through resolutions adopted in 2012 INTO Annual Congress in Killarney and reiterated at the 2016 INTO Annual Congress in Wexford: to progress the issue of pay equality imposed by government on new entrant teachers under the 2009 Financial Emergency Measures in the Public Interest Act.

These demands were again reiterated at the 2017 INTO Annual Congress in Belfast, as registered by the INTO Standing Committee responsible for Congress resolutions:

> [That] Congress:
>
> a   deplores the cuts to teacher pay, North and South;
> b   condemns the unilateral approach to recent pay determination in Northern Ireland;
> c   demands full reversal of pay cuts and the re-establishment of pay equality in the Republic of Ireland; and
> d   instructs the CEC to maximise cooperation between members in both jurisdictions to fight for the pay rises that both the workers and the economies require, North and South.

Notes

1 Following the success of Fianna Fáil in the 1957 general election, Séan Lemass took over from de Valera as Taoiseach in 1959. He, along with Secretary of the Department of Finance Ken Whitaker, realised the need to adopt a new government policy to halt economic decline. Together they set about to abandon the notion of 'national' capitalism and self-sufficiency policies and instead rebuild the Irish nation on the basis of foreign direct investment in order to create a more industrialised society. According to Fennell (1983), Lemass articulated the new policy in patriotic and nationalistic terms: 'The historical task of this generation is to secure the economic foundation of independence'. The course of Irish history was changed forever.
2 Other members of the Committee were Ernest Benson, Employers Representative from the Labour Court, Maurice Cosgrave, General Secretary of the Postal Workers' and Trade Union Representative from the Labour Court, Union, Cathal O Shannon and Louis Fitzgerald, former Assistant Secretary in the Department of Finance. Art O'Callanáin, an officer from the Department of Education, acted as Secretary to the Tribunal.
3 The Royal University was the degree awarding body in Ireland operating from 1880 until it was dissolved apropos the 1908 Universities Act. On 31 October 1909, it was replaced by the NUI, which became a federal university situated in Dublin but involving three constituent Colleges: University College Dublin, University College Cork and University College Galway.

4 The HEA was established on an ad-hoc basis in 1968 as a planning, co-ordination and financial body liaising between government and the universities. It was placed on a statutory basis in 1972 and funds the universities, institutions of technology and other third level institutions; see Mulcahy and O'Sullivan (1989).

5 The HEA, established on a statutory basis in 1972, comprised a chairperson, and not more than 18 members, all appointed by the government on the recommendation of the Minister for Education. At least seven of the ordinary members were academic members and at least seven non-academic members; see Mulcahy and O'Sullivan (1989).

6 Co-author John Carr made the connection that many of the duties subsequently assigned to The Teaching Council (2001) were contained in the proposal to establish *An Foras Oideachais*.

7 Barretstown Castle in Kildare was in the estate of the Eustace family, who acquired the castle in the sixteenth century, though it was originally confiscated from the Archbishop of Dublin during the Anglo-Norman invasion in the twelfth century. The castle went through several owners until the British and Canadian business and philanthropist Galen Weston acquired it in 1967. After completing extensive renovations to the house and grounds, he presented the castle and the estate to the Irish Government in 1977. It was used as a meeting and conference centre by the Department of Education until 1994 when it was leased by the Government to Barretstown Gang Camp, part of Paul Newman's 'Hole in Wall Camp' serving children with special needs.

8 The agreement to establish a Review Body formed part of a settlement following a campaign of industrial unrest conducted by the INTO, in conjunction with parents and management authorities, arising from a government decision in 1987 to increase class sizes and impose cuts on primary education. The 21-member Review Body was established in 1987 and reported to government in 1990.

9 In regard to this matter, the issue of teacher status in a state-regulated system had already been raised in the *Irish School Weekly* of 7 September 1907, in an article entitled 'A Profession or a Trade – The Teachers True Mission'. Deploring the fact that 'in the boasted advancement and civilization of the twentieth century the operation of Education Departments are conducted on the principle that education can be produced in quantities like a manufactures commodity, and that the moral side of education is a valueless or negligible element'. The article goes on to outline unfavourable conditions that were hindering the development of teacher professionalism, gender bias notwithstanding:

'The conditions under which they work are unfavourable to development into professionalism. Teachers are too much handicapped and harassed by drastic and unwise rules and regulations and red-tapeism. The teacher is not permitted the scope for the development of his individual view; he has no independence as a teacher. No matter how noble his efforts, how fertile his schemes of working, how self-sacrificing his devotion, he is condemned to hide them from view; he is repressed by the irrepressible'.

10 This is all recounted in the INTO (1994) published booklet, *Comhairle Múinteoireachta: A Teaching Council*.

11 The ongoing commentary in the *Irish School Weekly* indicated that despite INTO disappointment at not being represented on the Registration Council, it had accepted the establishment of the Registration Council as 'a step in the right direction' on the basis that it would 'confer upon the Intermediate (Secondary) teachers a status which otherwise they could not possess'.

12 Three major campaigns were waged by the INTO against government austerity measures during the 1980s, the 1981 Age of Admission to National Schools Campaign (known as the 'Age of Entry Campaign'), designed to reverse the Minister for Education's attempt to increase the school going age from 4 to 4.5 years,

the Teachers' Pay Dispute campaign (known as the 'Teachers United' campaign) calculated to enforce the implementation, in its entirety, of a recent arbitration pay award and the dispute over the infamous Circular 20/87 from the Department of Education to schools promulgating significant increases in pupil teacher ratios, thereby potentially reducing the overall teacher salary budget.

13 This was INTO Education Officer Charlie Lennon's (1988) *Primary Curriculum and Related Curriculum Matters: Report of Conference*, which was an edited document that contained numerous essays organised under a table of contents: introduction by Charlie Lennon; 'They Are Never Idle – Current Concerns about the 1971 Primary Curriculum by Padraig Hogan'; 'Primary Curriculum Survey' by Kieran Griffin on behalf of the INTO Education Committee; 'Recommendations from the Survey' by Patrick Hurley, Cathaoirleach, Education Committee; 'Multi-grade Teaching' by Paul Brennan and Ita McGrath, Education Committee; 'The Educational Implications of Demographic Changes' by Declan Kelleher and Andrew Fenton, Education Committee; 'Reports of Discussion Sessions – Rapporteur's Report, Section One' by Joe Carroll, Education Committee; 'Rapporteur's Report, Section Two' by Teresa Curley, Education Committee; and an appendix on the Bundoran Conference Programme.

14 The Naí-scoil advocated that infant teachers should adopt a more child-centred curriculum approach to teaching: 'Individual differences should be recognised and catered for; 'there should be in the infant school curriculum a blend of individual and group and class activities, individual and group work should predominate'

6 Teachers' case for the defence

Introduction

The INTO invested much in its policy document on the subject of a Teaching Council, but this is not to ignore dissenting voices in the INTO and beyond. There was a 'battle of ideas' over the establishment of a Teaching Council throughout the best part of the twentieth century, marked at the end by the 1998 Education Act.[1] The INTO (1994) booklet *An Chomhairle Mhúinteoireachta. A Teaching Council* was itself a model of policy advocacy. As the INTO General Secretary Joe O'Toole (1994) claimed in the acknowledgements:

> *It could prove to be of the most extraordinary significance for teachers and for educators. Its production was a mammoth task. The research, drafting, discussion, preparation and writing required determination, accuracy, judgement and a lot of raw energy . . .*
> *Michael McGarry chose this as his special project during his Vice Presidency. For John Carr it is the culmination of years of work and study on the professionalism of teachers. Deirbhle Nic Craith, Executive Officer guided and directed progress through many important sections.*

It happened that co-author John Carr wrote and co-wrote many of the documents that informed the development of the Teaching Council during the 1990s. This was during his time as INTO Education Officer (1989–1992), which preceded his term as INTO Assistant General Secretary (1992–1995), Deputy General Secretary (1995–2001) and General Secretary (2001–2010). At the time, Gerry Quigley (1978–1990) then Joe O'Toole (1992–2001) held that office. In fact, Carr wrote a series of papers for the INTO (1992) that proved crucial to the rationale and conceptualisation of the Teaching Council, which intersected with the INTO policy visions for social partnerships and collaborative professionalism.

These are seriously under threat in the present, which brings into focus the policy debates about the (neoliberal) past, present and potential (progressive) futures in regard Ireland's development and modernisation. This includes the empirical particularities of what teachers see in local school communities, which are acute in this present age of globalisation. This is to make the point that the status of teaching even when allied to new visions of teachers' democratic professionalism is not just academic; it is social and political. The evidence to date shows that in Ireland what is now required of teachers is the regulated-regulation of teaching apropos the National Economic and Social Council (2012) 'Smart Regulation' agenda advanced at European level under Ireland's EU presidency in 2013.

Any wonder teachers are feeling overwhelmed with workload and frustrated by the visible turning of events away from the historical record. Part of the problem in Ireland is that there is a dearth of teachers and academic partners doing practitioner research, including documentary research, despite the fact that the INTO not only has a long-standing track record of supporting research-active teachers sharing and publishing reports of teacher inquiries.[2] These are required to strengthen the teacher union's stand on different matters, consistent with the INTO Education Committee and the work of Director of Education and Research Dr Deirbhle Nic Craith (2013–present). She organises annual education research conferences that encourages teachers' research efforts, builds research capacity and uses this research output intelligently.[3] For example, feeding into the Department of Education and Skills (2015) consultation paper, *Advancing School Autonomy in the Irish School System*, the INTO submission noted, 'There has been no call among the education community in Ireland for greater autonomy for schools and there is no evidence to support the proposal that granting schools in Ireland greater autonomy will be of benefit to school communities'.

This chapter comes back to *An Chomhairle Mhúinteoireachta. A Teaching Council*, which provides the backstory to the regulated-regulation of teaching that effectively undermines that earlier edu-political settlement. The aim is to encourage teachers' intellectual activities and boost teacher union research for the INTO communicating grassroots perspectives into consultations and to foreshadow teachers' professional research-informed responses to the never ending stream of government policies. This is intended to apprise both nationally and locally determined comebacks to politicians, policymakers and power brokers and to better equip teachers to 'speak truth to power' and reclaim their stake in Irish national schools and third-level teacher education.

This last tranche of documents homes in on the extant policy ideas amenable to critical policy analyses and includes the following:

- 1990 INTO letter on the Teaching Council
- 1994 *Comhairle Múinteoireachta. A Teaching Council*
- Bruton's *Action Plan for Education* :

    Select items

    1   School self-evaluation
    2   *Droichead* or induction
    3   *Cosán*, the first national framework for teachers' learning

These rhetorical devices are the cornerstones for teachers' 'case for the defence'. In fact, our title for this chapter takes a cue from research-active teacher partners in the north of England,[4] who have not only witnessed the demise of the General Teaching Council in England (2000–2012) but also have to respond to Ofsted inspectors who parse their judgements on school performance with reference only to SATs and GCSE exam results. In response, these teacher partners build their own evidence on the complexities of performativity including poverty effects on students' learning and teachers' working lives. The phrase 'case for the defence' was actually coined by two school Heads and an academic partner who wrote for publication (Gorton, Williams, and Wrigley, 2014).

1990 letter on *Comhairle Múinteoireachta. A Teaching Council*

This letter[5] was ordered by the INTO CEC and prepared by co-author John Carr when he was INTO Education Officer (1989–1992). It was then signed by INTO General Secretary Gerry Quigley (1978–1990) and sent to the Haughey/Reynolds Fianna Fáil Progressive Democrats Coalition Government (1989–1994) Minister for Education Mary O'Rourke in January 1990. As McCulloch (2004) noted, a letter could be categorised as a personal document given they are produced by individuals and because they shed a great deal of light on personal and private attitudes, aspirations and ambitions. But on this occasion, this letter provides documentary evidence of the INTO's goals and objectives in regard to teacher status as well as the sequence of events when the CEC discussed a draft European Council Directive[6] entitled A *General System of Recognition of Higher Education Diplomas Awarded after a Minimum of Three Years Professional Training*[7] at its meeting on 22 October 1988. At issue was the potential implication of upholding the professional status of Irish teachers in the light of its proposals.

Carr remembered that the members of the INTO CEC expressed concern that recognition of qualifications would be based on mutual confidence between Member States in the EU without prior coordination of the education and training systems for different professions. More importantly, as a basic principle, a Member State could not refuse access to a regulated profession to a national of another Member State holding the required certificate for the exercise of such a profession. The CEC noted that Member States would have a period of two years from the publication of the directive to bring its provisions into force and, more significantly, that each jurisdiction would be obliged to designate a competent authority to recognise the qualifications of the various professions, including teachers.

A particular concern for the INTO was the fact that the Secondary Registration Council had already been recognised as the competent authority to regulate the qualifications of secondary teachers since its inception in 1914, but it had not been given powers to regulate the qualifications of primary teachers which raised concerns among primary teachers at the time.[8] Their exclusion from the Secondary Teachers Registration Council enabled the Department of Education to exercise professional and regulatory control over primary teachers' practices and procedures. For example, the state-regulated entry requirements into primary teaching, prescribed recruitment procedures, enforced norms of behaviour, monitored standards of practice, evaluated the work of teachers and assumed responsibility for their ongoing professional development. In effect state-regulated control, sometimes described as state mediated control, fostered dependence on the State and its various agencies rather than independence and professional autonomy.

Meanwhile, Carr, who had been a member of the INTO CEC since 1982, had been appointed as the sole representative of the primary sector on the Secondary Registration Council in October 1988, which was just before his appointment as INTO Education Officer (1989–1992). He informed the CEC at its meeting on 8 December 1989 that a proposal from the Department of Education was under consideration by the Registration Council to extend its remit to include the registration of primary and vocational teachers. This effectively enabled the Council to act as the competent authority for the recognition of the qualifications of teachers under the European Council Directive noted earlier.

This ran contrary to the INTO's long-standing demand for the regulation of teaching. It could not countenance the designation of the Secondary Registration Council as the competent body to regulate the qualifications of primary teachers, especially as there was only one primary representative entitled to sit on that Council. More to the point, the INTO had been pursuing without success since 1966 the establishment of a self-regulatory Teaching Council for all teachers, which then seemed to be abandoned by the Department of Education. Not surprisingly, the INTO CEC rejected any proposal to extend the activities of the Secondary Registration Council to encompass the primary sector.

The INTO had looked to the recognition of teachers trained in England and Wales under the 1989 Articled Teacher Scheme, which certified teachers based on practical classroom experience, and the 1989 Licenced Teacher Scheme, based on a two-year, school-based training (Galvin, 2008). More worryingly, the Initial Teacher Training: Approval of Courses (Department for Education and Skills Circular 24/89) was already deemed to be usurping the status of the teaching profession in England and Wales. The INTO concluded that the Haughey Fianna Fáil Progressive Democrats Coalition Government (1989–1992) could no longer be trusted to uphold teachers' professional status in the context of the European Council Directive on mutual recognition of qualifications.

It was a strategic move on the part of INTO General Secretary Gerry Quigley to write to Minister Mary O'Rourke at the end of 1990 before the enactment of regulations to give legal effect to European Council Directive No. 89/48/EEC. Quigley reminded her of the impending implementation and the necessity to introduce relevant regulatory instruments:

> *You will be aware that the European Council Directive on the general system for the recognition of higher education diplomas awarded on competition of professional education and training of at least three years duration is due to come into effect on 4 January, 1991.*
>
> *Member states are required to take the measures necessary to comply with the directive before the end of 1990. In Ireland's case this will necessitate the passing of a statutory instrument by the Oireachtas.*

O'Rourke was also reminded that the State would be required to designate a competent authority to undertake the task of recognising the qualification of teachers:

> *Each member state will be obliged to incorporate in its legislation provision to empower competent authorities to receive applications for membership and the authority to practice or to use a professional title or designatory letters.*
>
> *The current competent authority for primary and vocational teachers in this country is the Department of Education. The Secondary Teachers' Council is the statutory authority for Secondary schools. This council is also the body that regulates the professional qualifications of community and comprehensive teachers.*

The provision to empower a competent authority raised concerns for the INTO because for primary teachers this could either be the Department of Education continuing in its role as heretofore but now with added responsibility for the mutual recognition of the qualifications of teachers from Member States. The other possibility was put to the CEC by Carr at its 8 December, 1989 meeting, in regard to extending the remit of the Secondary Registration Council to include the recognition of the qualifications of primary teachers. Neither of the two options were acceptable to the INTO.

The requirement to designate a competent authority brought into sharp focus the continuing control that the Department of Education exercised over the professional status of primary teachers. It also underlined the failure of previous attempts between the Department of Education and the teacher unions working cooperatively to establish an independent self-regulatory body. It was now more apparent that the only way to uphold the professional status of teachers, in the context of the enactment of regulations to implement the requirements of the European Directive, was to pursue the establishment of a statutory self-regulatory Teaching Council for all teachers. As Quigley put it in the letter:

> *In view of the impending legislation on the E.C. directive the INTO demands that a Council for all teachers be established on a statutory basis without delay. The new Council would act as the competent authority for determining the qualifications of teachers at both primary and secondary levels.*
>
> *I wish to request, therefore, that you convene a working party, as a matter of urgency, to bring forward proposals for the establishment of a Council for all teachers.*

There was some urgency because the INTO wished to have the Teaching Council established prior the enactment of statutory instruments scheduled for the end of 1990. Despite the failure of previous attempts to secure teacher agreement, O'Rourke agreed to the INTO request and established a Working Party in May 1990 under the chairmanship of Department of Education Secretary Liam O'Laighin. The task, according to CEC Report 1990–1991, was 'to examine and make recommendations on the establishment of a Council for Teachers to consider and recommend on the composition, structure, function and financing of such a Council' and 'to report to the Minister within six months'.

1994 *Comhairle Múinteoireachta. A Teaching Council*

At the 1993 INTO Annual Congress in Waterford the Reynolds Fianna Fáil and Labour Coalition Government (1993–1994) Minister for Education Niamh Breathnach openly acknowledged her support for the establishment of a Teachers' Council. Interestingly this was the working term at the time:

> *I believe that the teaching profession in this country is ready for a Teachers' Council. A self-regulating body is possible only in a mature profession with a real sense of responsibility. The monitoring of the professional conduct of teachers by the profession itself brings obligations as well as privilege. I am confident that the profession is equal to the task.*

In her closing remarks to the National Education Convention in the Dublin Castle in October of the same year, Breathnach showed she had been impressed by the strength of support for a Teachers' Council when she reiterated her commitment to the establishment of a Teachers' Council adding,

> *This Convention has dramatically advanced the potential for rapid progress on this issue.*

According to co-author John Carr's recollections, the INTO seized the moment to respond to the Minister's expressed commitments. The time was right. By the early '90s, teachers were highly regarded, teaching continued to attract people of the highest calibre, and teachers' contributions to society and the 'knowledge economy' were highly valued. The quality of the Irish teaching force also received international recognition. The OECD (1991) in its report entitled *Review of National Policy on Education* stated, 'Ireland has been fortunate to maintain the quality of its teaching force' and recommended that the establishment of a statutory national council for teaching would be a valuable agency.

At the 1994 INTO Annual Congress in Bundoran, a resolution was adopted (see INTO CEC Report, 1994–1995) that clearly set out the INTO's position in relation to the duties, functions structures and composition of a Teaching Council:

> *Congress demands the establishment of a statutory Teachers' Council*
>
> a   to promote the educational and professional interests of all teachers;
> b   consider all matters relating to the supply of teachers;
> c   determine the minimum standards of education necessary for entry to the profession including the nature and length of initial training;
> d   establish and monitor criteria for the satisfactory induction into teaching;
> e   ensure the maintenance of standards within the profession;

Figure 6.1 Comhairle Múinteoireachta: A Teaching Council (1994)
Source: https://www.into.ie/ROI/Publications/PublicationsPre2000/Title,17313,en.php. Reproduced by permission of INTO.

f   make regulations governing the conditions under which registration should be accorded, withheld suspended of withdrawn; maintain a register of qualified teachers; and issue certificates for registration;
g   devise and monitor a code of professional conduct;
h   develop, organise, arrange and monitor a range of inservice courses for teachers;
i   promote educational research and innovation; and
j   function as an information centre on all matters pertaining to the teaching profession.

The motion further demands that teachers shall constitute a majority of the membership of a statutory Teachers' Council.

This was a strong mandate, and it followed that the INTO CEC designated newly elected Vice-President Michael McGarry (1993–1994), Assistant General Secretary John Carr (1992–1995) and Executive Officer Dr Deirbhle Nic Craith (1992–2001) to prepare a comprehensive policy document on the establishment of a Teaching Council. The 207-page, A5-sized document, *Comhairle Múinteoireachta. A Teaching Council, Accessible, Accountable Autonomous*, was sold for £3. In the foreword, General Secretary Senator Joe O'Toole (1990–2001) outlined how the roles of elected Government, parents and teachers could be 'easily contextualised and accommodated in the discussion on the need for a Teaching Council' adding, 'Each of the interests must ponder on its own role':

The Government must recognise that their responsibility to provide an educational service is not a carte blanche to fashion an educational system reflective of the narrow ideology of the party or parties in power.

Parents, students and pupils must recognise that their demands, however just, must show deference to the professionalism of the educators and be restrained or constrained by the demands of the common good as determined by Government.

And we as teachers must recognise that our role is to provide the professional input and that control of the profession does not mean and can never mean, control of the educational service.

That party-political ideologies were called is hugely significant, indicative of a critical understanding that they are actively constituted. As Apple (1982) put it, they do not appear fully blown out of thin air, but need to be ongoingly built in a variety of specific places. This incrementalism holds in the present in the face of the myriad actions and sub-actions in Bruton's *Action Plan for Education*. A quarter century ago, there were clearly checks and balances in the form of triangulation between government, parents and teachers. As if to emphasise the point, O'Toole had delivered two emphatic messages on behalf of the INTO, on the one hand to its own members, and on the other to the general public:

1. The organisation 'must recognise' the role that it has in providing a professional input into the debate on the establishment of a Teaching Council;
2. That control of the profession 'does not mean and can never mean', control of the education services.

In their introduction, the co-authors McGarry, Carr and Nic Craith (INTO, 1994) set out the purpose of the document: to 'analyse the implications and issues which are germane to the topic, and then to place on record the INTO's specific proposals on the function and composition of a Teaching Council'. The report was then presented in four chapters, each with its own distinct focus, and each one worthy of close study to tease open the production of such an important cultural text for teachers' practices in Ireland.

Chapter 1 outlined the historical background to the proposed Teaching Council designed to 'shed light upon the social and professional views which [are] still reflected in attitudes towards teachers' acquisition of greater self-regulation and control'. It traced the history of the development of the Teachers' Registration Movement and the various efforts from the mid-1960s onwards to establish a Teachers' Council made by the INTO, in conjunction with the Teachers' Union of Ireland and the ASTI. It also documented the failure of the various working parties, set up by successive governments at the behest of INTO, to reach agreement on the composition, functions and duties of a Teachers' Council. This was mainly due to the persistent failure to achieve consensus among the teacher unions and the lack of leadership and sponsorship by Government.

Significantly, the first chapter ended with the revelation that legal senior counsel advice had been sought by the INTO regarding the perceived obstacles to setting up a Teachers' Council which caused the collapse of previous attempts. This focussed on matters of compulsory registration, contractual property rights, the charging of registration fees, the withdrawal of recognition procedures in other professions, disciplinary powers, teacher dismissals, the withdrawal of recognition and the European Directive on the mobility of teachers. The co-authors of the report were of the view that unless these issues could be resolved progress could not be achieved in any future negotiations, and it was a strategic move to have sought legal opinion.

The senior counsel advice represented a significant breakthrough for the INTO, which was now 'fully satisfied that no difficulty of a constitutional nature arises in respect of the establishment of a Teachers' Council provided the broad procedures established in respect of doctors, nurses and solicitors are followed in any proposed legislation'. Another strategic decision was made by the co-authors of the report to change the working title and substitute the Teaching Council for the Teachers' Council, which was the term used earlier. Their reasoning was sound. The term Teaching Council for teachers resembled the term Medical Council for doctors. There was no such thing as a Doctors' Council in existence so why a Teachers' Council? This paved the way for the co-authors to frame their proposals in subsequent chapters by adhering to the duties and functions that had been established in other professions.

Chapter 2 outlined the Rationale for a Teaching Council under the following headings: 'The Challenge of Social Change', 'Professional Development and Teachers', 'Professionalism and the Teaching Council' 'The Contribution of a Teaching Council to Quality in Education'. In developing the rationale, the INTO had to answer the major question: in what sense would a Teaching

Council benefit the general public? An answer was mooted by the co-authors: 'The establishment of a Teaching Council is one of the structures which should be put in place as a means of recognising teacher professionalism and of improving the quality of pre-service and in-service provision'. Significantly, under the heading 'The Challenge of Social Change', it was recognised the pivotal role that teachers played in the process of a rapidly changing Irish society.

Also significantly, under the heading 'Professional Development and Teachers', it was noted some aspects of teaching had been identified by the OECD (1991) examiners in their *Review of National Policies for Education: Ireland 1992*. These were impediments to the development of teaching as a profession in Ireland particularly the close monitoring of primary schools which was viewed as one of the characteristics which was inimical to teacher professionalism. The INTO at the time seemed content this close monitoring would reduce by the changing role of the inspectors:

> *Admittedly, the scrutiny to which primary teachers were subjected in former times by the Inspectorate was not an augury for professional development, but with the introduction of "Circular 11/76" and "Circular 31/82", Inspectors' advisory functions as distinct from their investigative role have been emphasised, and the [basis] of reporting has changed from an examination of individual teachers to an examination of the functioning of the whole school.*

The co-authors of the report again sought to allay any public concerns regarding what the teachers mean by taking control of their profession, under the heading 'Professionalism and the Teaching Council':

> *Extending control to a Teaching Council is not about establishing a monopoly for teachers. On the contrary such a body would complement rather than compete with democracy, in that it would propose a degree of autonomy in exchange for the obligation to develop and enforce standards of good practice free from bureaucratic or external regulation. It would, in fact, provide teachers with sufficient insulation from external control as would be necessary to enable them to fulfil their democratic and social functions to society.*

Once again an emphatic message on behalf of the INTO had been articulated, this time about the complementarity of teachers' professional control with democracy. This was a crucial public statement about teachers' preparedness to exchange a degree of autonomy though not total autonomy for the 'obligation to develop and enforce standards of good practice'. This penchant for democratic national schooling equally holds in the present in view of the ground being laid for new patrons or sponsors. If Anglo-American style system reforms are anything to go by, these are likely to be non-educationalists who are apt to dictate the terms and conditions of teaching and teacher education. This paves the way for multinational business opportunities at the expense of the democratic public interest inclusive of the needs and interests of diverse children in local school communities.

Chapter 3 of the report specified in great detail the duties, functions, composition and structures of the proposed Teaching Council under the following headings, which are here annotated with explanatory notes:

a   Constitution for a General Teaching Council or *An Chomhairle Mhúinteoireachta* (containing guiding principles in regard to obligatory registration of all teachers; majority teacher representation, constituted in a manner which would 'reconcile parliamentary responsibility for protecting the public interest with the legitimate professional aspirations of teachers to exercise a large measure of control; and responsibility for the quality and standards of the professional service they provide to the general public');
b   *An Chomhairle Mhúinteoireachta* (an independent statutory body representative of the teaching profession, the interests of education and the general public);
c   Functions of *An Chomhairle Mhúinteoireachta*;
d   Composition of *An Chomhairle Mhúinteoireachta* (which included majority teacher representation);
e   Structure of *An Chomhairle Mhúinteoireachta*;
f   Duties and responsibilities of the various academic and registration committees established under the board;
g   Duties and responsibilities of disciplinary committees;
h   Health and Welfare Committee;
i   Duties and responsibilities regarding the administration of the Teaching Council;
j   Registration of teachers;
k   Finance;
l   Professional discipline;
m   Relationship with outside bodies;
n   Research and innovation;
o   Organisation of the council;
p   Proposed structure of *An Chomhairle Mhúinteoireachta*.

Each and every one of these sections requires close study to inform contemporary teachers' critical analyses of the regulation of teaching by the Teaching Council and the regulated-regulation of teaching in Bruton's *Action Plan for Education*. A quarter century ago, the INTO engaged in the practical politics of teachers' organising by engaging intellectually and operating politically and strategically in edu-politics. There are lessons to be learned here about ways to channel contemporary teachers' protests and challenges to regulated professionalism in the global neoliberal policy context, which would do well to be politicised.

Chapter 4 presented a draft parliamentary bill entitled the Teachers' Act. The INTO commissioned a parliamentary draftsperson to draft a bill for the enactment of legislation to establish a Teaching Council modelled on the practices and procedures of other self-regulatory bodies and including the structures, duties, function and composition outlined in Chapter 3, which were submitted by the INTO to the draftsperson in advance. The purpose of the draft legislation was to exert pressure on the government to introduce its own parliamentary bill, which was exemplified in a draft Arrangement of Sections:

Part I Preliminary
Part II *Chomhairle Mhúinteoireachta*
Part III General Functions of the Council
Part IV Registration
Part V Fitness to Teach
Part VI Miscellaneous

Three appendices were added to the report: Appendix I outlined the historical development of Teacher Councils in England and Wales, Scotland and Northern Ireland. Appendix 2 traced the establishment of the Registration Council in Ireland and Appendix 3 looked at professional associations in Ireland, under the headings 'Purpose of Legislation', 'Objects of Association', 'Education and Training', 'Categories of Membership', 'Registration, Registration and Retention Fees', 'Professional Conduct', 'Fitness to Practice and Rules' and 'Bye-laws'.

Bruton's *Action Plan for Education* 2016–2019

Bruton's vision that Ireland would be the lead in Europe was then followed in his *Action Plan for Education* by an elaboration of the five high-level goals with two pages of bullet-point lists of 'Objectives and Outcomes' and 'Some Key Actions' that ended with an explanation of 'The Action Plan Process':

> *The Action Plan is the start of a process. It is not an exhaustive list of everything that will be done to deliver our ambitions in education over the next 3 years. Updated annual Action Plans will be published in December each year, covering the actions that will be implemented during the subsequent 12 months. As part of this process:*
>
> - *Actions will be monitored against published timelines*
> - *Each year a new Action Plan will be developed and published to further our goals in consultation with stakeholders*
> - *Responsibility for actions will be clearly assigned.*
>
> *Furthermore, the Department will publish progress reports each quarter that will evolve and improve from the experience of implementation.*

It must be said this is ambitious, but 'The Action Plan Process' outwardly negates teachers' sense of professionalism, which calls into question the evaluative research component of the Kenny-Varadkar Fine Gael led Coalition Government (2016–present) plans along with previous consecutive neoliberal governments' plans. Having learned the lessons in 'analysing the present' (Carr and Beckett, 2016), it is crucial to be focussed on the history of ideas with some sensitivity to historical, social, cultural, political and economic contexts to realise the ambitions, which demand interrogation. There is need for quality evidence in regard to teachers' practice (Groundwater-Smith and Mockler, 2007), but there is also need for a research-informed evaluation of the *Action Plan for Education (2016–2017)*. This goes past departmental progress reports to interrogate the Kenny-Varadkar Coalition Government's promise of achievements, which means research-active teachers need to wrestle with conceptual issues: in regard to evaluation in education, different approaches to evaluation, standards of self-evaluation, quality of evaluation data, quality assurance, interpretations of teachers' work, criteria used in judging the worth of teachers' work, and conflicts that might arise (see Kemmis and Stake, 1988; McNamara and O'Hara, 2008a, 2008b; Sugrue, 2009a, 2009b; Lynch, Grummell, and Devine, 2012; Mooney-Simmie, 2012; Grummell and Lynch, 2016; O'Donnell, 2017; Gallagher, 2017; Wall 2017).

This then puts the spotlight on Bruton's opening statement:

> *The basic aim of this Government is to use our economic success to build a fair and compassionate society. Few areas are more pivotal than education to our ambitions as a nation. The quality of the service we provide through our education system will determine whether we can deliver our most important goals:*
>
> - *To break cycles of disadvantage and ensure that every person has an opportunity to fulfil their potential*
> - *To create sustainable well-paying jobs and strong economic growth*
> - *To solve the great problems through research and innovation, and excel in culture, art and every other field of human endeavour*

This was more or less a reiteration of Bruton's (1999) earlier vision rehearsed some 20 years ago that hinted at the economic-educational complex, neoliberal ideologies notwithstanding. In tandem with a research evaluation of the present if not past governments' plans, critical questions need to be asked about whose economic success and whose ideas about a fair and compassionate society underpin 'our' ambitions as a nation. Likewise critical questions need to be asked about cycles of disadvantage, equality of opportunities and equality of outcomes, not to forget consecutive governments' social and economic policies; sustainability and economic growth along with the beneficiaries; and who determines 'the great problems' if not teachers with a keen sense of the hard lived experiences of their students, families and local school communities in particular contextual locations.

Bruton's *Action Plan for Education 2016–2019* (Department of Education, 2016b) was updated and re-issued online[9] as the specific *Action Plan for Education 2017* and again as *Action Plan for Education 2018* (Department of Education, 2017, 2018), respectively launched on 6 February, 2017 and 7 February, 2018. Noticeably lengthier, the 2017 version was an 83-page, A4 document that incorporated much the same content, format and graphic design. The introduction contained the Department of Education's Statement of Strategy, a foreword by Bruton, a statement by Secretary General Seán Ó Foghlú, and a four-page statement headed 'Our Ambition for Education and Training'. This was inclusive of graphics on 'our strategy', 'themes for 2017' and a final note titled 'The Action Plan Process'.

Once again, Bruton evidently showed concern about the economic uses of education, as noted in the opening to his foreword:

> *Education is at the heart of all of our ambitions as a nation. No other area of Government activity has greater capacity to change our country for the better. It is crucial to all of our ambitions to support a fairer society, and it is crucial to all of our ambitions to deliver a stronger economy.*

Significantly, Bruton reiterated his belief in representative fashion about 'all our ambitions' if not presumptuously on behalf of the whole population in line with his previous tract as opposition spokesperson (see Bruton, 1999). Again, there needs to be critical questions asked about whose conceptions of the Irish nation and also fairness in society are brought into play. Fortuitously, these matters were brought to public attention in 2016 during the centenary commemorations of the 1916 Easter Uprising, said to have been seen differently and contested in every generation (Fennell, 2009; O'Toole, 2009; Leahy, 2013; Ferriter, 2015; McAullife and Gillis, 2016, McGreevy, 2016; Biagini and Mulhall, 2016). All the subsequent lengthy consecutive versions of Bruton's *Action Plan for Education* demand investigation, given the details will be compounded by yearly updates over its three-year lifespan. These too will no doubt be marked by an expectation the hundreds of actions and sub-actions are to be implemented during the year and cumulatively over 2016–2019.

For the purposes of this sample documentary research, it was necessary to be selective about certain actions and sub-actions to be found online, but at the same time provide the backstory to encourage teachers' intellectual activities and work with academic partners. The challenge for the INTO is to tap practitioners' research-informed responses to centrally imposed policies so they can ascertain the most appropriate nationally and locally determined comebacks to politicians, policymakers and power brokers: on increased accountability, quality teaching and quality assurance mechanisms, performance management systems and in the case of de-contextualised school improvement, the focus on outcomes, data collection, performance and improvement.

Select item: school-based evaluation

Action 69 of the initial *Action Plan for Education 2016–2019* charged the Inspectorate with the newly issued *Looking at Our Schools 2016*, the new quality framework for school self-evaluation; it contained standards for teaching, learning, leadership and management, intended to help schools to plan for continuous improvement.[10] The Inspectorate were to issue revised school self-evaluation guidelines to all primary and post-primary schools and manage a programme of school self-evaluation advisory visits to schools. In addition a circular was to be issued by the Department of Education and Skills setting out simplified requirements on schools for self-evaluation and for annual reporting to parents for the period 2016–2017. Action 69 was repeated in the follow-up *Action Plan for Education 2017*, this time committing the inspectorate to conducting school self-evaluation advisory visits to 400 schools.

The backstory is such that in March 2012, Chief Inspector Dr Harold Hislop did an interview for Seomra Ranga, which is Gaelic for classroom and which is an online hub and repository for quality-created resources for primary schools.[11] He indicated that the Inspectorate had been developing draft materials to support better and more systematic school self-evaluation procedures and added a purpose for self-evaluation:

> *Our (the Inspectorate) goal is for schools to conduct their own evaluations transparently and accurately and for inspectors to visit schools to evaluate the school's own self-evaluation.*

The intention that the Inspectorate weighs in evaluating a school's self-evaluation gives pause for concern, and it is well to heed MacBeath's (1999; cited by McNamara and O'Hara, 2008a) advice in *Schools Must Speak for Themselves: The Case for School Self-Evaluation*. The role of external evaluation and inspection is to focus 'primarily on the school's own approach to self-evaluation' in order 'to ensure that internal systems of evaluation and self-evaluation are implemented effectively'. So far, so good. This accords with Nevo's (2002; cited by McNamara and O'Hara, 2008a) claim 'that there is, in most of Europe, a perhaps surprising emphasis in school and teacher autonomy and on self-regulation and internal evaluation as the best way forward'. The subtle shift in terminology notwithstanding, it is as well to give Hislop the benefit of the doubt as long as the classic strategy of sound educational management and decision making is not conflated with the new managerialism. This is distinctly political in terms of the values and mores incorporated into systems of governance, regulation and [public] accountability (Grummell and Lynch, 2016). Otherwise, the likely result of Hislop's actions would be regulating the self-regulation of teachers' work. This adds another dimension to the expression regulated-regulation of teaching used throughout this anniversary book in regard Bruton's *Action Plan for Education*.

Hislop (2012) considered quality assurance of Irish schools 'through external inspection and school-based self-evaluation'. This was confirmed in November 2012, when the Kenny Fine Gael-Labour Coalition Government (2011–2016) Minister for Education Ruairí Quinn authorised *School Self-Evaluation: Guidelines for Primary Schools*. These drew on school effectiveness research, designed to complement the new range of inspection models being developed at the time.[12] School self-evaluation became a mandatory requirement in schools in 2012, and it facilitated a reduction in the number of Whole School Evaluations towards a greater reliance on an internal School Evaluation System with the 'consequent change in language from 'school development' to 'school improvement', from 'inputs' to 'outputs', which suggested 'a stronger focus on public accountability for educational outcomes' (see O'Donnell, 2017).

However, despite these departmental research-informed guidelines, the standards proved unwieldy and unmanageable and, according to Hislop (2017), schools struggled to handle the data generated and to communicate the outcomes of self-evaluation to parents. As noted in Chapter 1, a 'radically different' set of guidelines, informed by further national and international research, was published by the Department of Education and Skills (2016e): *Looking at Our School: A Quality Framework for Primary Schools.* According to Hislop (2017), these are the first fully comprehensive set of published standards for Irish Schools. The content of the standards had been paired back considerably:

> *The standards are presented as statements of practice (or descriptors) that provide an accessible picture of what each standard means. More significantly, however, each standard is now presented at two levels of practice: what constitutes 'effective practice' and what might be expected at the level of 'highly effective practice'. The decision to present the standards in this way is deliberately intended to encourage schools to think about and improve aspects of their practice from, 'good' to 'excellent'.*

This raises alarm bells, and no doubt informed the INTO stand of non-co-operation with school self-evaluation in the same year. The statements of practice are in effect specifications for teachers' work and make explicit the standards that inspectors will use in coming to judgements about the work of the schools. This harks back to a new government policy discourse in the Department of Education and Skills (2016a) *Minister's Brief* and risks putting paid to teachers developing evaluative research perspectives. This should come as no surprise. More than a decade ago, McNamara and O'Hara (2006) warned 'that by and large, schools and teachers [are] in fact for the most part unable to undertake systematic self-evaluative research'. They referred to Elliot (1995), who had declared even earlier that neither training, experience nor professional culture had 'allowed teachers to develop the discursive consciousness necessary to become reflexive, self-aware, and thus able to self-evaluate'. This was a salutary reminder that teachers were 'methodologically adrift', unsure of what questions to ask, what kind of data to collect, by what methods and how to analyse it when it had been collected (McNamara and O'Hara, 2008a, 2008b).

Hislop (2017) went on to say that the standards were written in a way that respects the professional autonomy of the teacher rather than as a checklist of mandatory requirements, and hastened to add, 'Of course, over time, we have work to do to ensure the ongoing validity of the framework and indeed of the inspection models linked to it'. The emphasis on professional autonomy might be the 'get-out' clause, but it remains to be seen if national schools have really been given the freedom to identify their own issues for self-evaluation with the proviso they relate to teaching and learning.

This is of the utmost importance, and not only for teachers' politicisation. For teachers to assume greater control over their professional domain, they need to collectively design their own self-evaluation standards. This could be based on reintroducing school development planning on the basis of inputs back into schools: planning, implementing, and reviewing so teachers are not caught in the trap of evaluating outcomes based on standards developed elsewhere. INTO Director of Education and Research Dr Deirbhle Nic Craith (2013–present) said as much to the 2014 INTO Conference on Quality in Education in Armagh: 'Professionals need to redefine their profession in the context of the 'New Public Management' if they are to retain the trust and respect of the public'. Then the teachers' salaries dispute took precedence and the INTO lifted its directive on the non-co-operation with school self-evaluation, effective February 2018. The Department of Education and Skills responded by issuing Circular 16/2018 in March 2018 clarifying how schools should re-engage with school self-evaluation.

Select item: *Droichead* or induction

Action 65 of Bruton's *Action Plan for Education* under the heading, 'Regulate the Teaching Profession', the Department of Education is said to aim to progress the 'growth phase of Droichead through the Teaching Council and to assess and scope the policy implications that the Teaching Council may put forward on the revised Droichead policy'.

The backstory is such that in July 2010 the Cowen Fianna Fáil, Greens and Progressive Democrats Coalition Government (2008–2011) Minister for Education Mary Coughlin informed the Teaching Council that she intended to commence section 7(2) (f) and (g) of the 2001 Teaching Council Act no later than September 2012, which empowered her

> (f) to establish procedures in relation to the induction of teachers into the teaching profession;
>
> (g) to establish procedures and criteria for probation of teachers including periods of probation.

The Teaching Council welcomed the Minister's proposal and proceeded to develop procedures for the induction and probation of teachers resulting in the issuing of a consultation document Career Entry Professional Programme (CEPP) on 24 February 2012, which shows that the edu-politics was agreeable. However, six months after Coughlin's announcement and before any actions could take effect, Chief Inspector Dr Harold Hislop announced in January 2011 at the Irish Primary Principals Conference that responsibility for the probation of teachers would transfer from the Inspectorate to the principals of primary and post-primary schools. This seemingly disturbed an apparent settlement. By signalling the Inspectorate's intention to withdraw from the probation process, this effectively pre-empted any decision which might be made by the Teaching Council in relation to how the induction of new teachers into the profession and the probation processes were to be conducted.

It happened that during the drafting of the Teaching Council's procedures and criteria on the induction and probation of teachers, the three teacher unions' representatives[13] became aware that a proposal to transfer the responsibility for the probation of teachers from the Inspectorate to the principals of primary and post-primary schools was under active consideration. Moreover, it was likely to receive widespread support at the Teaching Council, which indicated Hislop's announcement had had an effect, which suggests power plays at work. The general secretaries of the Teacher Unions wrote to the Teaching Council in a letter dated 16 November, 2011:

> *From our knowledge of the proposed new CEPPFR (Career Entry Professional Programme [For review]) policy the three teacher unions are gravely concerned that it incorporates an evaluation process akin to the current system of probation into the profession, notwithstanding the extended length of teacher education including significant additional time for school placements. We are gravely concerned that this proposed draft CEPPFR policy in effect would simply facilitate the transfer of responsibility for probation from the Inspectorate to schools and particularly school principals.*

This was the nub of the teacher unions' objections, which subsequently developed into a major confrontation between the INTO and the Teaching Council, which requires close study to critically understand the disputes. This is not just in relation to the edu-politics but also to teaching as an intellectual activity and the professional conversations about professional learning (see Philpott, 2014). The INTO held seven regional meetings during the month of February 2012 to ascertain the views of members in relation to the CEPP. Shortly afterwards, the INTO conveyed its concerns to the Teaching Council and sought a rethink of its strategy and demanded that it retain the facility of external evaluation of Newly Qualified Teachers (NQTs). Following consultation with stakeholders, the Teaching Council published a new model of induction and probation in February, 2013, entitled *Droichead: Teaching Council Policy on a New Model of Induction and Probation for Newly Qualified Teachers.*

The INTO rejected the proposal following a resolution passed at the 2013 INTO Congress in Cork objecting to any induction and probation pilot project such as *Droichead* and demanding that the CEC investigate alternative methods of probating teachers. In response to the resolution, the INTO held a further seven consultation meetings and the CEC decided at their June 2013 meeting to issue a directive to members not to participate in the Droichead pilot scheme. However, an agreed settlement was reached between the INTO and the Teaching Council in January 2014, and the CEC decided to lift the directive on Droichead at its meeting in February, 2014.

In March 2016, the Teaching Council published a revised *Droichead: An Integrated Induction Framework for Newly Qualified Teachers*, but the INTO rejected this version following a resolution adopted at the 2016 INTO Annual Congress in Wexford demanding that induction and probation should be evaluated externally through panel of seconded teachers and/or principal teacher funded by the Department of Education and Skills. The INTO then conducted a ballot for industrial action which was carried by 91%, and so the CEC directed 'members not to participate in, or cooperate with, *Droichead* or any form of probation/induction that does not include fully external evaluation of all NQTs with effect from 1 July 2016. From September 2016 onwards the INTO took part in a 'talks process', in the context of securing the restoration of qualification allowances payments for post-2011 entrants to teaching, with a view to resolving the *Droichead* dispute. The process involved a series of engagements which led to an agreement in the Teaching Council to adopt and subsequently to commence a revised *Droichead* policy. In March 2017, the Teaching Council issued a new revised *Droichead: The Integrated Professional Induction Framework*[14] marked 'for information purposes only' pending agreement with the Department of Education regarding the provision of resources to implement the new induction and probation arrangements. The online site provides substantial information, but its introduction is worth quoting at length:

> *Droichead has been designed in collaboration with the profession to reflect the importance of induction for new teachers as they are formally welcomed into the most important profession in society. It is grounded in the belief that those best placed to conduct this formal welcome are experienced colleagues who have relevant and in-depth knowledge of teaching and learning in their respective schools.*
>
> Droichead *recognises the effectiveness of the reconceptualised programmes of initial teacher education and particularly the extended school placement, in the professional preparation of student teachers. It builds on that phase, taking as its starting point the areas for further learning that have been identified by the NQT in collaboration with the HEI (Higher Education Institutions) as part of the school placement experience. At the same time, it recognises that induction is a distinct phase of the continuum of teacher education, a socialisation process into the teaching profession. This integrated framework includes both school-based and additional professional learning activities to address the needs of teachers as they begin their careers.*

The revised *Droichead* document was finally approved by the Teaching Council at its meeting on 8 May 2017. The INTO CEC announced on 12 May the lifting of its directive, which prohibited co-operation with *Droichead* claiming that, on balance, the directive had served its purpose in bringing about significant changes (INTO Website News 12 May 2017). In response to the INTO announcement, a special regional conference was convened on the basis of the required number of INTO District Committees in attendance, as specified under INTO Rule 20,[15] to consider the following motions:

Congress

1. *Demands that participation in PST (Professional Suppot Team) must be properly resourced, funded and remunerated;*
2. *Instructs the CEC to ballot all members, within the next school calendar month, on a directive not to participate in, or cooperate with, Droichead or any form of probation/induction as part of the Teaching Council registration process unless and until appropriate resourcing and remuneration is agreed.*

The first motion superceded the second to become the substantive motion that was adopted. This enabled a settlement to be reached on the introduction of the revised *Droichead* programme into schools. This had been fundamentally changed from the original version which INTO opposed. For example,

- Probation has been replaced by a positive, supported induction system which will serve the interests of NQTs and of our schools.
- The Council has explicitly stated that *Droichead* is a non-evaluative process.
- There are enhanced specific supports, including substitute cover for release time and for training for the Professional Support Team.
- Principal teachers are not obliged to be part of the Professional Support Team.
- There is a gradual introduction of the revised system, starting with schools of 24 teachers and more next school year, extending to 2020/2021 for all schools.
- The new version of *Droichead* takes account of the extension to initial teacher education and the extended periods of school placement.[16]

The 'battle of ideas' over teachers' induction had continued for seven years, but the timing of this conflict was unfortunate. It coincided with the enforcement of salary cutbacks, the decimation of middle management posts of responsibility in schools because of austerity measures, the failure to address the principals' benchmarking award, the intensification of teachers work arising from relentless government policy initiatives, the difficulties with evaluating NQTs in small schools and the perceived shedding of workload by the Inspectorate, thus freeing up more time for incidental or unannounced inspection visits. Finally there was the matter of the transfer of the responsibility for probation including evaluation of NQTs on to principal teachers. Perhaps it was unfortunate too that the Teaching Council did not, from the beginning, devise a new induction and probation arrangement different from the external evaluation model which was operated by the Inspectorate for decades. At issue is the fact that the 2001 Teaching Council Act always envisaged that the responsibility for induction and probation would be the responsibility of the Teaching Council under section 7(2) (f) and (g), noted earlier. In view of this long-waged campaign, it is imperative that the new settlement be sustained.

Select item: *Cosán*, the first national framework for teachers' learning

Action 65 of Bruton's *Action Plan for Education* under the heading, 'Regulate the Teaching Profession', the Department of Education is said to 'assess and scope the policy implications of the proposals that the Teaching Council may put forward for the development of Cosán'. *Cosán* is the Gaelic word for pathway.

The Teaching Council also has a statutory function, under Section 7(2) (h) (iii) and Section 14 (d) (i) of the 2015 Teaching Council (Amendment) Act to advise the Minister for Education on the professional development of teachers. Section 14 refers specifically to the renewal of registration of registered teachers on 'satisfactory completion of programmes of continuing education and training accredited under section 39'. The backstory indicates that throughout 2014–2015 the Teaching Council orchestrated a consultation process with stakeholders in relation to a draft framework for the CPD of teachers. It invited teachers to submit their initial views before the drafting process commenced. Then in May 2015, the Teaching Council published the first phase of the consultation process in the form of a draft framework document for teachers' learning entitled *Cosán at a Glance: Draft Framework for Teachers' Learning*.[17] Again, stakeholders were invited to submit their views to the Teaching Council by December, 2015. In its submission to the Teaching Council on 4 December 2015, the INTO appealed for trust in the teachers' own professional responsibility to engage in professional development as their needs dictate, whether through formal or informal engagement:

> *It is the view of the INTO that a mandatory requirement could lead to a box-ticking exercise to ensure compliance with regulations at the expense of teacher goodwill which underpins teachers' current engagement in ongoing professional development.*

The INTO submission stated, 'Teachers' professional autonomy to identify and determine their own professional development journeys is a core principle of teacher professional development'. In response to the feedback received from stakeholders, the Teaching Council issued a revised framework on 15 February 2016. The INTO conducted a consultation process facilitated by members of the INTO Education Committee during 2016, where a clear message emerged that CPD is a right and a responsibility, but that it should not be compulsory for teachers' (INTO CEC Report, 2016/17). At the 2016 INTO Annual Congress in Wexford a resolution was adopted 'demanding that any effort by the Teaching Council to introduce mandatory element of CPD [continuing professional development] for the purposes of Registration be rejected outright by this Organisation by all means necessary up to and including industrial action'. Further, 'that the CEC inform the Teaching Council that members will not be engaging with the proposed arrangements as laid out in Cosán' (INTO CEC Report, 2016/17).

Conclusion

This chapter has also done much to demonstrate teachers' politicisation marked by the practical politics of campaigning, and there is substance here for documentary research intertwined with school-based practitioner research activities on matters of immediate concern to teachers: policy visions for national schools, teachers' workload and teachers' salaries, the role and function of *Chomhairle Mhúinteoireachta* or a Teaching Council equipped for the twenty-first century, (social) partnerships with stakeholders and collaborative professionalism, school self-evaluation coupled with developing teachers' capacity for evaluative research, an induction and probation arrangement different from the external evaluation model and, finally, teachers' learning. This needs to include professional conversations about any number of important theories (see Philpott, 2014) as they relate to the edu-politics in Ireland in the present. This is all crucial to engage the 'battle of ideas' and ground any confrontations with the Teaching Council, including rejections and revisions of aspects of Bruton's *Action Plan for Education*. This is the nub of teachers' 'case for the defence'. As Gorton, Williams, and Wrigley (2014) pointed out, it is imperative to look at how summative inspection judgements gloss over the complexities of students' lives and teachers' work, and ignore school-generated evidence of what is actually being done to meet policy expectations.

Notes

1. It must be said Irish teachers' sense of professionalism became more challenging with the 1998 Education Act, which consolidated the Minister's locus of power despite consultations with the relevant stakeholders.
2. There are many, not least the *The Irish Teachers* Journal, Vol I, II, III, IV, particularly the 2014 volume *Quality in Education: Accountability & Responsibility*; see also Colgan (2001).
3. See the INTO's publications: www.into.ie/ROI/Publications/, as well as copy of Dr Deirbhile Nic Craith's presentations from 2009 to 2015 Education Conferences, available at this link: www.into.ie/ROI/NewsEvents/Conferences/EducationConsultativeConference/.
4. Co-author Lori Beckett worked with these teacher partners culminating in the publication of their teacher inquires, co-authored with academic partners: see *Urban Review*, 2014, 46, 5.
5. A copy of the letter, while undated, was reproduced in its entirety under the sub-heading 2.6.2 Council of the European Communities – Directive in the proceedings of the 122nd INTO Annual Congress held in Tralee on 16–20 April 1990. These proceedings contained the 1989/1990 reports of the Central Executive Committee, the Education Committee and Equality Committee.
6. This was Directive No. 89/48/EEC issued on the 22 June 1988; see www.google.ie/search?rls=aso&client=gmail&q=directive+89/48/EEC&authuser=0&gws_rd=cr&ei=Moh4WczMIufJgAby8o6wBA.
7. This was to give legal effect to Council Directive No. 89/48/EEC on 21 December 1988. This introduced, for regulated professions, a general system for the recognition of higher education diplomas awarded on completion of professional education and training of at least three years' duration. A Member State which regulates a profession is obliged to recognise the qualifications obtained in another Member State and allow the holder of the qualification to practice his or her profession in the particular Member State on the same conditions as apply to the citizens of that Member State. The diplomas held by EEC nationals which they obtained in a third state are also recognised under the directive in certain circumstances.
8. This was ironic because the evidence shows that teachers and their representatives had long equated teaching with doctors and lawyers and presumably other professionals, no doubt a reflection of the class- and gender-based social order in Ireland at the time. This was before the start of the First World War and the 1916 Easter Uprising. See the full quote in *the Irish School Weekly* dated 20 June 1914: 'Why

should they not, like the medical profession and legal profession, hold their own examinations and take care that only the qualified pass through the entrance gate to the profession?'
9 See Department of Education and Skills (2017) Action plan for Education 2017. Dublin: Department of Education and Skills https://www.google.com.sg/search?rls=aso&client=gmail&q=See+www.education.ie/en/Publications/Corporate-Reports/Strategy-Statement/Action-Plan-for-Education-2017.pdf
10 See Department of Education and Skills (2016e) Looking-at-Our-School-2016 A Quality Framework for Primary-Schools https://www.education.ie/en/Publications/Inspection-Reports-Publications/Evaluation-Reports-Guidelines/Looking-at-Our-School-2016-A-Quality-Framework-for-Primary-Schools.pdf
11 See www.seomraranga.com/. Lori, Seomra Ranga is an online hub for Primary School Resources run by Quinn, D.F.
12 The promotion of school self-evaluation is not peculiar to Ireland. It is also a European-wide phenomenon. For example, the *European Parliament and Council on European Cooperation in Quality Evaluation in School Education* (2001) called on Member States 'to clarify the purpose and the conditions for school self-evaluation; to ensure that the approach to self-evaluation is consistent with other forms of regulation; to develop external evaluation in order to provide methodological support for school self-evaluation and to provide an outside view of the school encouraging a process of continuous improvement and taking care this is not restricted to purely administrative checks'. Further recommendations included involving all school stakeholders in the process of external and self-evaluation in schools, training in the management and use of self-evaluation instruments in order to make school self-evaluation function effectively as an instrument strengthening the capacity of schools to improve.
13 The Teaching Council comprises 37 members: 11 primary teachers, 9 of whom are elected and 2 of whom are teacher union nominees; 11 post-primary teachers, 7 of whom are elected and 4 of whom are teacher union nominees; 2 nominated by colleges of education; 2 nominated by specified third-level bodies; 4 nominated by school management (2 primary and 2 post-primary); 2 nominated by parents' associations (1 primary and 1 post-primary); and 5 nominated by the Minister for Education and skills, including one representing each of IBEC and ICTU.
14 See The Teaching Council (2016) *Droichead: The Integrated Professional Induction Framework* Maynooth: Teaching Council http://www.teachingcouncil.ie/en/Teacher-Education/Droichead/
15 As the matter to be discussed was relevant only to the INTO members in the Republic of Ireland, the meeting, attended by over 500 delegates, was deemed to be a regional conference with the same decision making power as Annual Congress, aka Rule 20 of the Rules and Constitution of the INTO 2014/2015:

   A. A special Congress constituted under Rule 6 shall be called by the CEC on the requisition of six district Committees, which have held special meetings to discuss the proposal, the majority of those present and voting at those meeting being in favour of such Congress;
   B. A special congress shall, in regards the special matter for which it was summoned, be vested with the same power and authority as an Annual Congress.

16 See INTO Website May 2017: www.into.ie/ROI/NewsEvents/LatestNews/NewsArchive/NewsArchive2017/May2017/Title,41821,en.php.
17 See The Teaching Council (2015) Cosán at a Glance Draft Framework for Teachers' Learning. Maynooth. The Teaching Council www.teachingcouncil.ie/en/Publications/Teacher-Education/Documents/Cosan-at-a-Glance.pdf.

Co-authors' closing: the rebuttal

Introduction

The hope for this anniversary book, written for the occasion of the INTO's sesquicentenary in 2018, is that it will encourage teachers and academic partners with allegiance to the INTO to be intellectually and politically engaged in teachers organising. This major idea has been teased open in terms of its history, theory and practical politics in an effort to make some approximations towards historicising teachers organising or tracing its development back to Vere Foster (1819–1900), who was instrumental in founding the INTO in 1868; theorising teachers organising, particularly in regard teacher activism, in effect operating astutely, working collectively and mobilising around particular concerns that need attention; and politicising teachers about ways to go about raising their professional voice cognisant of its strengths and limitations, not to forget the INTO's reputation as a part of 'networked' state power or 'governed interdependence' (see Hardiman, 2012).

This closing chapter distils the lessons to be learned about teacher union research from the samples of documentary research in previous chapters. These spanned the INTO's history insofar as these select studies shore up the INTO in the present so that it can operate politically and strategically, that is, professionally. They also provide an indication of the evidence to be gleaned from the INTO archives on teacher status allied to deliberations on different forms of professionalism (see Whitty, 2008; Stevenson and Gilliland, 2016). The INTO has been evidently much engaged in edu-politics over the years, which speaks to the historical significance of teachers organising around the major ideas of the time and how they came to take particular stands in their day. These insights are crucial to forging a response not only to current neoliberal policy challenges for the INTO but also the threats to teacher status and their professional standing that come from politicians, policymakers and power brokers as well as ill-considered forms of teacher activism.

The 'rebuttal' is a euphemism for the tasks at hand. Central to this anniversary book are teachers' disquiet, resistance, protests and challenges, especially in regard to the situation where teaching and teacher education has experienced incremental shifts towards being tightly controlled and regulated. It happened over time, but more recently, Bruton's *Action Plan for Education* signalled the regulated-regulation of teaching and Hislop's (2012, 2017) reforms attended to likely regulating the self-regulation of teachers' work. This could be called a notion of regulated professionalism (see Whitty, 2008; Stevenson and Gilliland, 2016).

On the face of it, Bruton was an obvious choice for Minister of Education and Skills in the neoliberal Kenny-Varadkar Coalition Government (2016–present) because he brought economic and business credibility to the portfolio. His *Action Plan for Education* seemingly sits well with the dominant global neoliberal ideology but also the mandate that elected governments have, say, to institute system reforms for 'school improvement'. Just in passing, Varadkar's liberal-conservative values and appeals to populism notwithstanding, the main question stands about who decides these regulated ends in Ireland's national schools because regulated professionalism has the potential to go past 'school improvement' towards performativity.

Likewise the subsidiary set of questions stand about the opposition from teachers and the INTO to the imposition of centrally determined, top-down policies despite being involved in numerous consultation processes. The responses more than ever need to draw on teacher union research peculiar to Ireland, especially in view of the concern that performativity likely heralds Anglo-American style corporatised school system reforms. This would not only reinforce regulated professionalism. It would scupper any traces of collaborative professionalism never mind any vision of a new democratic professionalism with teacher unions at its heart (Stevenson and Gilliland, 2016).

The co-authors' point of departure on 'flipping the system' (Evers and Kneyber, 2016; Stevenson and Gilliland, 2016) is that throughout its history, the INTO has developed great insights and keen perspectives on what needs to be done in and for education and national schools. So it does in these hard times, but the INTO's work in the present is best harnessed to the republic's development and modernisation, indeed to Ireland's democracy.[1] There are complexities to be identified and indeed negotiated, and the INTO is well placed to harness teachers' professional knowledge about national schooling situated in local school communities but also nationally across the island of Ireland. This includes a sense of Ireland's place regionally and globally in the wake of the collapse of the Celtic Tiger, GFC, Troika bailout, austerity politics, Brexit and other insecurities including terrorist threats. These major concerns are clearly an issue for INTO members going by an item on the conference agenda at the 2016 INTO Congress in Wexford, held just before the UK June referendum[2]:

> *Congress notes with concern the exit of the UK from the EU (Brexit) and the effect that it could have on:*
>
> *(i) the relationship between education partners across the island of Ireland; and*
> *(ii) teachers' conditions of employment in areas such as mutual recognition of qualifications/mobility and loss of EU employment protections e.g. fixed-term and part-time teachers.*

> Congress calls on Northern Committee[3] to work with CEC to develop a strategy which reaffirms the need for unity within ICTU and in particular INTO, including protection of teachers' terms and conditions should such an exit take place.

This is but one of many 'battles of ideas' played out over the sesquicentenary years of the INTO: these are showcased in this anniversary book in the samples of documentary research, intended to fuel historically informed research intelligence feeding into the INTO. It all comes back to teachers' intellectual activities and campaigning for teacher status tied to different forms of professionalism that are responsive to the transformations in Ireland's political economy, whatever the era.

'Battles of ideas'

Chapter 1 began with critical reflections on 'analysing the present' (Carr and Beckett, 2016) and the necessity to focus on the provenance of the ideas for the reform of Ireland's national schools. This better informs the current penchant for vernacular forms of global neoliberal polices that take directions from regional and global power blocs: 2012 Hislop's lecture Quality Assurance of Irish Schools, Department of Education and Skills' (2016a) *Minister's Briefing* and Bruton's *Action Plan for Education* with specific reference to the Inspectorate.

Chapter 2 backward mapped to Foster's efforts working with teachers in national schools and the early inexpert efforts of the INTO in the years before it assumed the mantle of a registered teachers' trade union: 1868 letter from Vere Foster in *The Irish Teachers' Journal*, 1868 Chamney's inaugural editorial in *The Irish Teachers' Journal*, the 1869 teachers' evidence to 'Primary Education Commission (Ireland) and the 1878 newspaper report on teachers' protests on performance-related pay, which had to do with Foster's demise.

Chapter 3 aligned with Ferriter's (2016a) keynote for INTO Congress on some watershed moments of early twentieth century Ireland. This was a time when Anglo-Irish power relations were ever more fraught and complex: 1916 Padraic Pearse's *The Murder Machine*, 1916 Catherine Mahon and women's struggles, 1922 National Programme of Primary Instruction and the 1941 INTO inquiry into the Irish language question.

Chapter 4 again followed the contours of Ferriter's (2016a) INTO keynote on some watershed moments of mid-late twentieth century Ireland: 1946 teachers' strike, 1947 INTO Plan for Education, 1957 INTO presidential address by Margaret Skinnider and 1968 INTO centenary history book *100 Years of Progress*. McCormick's summation of the teachers' strike, having disturbed the peace as it were at the end of World War II, is worth revisiting:

> It did, however, mark the emergence of a force of increasing power in the field of education in the 1950's and since.

Chapter 5 came to the forerunners to the present in the late twentieth century and spanned co-author John Carr's term as teacher and trade union official in the INTO (1967–1989) with a particular focus on what could be described as progressive thinking: 1969 INTO submissions to the Tribunal on teachers' salaries, 1970 INTO Comments on HEA report on teacher education, 1971 curriculum and 1988 INTO position paper on curriculum prescription.

Chapter 6 continued with the forerunners to the present and spanned co-author John Carr's term as trade union official in the INTO (1989–2010) as it mapped the backstory to the conflicts and controversies that confront contemporary teachers: 1990 INTO letter on the Teaching Council; 1994 *Comhairle Múinteoireachta. A Teaching Council*; Bruton's *Action Plan for Education* with a focus on select items including school self-evaluation; *Droichead* or induction; and *Cosán* or the first national framework for teachers' learning.

It is the argument of this anniversary book that teachers and academic partners working solidly in unison to support the INTO is a worthy strategy to defy the shifts towards regulated professionalism. This suggests successfully holding fast in its quest for teacher status tied to deliberations on forms of professionalism. Taking a cue from the archival records, this should be fortified by rigorous historical 'truths' to be found not only in the documentary sources but also in teaching practices. For example, Ministers of Education and Skills in successive neoliberal governments have used rhetorical devices and engineered consent in regard to teaching quality and accountability. This is particularly worrying for DEIS schools.[4] With any moves towards an over emphasis on assessment and performativity they could potentially be targeted in the future as underperforming schools. If Ireland was ever to go the way of England and the USA, these schools could be 'named and shamed' for not meeting mandatory floor targets and then deemed 'failing' schools in need of 'structural solutions'. These could be new school patrons in the form of corporate sponsors (see Beckett, 2014, 2016).

Historical 'truths'

The truth, often distorted for ideological purposes, is comprised of the 'witnesses of fact' (Apple, 1982/2017) to be marshalled as evidence that then empower practitioners armed with historically informed research intelligence. This has long roots going back to Vere Foster's era and the early days of the INTO when nascent (practitioner) research efforts underpinned teachers' democratic representation of their professional concerns about their working lives. Now as then, by channelling into the INTO, it is then in a strong position to work with members and other stakeholders but also to contest if not rebut assertions about myriad issues that are not always well-advised or skewed in intent: 'Smart Regulation', 'Responsive Regulation', external inspection, school self-evaluation, standards, *Droichead, Cosán,* equal pay issues for young teachers and school autonomy. None of this is to forget standardised teaching and learning and school improvement and the reversals to 'intelligent accountability'. Without a match, politicians, power brokers and policymakers will win the day by default.

The sketches of sample documentary research projects laid out in previous chapters need to be supplemented with other research strategies and methods (see McCulloch, 2004). For example, in regard to *Cosán*, teachers' learning lends itself to opportunities for teachers and academic partners to co-develop

Figure 7.1 Droichead: an integrated induction framework for newly qualified teachers (March 2016)

Source: http://www.teachingcouncil.ie/en/Publications/Teacher-Education/Droichead-Pol icy.pdf. Reproduced courtesy of the Teaching Council.

contextually sensitive and locally responsive CPD programs, either accredited or non-accredited. This model of teacher learning was successfully trialled in the north of England.[5] Teachers and academic partners working in so-called failing schools co-developed a long-term, sustained CPD twin-pack designed as a sociology of action twinned with practitioner research methods to help devise democratic 'local' solutions' as practical actions (see Beckett, 2016). In turn, such opportunities for contextually sensitive and locally responsive joint work lend themselves to a 'multi-method approach' to the INTO's archival records and policy advocacy. As INTO General Secretary Sheila Nunan (2010-present) said in the preface to *Learning Communities*, a discussion paper on the proceedings of the 2010 Consultative Conference on Education in Cork, 'Our school leaders must also be enabled, through supportive infrastructure and professional development, to nurture learning communities'. Now more than ever the INTO has a role to play in nurturing a research-informed teaching profession.

Mention was also made of co-author John Carr's recollections from memory work,[6] which proved fruitful particularly when it came to his research-informed strategy 'internal struggle and external persuasion'. As he explained, this was used on numerous occasions and in different campaigns. For instance, in regard to the establishment of *An Chomhairle Mhúinteoireachta. A Teaching Council*, the achievement and maintenance of self-regulation was based on the premise of internal struggle which involved convincing teachers of the value of self-regulatory control. At the same time, it encompassed persuading the general public and particularly the government that a self-regulated profession contributes to the development of a sound education system and enhances children's learning. Such a research-informed strategy should hold in regard to Cosán, Droichead and myriad other issues of professional concern in the current conjuncture.

In addition, these recollections were triangulated with other qualitative research methods, notably interviews with INTO senior officers past and present and school principal teachers. Also, as it happened, a research-active colleague in Dublin interviewed co-author John Carr prior to starting the documentary research for this anniversary book. This not only augmented his research output throughout his terms as teacher and INTO trade union official (see INTO 1994), but it provided insights into his work experiences, particularly his commitments and views of teachers organising:

> *The idea of a teachers' professional community is vital because of the fact that we need to work together as a profession and indeed as other professions do like doctors, lawyers, accountants etc. They continually upgrade themselves and it is vital therefore that teachers act as a professional community, that they assume responsibility for on-going professional development. In the past we relied on the State to do it [but] we need to become closer together and it probably manifests itself in our [INTO] associations like the 'special needs' groups, teaching and learning groups, the Principals' group, and the groups for Travellers. The people who work within a particular area of education feel that they need support themselves and the idea then of professional communities emerges.*

The conviction that teachers learn best in their own work communities (see Lieberman and Miller, 2008) was central to a sense of the real lived experiences of teachers' organising, albeit at senior leadership levels. Carr indicated that the teachers' union was actively involved in building professional learning communities, but that it too was a learning community with potential for improving teaching and learning. In 1994, under the direction of Catherine Byrne, assistant general secretary (1992–1995), the INTO set up its own Learning Unit to deliver courses for teachers and since then it has grown into a major learning resource for INTO members, providing, for example, 20 summer courses alone in 2017. These were delivered in the northern summer holiday months of July and August, with an attendance of almost 5,345 teachers involving online and face to face courses. This is significant because the INTO has the potential to become a major player in the provision of CPD courses for teachers; by working closely with the Teaching Council, this would be a major contribution to the ongoing development of teaching as a profession.[7]

This is critical intelligence, particularly when it comes to teachers' disquiet, resistance, protests and challenges in regard to the Teaching Council in the present. For example, Gregor Kerr, an INTO representative on the Teaching Council and one of the candidates in the 2017 INTO presidential election, alerted teachers to his own disquiet with the Teaching Council in his online campaign statement in an interview for *Voice for Teachers*[8]:

> *Their attitude is to ram changes down our throats, in some cases going through a sham of pretended 'consultation' first.*

This creates a false sense of 'them and us' and makes a mockery of the Teaching Council as a representative group, but it is not to dismiss tensions and contradictions in the current edu-political climate where teacher representatives are under pressure from neoliberal governments. It would have been interesting to follow through to ascertain what research and practice have to say about how such a representative learning community grows and develops and how it negotiates the tensions and contradictions. This would help show the depth and breadth of the work of the INTO, which sits well with teacher union research. As Bascia (2015) said in opening her book, *Teacher Unions and Public Education. Politics, History and the Future,*

> *Teacher unions are at the crux of teachers' efforts to navigate the enduring tensions between their own lowly status in the educational system and the necessary autonomy and working conditions to teach effectively well.*

Bascia pointed out this was at a time when teaching, public schooling, and teacher unions themselves face unprecedented threats in the face of neoliberal reforms. The central principles in the global policy agenda at the heart of restructuring educational systems are choice, competition, incentives, performance and accountability. Any wonder the INTO and the Teaching Council in Ireland are confronted by a clash of principles when it comes to teacher status tied to different forms of professionalism, especially nowadays negotiating regulated professionalism. INTO Director of Education and Research Dr Deirbhle Nic Craith (2013–present) recognised these clashes when it came to the matter of *Droichead*, induction and probation:

> *It could be said that it is a professional responsibility to induct new members into the profession, and teachers have always supported new teachers. But if [others] make it that [there is] a specific way to do it, then it is an imposition: to be told that you have to do it [this way]; teachers don't like that. It is not that they don't support new colleagues; but you have to work with teachers [given] where they are and how it develops for them. We have to be careful that things are not imposed on teachers in a particular way, and that can sometimes be a challenge.*

Nic Craith was pointing towards the need for contextual sensitivity and local responsiveness, which is crucial to school improvement (Thrupp, 1999, 2005; Lupton, 2006; Beckett, 2014, 2016), but conceded there were pressures on the Teaching Council: 'It had a process like that but I don't think the teachers trusted it; at the moment the Teaching Council doesn't seem to have a good relationship with the teachers'. This can no doubt be traced back to consecutive government reform efforts and the tensions and contradictions experienced by teacher representatives. As Bascia (2015) recounted, 'New policies place tight controls'; 'new inspection practices affect teachers'; there is a 'crisis in teaching and teachers' work'; teachers' need for organised representation is more pronounced than ever (see Carter, Stevenson, and Passy, 2010; Verger, Altinyelken, and De Koning, 2013; all cited by Bascia, 2015). Nic Craith put her faith in the INTO's research efforts:

> *In terms of our own work we would also consider research important: the type of research that we can do is to gather teacher's opinions and views on issues to do with their immediate practice or even their thinking on issues. That is what we have access to – teacher's views and opinions and we do that and we have done that in our own research through the years. It is important to do that and to challenge teachers and give them opportunities to look at what is happening and to be exposed to broader issues in education.*

These efforts are clearly valued by teachers and school principals who are affiliated to the INTO. As one school principal put it in an interview, the INTO was 'more than just a union that looks after working conditions; it has a strong professional leaning as well; it also has a strong professional presence [which] is something that people can identify with positively'. This principal also had complimentary comments about the portfolio of the INTO Director of Education and Research:

> *I suppose I keep coming back to that, in terms of promoting research like the Education Conference, Special Education Conference, giving people a platform in the Intouch magazine[9] to share practice, professional development, providing opportunities for teachers to engage with others, to attend courses or to just further their own professional learning. That is a strong component of the INTO really.*

Edu-politics into the future

This penchant for practitioners' active involvement in research is a different strategy to disparaging the Teaching Council and replacing it with rhetoric about teachers' voice. As noted in Chapter 5, if it was all just a matter of giving voice to teachers, which is a seductive notion, without due regard to the edu-politics, there would be no need for teachers' organising. Moreover, as the samples of documentary research in previous chapters show, there are layers of complexities and intricate historical, theoretical and edu-political details to be uncovered about teachers organising. Yet by working collaboratively and cooperatively, practitioners are then able to uncover the evidence relevant to their arguments.

An example illustrates the point. The 2017 INTO Special Congress in October represented a milestone for the status of the teaching profession in Ireland. It had been seven years since the Cowen Fianna Fáil, Greens and Progressive Democrats Coalition Government (2008–2009) Minister for Education Mary Coughlin first announced that she was commencing the relevant section of the 2001 *Teaching Council* Act on probation and induction. There followed years of wrangling and rejections of proposals, as noted in the last chapter, but it got to a point where questions needed to be put: what would have happened if the Teaching Council did not agree to probate the NQTs entering the system? A potential major crises loomed if the INTO again rejected the most recent proposals or it was forced to block the most recent attempts at a settlement by the Teaching Council. What would have been the consequences if the Kenny-Varadkar Fine Gael and Independent Alliance Coalition Government (2016–present) did not allow its Inspectorate to participate in the probation process?

The risks were great, given the retention of self-regulatory control was at stake. Activist teachers and the teacher unions had to be careful not to create a situation where the Department of Education and Skills working with the Inspectorate had reason to step in and overrule their resistance, protests and challenges. For example, as it stands, there is a professional responsibility on the profession itself to develop procedures and criteria for the induction and probation of its NQTs. A prolonged standoff or period of dissent would not have been in the best interest of the Teaching Council nor of the teachers. At least under 'Responsive Regulation', Bruton was relying on the Teaching Council to implement probation procedures. Failure to reach a settlement on such fundamental professional issues like induction and probation could lead to calls for reform of the Teaching Council with the consequent potential loss of teacher majority representation. Then the government would inevitably be obliged to guarantee the public that NQTs were at least probated in order to continue practising their profession.

The point is that when it came to the pressing matter of *Droichead* in Ireland, brinksmanship needed to be avoided and renewed efforts were required to enable the Teaching Council as a representative body to reconnect with teachers and vice versa. As it happened, a major legal battle over teachers' probation procedures in Ireland did not ensue. The impasse, while averted, was the single greatest threat to teacher status this century and it will go down in history. Indeed, it will be interesting to see how it will be remembered given the conflicts and controversies, and if Brady's (1994) term *Historikerstreit m*ight still prove a useful term for edu-politics in the future.

In regard to thinking through what progressive contemporary education politics and policies might realistically look like in any potential (progressive) futures, it should be registered that the INTO enjoys the support of leading critical policy scholars. Notable are those who delivered the first series of the Vere Foster Trust public lectures conducted under the auspices of the INTO: Professor Bob Lingard (University of Queensland) did the inaugural public lecture on 10

September 2012 entitled 'Schooling and Pupil Progress: What Needs to Be Done in Policy, Schools and Classrooms'. Then came Professor Stephen Ball (UCL Institute of Education) with 'Neoliberal Education? Confronting the Slouching Beast' on 26 February 2013. Professor Kathleen Lynch (UCD) delivered 'New Managerialism in Education' on 27 September 2013. Professor Martin Mills's (University of Queensland) lecture was entitled 'Challenging the 'Tyranny of No Alternative'. Teachers and Students Working Towards Socially Just Schooling' on 7 November 2013. Finally, Professor Pamela Munn (University of Edinburgh) delivered 'Taking Research-Informed Teaching Seriously: From Aspiration to Reality' on 11 September 2014.

These public lecturers working at regional and global levels, had much to say for critical policy analyses in Ireland. They provided a good sense of the academic research community's reactions to the global neoliberal reform agenda. For example, Lingard (2012) considered multiple ways to address the pressing political and policy issue of inequalities in schooling, which he argued needed to be overcome to ensure pupil progress and secure improved learning outcomes for all. His argument began with an analysis of the macro systemic policy settings both within and external to education, which is worth reiterating. He drew attention to advice from Andreas Schleicher (2008), the OECD Division head and coordinator of the PISA and its Indicators of Education Systems programme (INES). In regard to high-performing schooling systems, 'informed prescription' was said to be combined with 'informed professionalism'. As Schleicher (2008) put it,

> *Ultimately, therefore, the challenge for modern education systems is to create a knowledge-rich profession in which those responsible for delivering educational services in the frontline have both the authority to act and the necessary information to do so intelligently, with access to effective support systems to assist them in serving an increasingly diverse client base of students and parents.*

A first reading might suggest this is a fair and reasonable statement, but it is important to maintain some distance in order to engage a critical-interpretive reading. Lingard went on to discuss the necessary community infrastructure of support: the required school leadership practices, school culture and the need to work with community 'funds of knowledge' to promote pupil engagement and achievement. He elaborated the importance of school-university partnerships as contributing to 'researcherly disposition' of teachers, which was in effect an argument for teachers working with academic partners. The point was the teaching profession needed to be research-informed and research-informing, but this relies on a recognition of both parties being equal partners and teachers as intellectual workers who contribute much to teacher professional learning communities. Lingard championed the idea of 'teachers as researchers', and after Stenhouse (1975), research as 'systematic inquiry made public'.

Similarly, Ball (2013a) was cognisant of Ireland's regional and global location and cited Lynch et al. (2012), who had noted that Ireland operates within the Anglo-American zone of influence for reasons of history, culture, language, colonisation and trade. It is not surprising therefore that it also displays many of the features of its powerful neoliberal neighbours in terms of its social, health and education policies. It was some comfort that she went on to say that 'despite all the changes occurring through the endorsement of neoliberal principles at management levels, evidence from schools suggest that not much may have changed at the classroom level'. Ball, however, underlined the point that the processes of neoliberal reform are legitimated, disseminated, sometimes enforced and indeed sometimes 'sold' by a set of very powerful and very persuasive agents and organisations. This included the OECD and World Bank, the World Trade Organisation, Irish International Financial Centre, EU and a whole plethora of market leaning Think Tanks, consultancies and policy entrepreneurs.[10]

In contemplating Schleicher's (2008) comments, it was useful to learn from Ball (2013a) that the changes in policy and educational reforms do not normally take place with grand flourishes or in single major *volte face* pieces of legislation. It followed they do not totally displace existing policy commitments because schools and teachers are often left to resolve the resulting contradictions between the old and the new within their situated practice. In using these terms for thinking about Ireland, he suggested the question is not *whether the education system is neoliberal or not*. The question is how neoliberal it is, and what lies in the future; what comes next in the processes of neoliberalisation. He explained the policy technologies and the reform processes:

These are not simply changes in the way we do things or get things done. They change what it means to be educated, what it means to teach and learn, what it means to be a teacher. They do not just change what we do; they also change who we are, how we think about what we do, how we relate to one another, how we decide what is important and what is acceptable, what is tolerable.

As Ball said earlier, these changes are both 'out there' in the system and in the institutions and 'in here' in practitioners' heads and in their souls (see Ball, 2013b). In other words, these policies of reform produce new kinds of policy subjects. And to a great extent, they do not make us do things; they do not oppress or constrain us; they enable us to do things differently; they create new roles and opportunities, the possibility of excellence, of improvement, of choice, of autonomy and of innovation. They recruit us as enthusiasts, but if we hesitate or demur then they quickly position us as unprofessional or irrational or archaic. They rework the meaning of professionalism, making it into a different thing. Professionalism becomes defined in terms of skills and competences, which have the potential for being measured, and rewarded, rather than a form of reflection, a relationship between principles and judgement. The 'new' professional is flexible and adept in the languages of reform.

It was also useful to learn from Ball (2013a) about what had happened in England, where neoliberalism is very effective in colonising and co-opting concepts from other traditions – partnership, reflection, lifelong learning and research-informed practice. Indeed, neoliberal government rests on a dialectical form of power relations that is both harsh and supportive, public and personal, technocratic and emotional. It is characterised by both the hard disciplines of measurement and visibility, and softer entreaties of mentoring, coaching, self-management and self-improvement. In all of this, new sensibilities are being developed, and new subject positions created, a new framework of accountability related to performance is being constructed. A discourse of quality is being articulated. It was then astonishing to learn that in a simple sense professionalism is the enemy of performance. As Ball said, while professionalism rests upon judgement related to principles, set within the context of practice, systems of performativity seek to pre-empt and displace judgement and de-contextualise practice with a form of responsiveness to external drivers. That is what Gleeson and Ó'Donnabháin (2009) call 'Contractual and responsive accountability'.

An oppositional consensus

Simultaneously these Vere Foster public lectures provided not only a good sense of oppositional consensus at global levels but also national level embracing the north and south of Ireland. For example, Lynch's (2013) public lecture held at Queen's University Belfast was focussed on the regulation and control of public sector professionals, which she considered central to the neoliberal 'New Managerial' project. A few salient points are worth reiterating. She hastened to add it is important to recognise the agency of teachers, academics and other educational professionals in education in the emergence of new managerialism. She cited McKinsey and Co's idea about *'war for talent'* (see Michaels, Handfield-Jones, and Axelrod, 2001), an idea that was developed and sold to governments and that created the myth of scarcity of talent. As Lynch put it, 'Shortage of Talent' is part of the 'knowledge economy' ideology with the goal of creating a global professional elite and greater State investment in same. She too was in accord with Ball's (2013b) Vere Foster public lecture when she said neoliberal and new managerial ideologies are translated into practices that frame people's lives and consciousness. Put more bluntly, ideologies of power and control masquerade as 'development', 'restructuring', 'innovation' and 'lifelong learning'. Under new managerialism, management systems focus on *the product* of education rather than the process.

In making the official 'thank-you' speech, Professor Ruth Leitch (Queen's University Belfast) made the comment that others present may have been a little less comfortable with aspects of the neoliberal scenarios expressed, having been saturated by the doxa of neoliberal-inspired new managerial changes over the past decades.[11] She was equally concerned about this being represented in such terms as 'marketisation', 'accountability', 'global competition', which have all reframed education. She was worried about the riposte to the New Managerialism, articulated by Lynch (2013), given one of the manifestations of the neoliberal project is that the profession had lost its way; colleagues had lost heart, lost motivation, lost a sense of the goals of education.

In the saturated world of the New Managerialism, Leitch argued, there was a ready concern with accountability, competition, deliverables, targets and improvement and almost impervious to a competing human inclination to be responsive and caring. She cited the old adage: what counts gets counted in the rush for accountability, but as a corollary, what can't be counted gets devalued or becomes valueless. Leitch argued that a dual rhetoric confuses the lived experiences of professionals: competing demands to endlessly improve quality and performance, but also to care for children who are less-abled, disadvantaged, and with complex needs, and who are all seemingly castigated for having lower market value! She finished with the words of the poet Seamus Heaney: 'Even if the hopes you start out with are dashed, HOPE has to be maintained'. She reiterated hope has to be maintained collectively for a new ideology for education in Ireland, north and south.

Mill's (2013) public lecture provided a sense of hope but also demonstrated an intuitive sense of the hard lived experiences in school-communities in Ireland. He sought to demonstrate how all schools can take up the challenge of addressing the economic, cultural and political injustices faced by young people from various backgrounds. It began from the premise that many young people and teachers experience contemporary schooling as less than satisfying, but that this need not be the case. It drew on data from a range of 'alternative' schools in Australia and England to explore the ways in which all schools can become more socially just. The data came from interviews with teachers and students in schools variously known as 'second chance', 'flexi-schools' and 'flexible learning centres' and schools sometimes referred to as 'democratic'. The first set of schools regularly caters to the needs of young people who experience severe social and economic disadvantage through, for example, poverty, homelessness and caring responsibilities. Many of these young people have been failed by the mainstream education system, yet now demonstrate a great enthusiasm for learning. The second group of schools cater to more middle-class students, but demonstrate how engaged young people can be when involved in schools' decision-making processes. In both sets of schools, teachers indicated that they were freed from many of the neoliberal pressures shaping education systems globally and that this made their work more productive and rewarding, which in turn benefitted their students.

Munn's (2014) public lecture was likewise pertinent to national level deliberations given she was party to Sahlberg, Furlong and Munn's (2012) *Report of the International Review Panel on the Structure of Initial Teacher Education Provision in Ireland*. She focussed on 'closing the achievement gap between rich and poor', declared as an aspiration of politicians of all parties. This was seen as the prime way of improving the life chances of children born into poverty and other forms of disadvantage. High quality teaching is now widely acknowledged to be the most important school level factor influencing student achievement. Munn drew attention to a substantial body of research identifying what counts as high quality teaching and noted that among the characteristics is research literacy – that is, teacher engagement with and in research. In her public lecture, she highlighted the growing international focus on improving the initial and continuing education of teachers, especially in OECD countries and the place of research literacy in that focus.

Munn argued that two key steps had to be taken if the profession was serious about making research-informed teaching a reality. As she put it,

> *Teachers share a common responsibility for the continuous development of their research literacy. This informs all aspects of their professional practice and is written into initial and continuing teacher education programmes, standards, and in registration and licensing frameworks.*
>
> *During the course of qualifying and throughout their careers, teachers have multiple opportunities to engage in research and enquiry, collaborating with colleagues in other schools and colleges and with members of the wider research community, based in universities and elsewhere.*

The conclusion, worth reiterating, was that if Ireland aspires to have a research rich, self-improving education system, as Munn thought it did, it started with a number of considerable advantages. These included the following:

- Highly qualified entrants to the teaching profession;
- National commitment to master's level of initial qualification;
- Belief in the importance of university led teacher education, both at policy level and among university presidents;
- A compact system which enables key decision makers to meet in one room and to have regular contact – formal and informal.

The rebuttal

In closing this chapter, we draw on these research resources from the first of the Vere Foster Public Lecture Series to elaborate what might be research-active teachers and academic partners' reply to what could be called the most pressing matter in Bruton's *Action Plan for Education*: school autonomy. This is singularly important and 'forewarned is forearmed'. This is what happened in England, especially given the construction of so-called failing schools, and the dismantling of its public system of schooling into isolated component parts that paved the way for corporate sponsors. If not politically astute and research-informed, Ireland could potentially follow suit, particularly given moves on school patronage not to forget DEIS and an over emphasis on assessment. Once again it is crucial to know something of the backstory.

The current interest in school autonomy first emerged in the Kenny-Gilmore Fine Gael-Labour (2011–2016) Coalition Government's *Programme for Government 2011–2016*. Under the heading 'Public Sector Reform' it was stated, 'Concrete mechanisms to improve performance, using a range of standards and benchmarks' would be introduced, as well as to 'deal with persistent underperformance'. The programme also stated, 'A new approach to government which empowers public servants by devolving more power' would be required.

The matters of public service reform and accountability are well rehearsed in the research literature published by Irish academic colleagues. O'Donnell (2017) indicated concern that many European governments are adopting, in the case of education, two key priorities: school autonomy and school accountability achieved through devolvement of greater responsibility for 'budgets, planning, self-evaluation and professional development' managed by the school and externally evaluated by the oversight body, the Inspectorate. Referring to the drive towards the autonomy and accountability reform agenda, Sugrue (2009a) called for a professional response:

> *This maelstrom of competing and conflicting policy agenda demands greater professionalism, on the one hand, while a climate of performativity due to decentralisation scripts, particularly regarding accountability, has become the flip side of this policy coin.*

In December 2015, the Department of Education and Skills published two consultation documents entitled '*Advancing School Autonomy in the Irish School System: Consultation Paper*' and '*Advancing School Autonomy in the Irish School System: Research Paper*'. The Department of Education (2015a) defined school autonomy as the 'freeing of schools from centralised and bureaucratic control' or, put simply, the decentralising of decision-making to schools'. The accompanying research document (Department of Education, 2015b) went on to quote two definitions found in the literature:

> *The concept of school autonomy is related to schools' ability to self-determine relevant matters, such as objectives and activities to be conducted. It refers to domains such as governance, personnel, curriculum, instructional methods, disciplinary policies, budgeting, facilities and student admission.*
> (Agasisti, Catalano, and Sibiano, 2013)

> *School autonomy is a form of school management in which schools are given decision-making authority over their operations, including the hiring and firing of personnel, and the assessment of teachers and pedagogical practices.*
> (Arcia and Macdonald, 2011)

On first reading, the first definition appears to suggest a form of school governance while the second a form of school management. A question to be asked is about the distinction, but it is likely these are different expressions of ideas about self-managing schools and/or local management of schools. Mortimore (2014) described what this looked like in England, following its 1998 Education Act that delegated to schools many of the management tasks formerly undertaken by their local authorities:

> *No longer exclusively educational, heads now had responsibility for their school's budget, appointing and dismissing staff, fixing pay, dealing with complaints, maintaining and extending the buildings and overseeing catering arrangements. Their educational knowledge had to be supplemented by financial*

know-how, health and safety regulations and building management expertise – including the benefits and snares of letting premises.

At once, the dilemmas for the respondents to the consultation were apparent, keeping in mind the concerns expressed by Ball (2013a) and Lynch (2013) about the colonisation of language for the neoliberal project. Not surprisingly, in its submission to the Department of Education (2015a) consultation paper, on the 15 February 2016, the INTO grappled with the language alert to the masquerade of the ideologies of power and control. It rejected the neoliberal decentralised nature of school autonomy but committed to protect the value of professional autonomy:

> *The INTO values autonomy in the areas of school ethos, the appointment and development of staff, pedagogical methods, freedom to teach within the curricular framework which can then be adapted to local needs and the freedom within SSE (School Self-Evaluation) to choose their own area for evaluation, set their own targets and decide on their own school improvement plan.*

Then on Wednesday 3 February 2016, president of Ireland Michael D. Higgins, at the request of Taoiseach Enda Kenny, dissolved the Dáil, and an election was called for Friday 26 March 2016. No further action was taken on school autonomy at the time. However, a resolution on autonomy in schools was then presented at the 2016 INTO Annual Congress in Wexford, which was significant for the immediate future of the teacher unions' ongoing campaigns:

> *Congress:*
>
> a *condemns in the strongest possible terms the December 2015 research document, 'Advancing School Autonomy in the Irish School System';*
> b *rejects the proposals to make changes in relation to the autonomy of schools over aspects of staffing, budget, curriculum, governance and ethos;*
> c *demands that the CEC alert the membership to the likely outcomes of such a model of autonomy and campaign against the introduction of measures that would undermine the full and proper resourcing of schools;*
> d *reaffirms that the responsibility for the funding and resourcing of staff allocation to schools lies with the DES;*
> e *further reaffirms that the funding and resourcing of in-school management, as school priorities require, is also the responsibility of the DES; and*
> f *demands the CEC reject all aspects of this document and vigorously campaign against it with the threat of industrial action up to and including strike action.*

The adoption of this resolution unmistakably shows the INTO were opposed to vernacular forms of global neoliberal school autonomy measures. These are inevitably embedded in national legal frameworks and unilaterally imposed on all schools, frequently accompanied by external evaluation and internal accountability measures. As Sugrue (2009a) stated,

> *When a neo-liberal economic agenda is overlaid on this prescription, it becomes as much an ideology as a policy, a juggernaut that on a downhill run is impeded in its momentum only by other dynamics within national borders – influence of teacher unions and the degree of consultation.*

The juggernaut was an apt metaphor but it was seemingly not impeded by the influence of the INTO or their submission in response to the consultation. Action 68 in Bruton's *Action Plan for Education* stated that the Department of Education and Skills will develop proposals to increase school autonomy. This will be achieved, according to the updated *Action Plan for Education*, through capacity-building measures regarding a proposed excellence fund, the Centre for School leadership, a post-graduate qualification for future leaders, changes to school leadership and middle management structures, a centre of excellence for schools and teachers, CPD and Education Training Board organisational design.

Conclusion

This pressing matter of school autonomy and the infrastructure for its implementation in Ireland's system of national schools throws a different light on teachers' disquiet, resistance, protests and challenges. This is not only in regard to the GERM or global educational reform movement (Sahlberg, 2011) but also the Teaching Council and the directions of the INTO in dealing with such matters. It is certainly not straightforward when confronting directions from national, regional and global power blocs that uphold the interests of neoliberal elitism, which is not to forget the republican promise! Yet given the strength of the INTO's sesquicentenary, teachers would do well to find ways to assert their professional authority based on research-informed evidence and become more proactive rather than reactive to government policies. To be sure, the current conjuncture is a different socio-historical context in comparison to the time of the 2001 *Teaching Council* Act, which was not so evidently marked by neoliberal regulatory control. As noted in the last chapter, the INTO made a significant point in its publication, *Comhairle Múinteoireachta*, which is worth reiterating:

> *Admittedly, the scrutiny to which primary teachers were subjected in former times by the Inspectorate was not an augury for professional development, but with the introduction of "Circular 11/76" and "Circular 31/82", Inspectors' advisory functions as distinct from their investigative role have been emphasised, and the bias of reporting has changed from an examination of individual teachers to an examination of the functioning of the whole school.*

However, in the past two decades, the role of the Inspectorate and its work in internal and external quality assurance in schools has changed with increasing emphasis on regulation of teachers' work, accountability and school improvement. Likewise, it is worth reiterating advice from INTO Director of Research Dr Deirbhle Nic Craith to the 2014 INTO Conference on Quality in Education held in Armagh: 'Professionals need to redefine their profession in the context of the "New Public Management" if they are to retain the trust and respect of the public'. This more or less squares with Hislop's (2012) advice in his Seamas Ó Súilleabháin Memorial Lecture entitled 'The Quality Assurance of Irish Schools and the Role of Evaluation: Current and Future Trends: that there is a necessity for

> *an increasing willingness of teachers and school leaders to set professional standards, to lead their own professional development and to seek to improve the educational experience for learners' by assuming greater control over their professional practices locally working with parents, students, and the wider community.*

The politically astute professional responses to these predicaments, as this anniversary book has endeavoured to show, is strategically best served by research-informed policy advocacy to carve a new professionalism best suited to the current regulatory regime. Teachers' resistances, challenges and protest voting against the INTO leadership is misplaced, never mind against extant government rhetoric and neoliberal policies. This is not sufficient without advocating researched-informed policy alternatives. The teacher representatives on the Teaching Council should ensure that they represent the professional concerns of teachers, and that they have the capabilities to put well-reasoned arguments. It follows these teacher representatives best find a mechanism to reconnect with teachers, perhaps through their union structures, and win back teachers' trust.

Then these teacher representatives best convince the public and incumbent governments, including the Department of Education and Skills and the Inspectorate, of their proposals. For instance, if professional self-regulatory control is the preferred option for teachers, then the Teaching Council must not assume the role of agents for respective government departments. Rather it must be independent and be seen to be independent, although this does not preclude building alliances with students, parents and the wider community.

The Teaching Council would do well to remember that trust in teachers is high in Finland, where teachers are expected and trusted to deliver intelligent accountability (see Sahlberg, 2011; Sahlberg, Furlong, and Munn, 2012). Teachers in Ireland, as a matter of principle, should be striving towards a similar type of system where trust is paramount. As in Finland, this would mean a ready engagement in 'intelligent accountability' (see Lingard, 2009), which would reduce the need for multiple new models of inspection and outcome-based approaches to school improvement. These stand in opposition to developmental approaches to school self-evaluation. Bruton's three-year *Action Plan for Education* (2016–2019) (Department of Education, 2016c) boasts it is aimed at making the Irish education and training service the best in Europe by 2026. This is certainly a challenge, but research-active teachers and academic partners, via the INTO and the Teaching Council, may need to convince politicians, policymakers and power brokers that this is best achieved with less inspection and more trust in teachers. Then teachers have to demonstrate that they can be trusted to deliver.

This sort of work requires an intellectual home for teachers and academic partners on the island of Ireland, and the co-authors will organise a second public lecture series and redouble efforts to resurrect Glyde Court or at least in what is left of the remains of the Foster family home in Tallanstown in County Louth. This is an ideal location equidistant between Dublin and Belfast for a world-class teacher union research centre with residential facilities for conferences, away-days, sabbaticals, and the like. A few years ago the Vere Foster Trust had prepared and presented an original proposal to existing and proposed new partner institutions as well as partners in Northern Ireland to seek support for Glyde Court. This had to reflect advice on a business plan, and the ideas developed into a plan for a Diaspora Study Centre to promote popular and accredited programs of study, coordinated with national and transnational institutions including universities.[12]

This business plan would have contributed a new dimension to Ireland's history and represented Ireland's new economy of the future that attracted global finance. It was hoped the follow-up, tracing Irish descendants through the *Irish American*, for example, would mobilise the diaspora to invest in this venture to purchase Vere Foster's derelict family home, save the remains, and re-develop the Glyde Court estate. In the spirit of Vere Foster, it may well require philanthropic investment to build a hub for popular and accredited programs of study on sponsored emigration, the family history industry and heritage tourism. It may also take a revised proposal to the teacher unions worldwide, via Education International, to consider an investment in re-establishing Ireland as a leader in mass education but also in teacher union research. This would go hand-in-hand with the historic and contemporary importance of national schools in the stimulation of the new economy: locally and nationally, regionally and globally.

Notes

1. A frightening article on threats to democracy emanating from James McGill Buchanan was authored by journalist George Monbiot, 'A despot in disguise: one man's mission to rip up democracy', *The Guardian*, Wednesday 19 July 2017. It referred to a new book by Nancy MacLean (2017) *Democracy in Chains: The Deep History of the Radical Right's Stealth Plan for America*. New York: Viking Press Inc.
2. For the source/location of INTO Annual Congress records see www.into.ie/.
3. Following a meeting in June 1921 in the Clarence Place Hall in Belfast of teachers in the six northern counties of Ireland, the INTO established a four-man Vigilante Committee on an interim basis consisting of three members of the Central Executive Committee and one from the Finance Committee. Soon afterwards, the Committee membership and powers were extended to include the chairperson of each county committee and an additional member of the Belfast Committee. The Northern Committee had been formally established by 1927 (Puirséil, 2017, p. 212).

4 This is an acronym for Delivering Equality of Opportunity in Schools, which is the signifier in Ireland for disadvantaged schools; the name gives it away because it is a compensatory strategy modelled on meritocracy, which is open to question in the academic literature (Littler, 2017; Beckett, 2018). In May 2005, the Department of Education and Skills launched the Action Plan for Educational Inclusion, said to remain the policy instrument to address educational disadvantage; but this was updated with a new 2017 DEIS Plan, which is supplemented by Action #47 in successive versions of Bruton's Action Plan for Education; see the four goals, the first foregrounding assessment, online at www.education.ie/en/Schools-Colleges/Services/DEIS-Delivering-Equality-of-Opportunity-in-Schools-/.

5 This was not without major resistances from power brokers including university management to initiatives outside the framework of extant neoliberal policies, but it must be said it was most welcome by teacher partners who came to be research-active in a network of disadvantaged schools in a deindustrialised city in the north of England and who published their work; see the special edition of *Urban Review*, 2014, 46, 5, and on the resistances, see Beckett and Nuttall (2017) and Beckett (forthcoming). Also it should be noted this work fed directly into the BERA Commission on Poverty and Policy Advocacy; see www.bera.ac.uk/project/bera-research-commissions/poverty-and-policy-advocacy.

6 See Frigga Haug (n.d) online: www.friggahaug.inkrit.de/documents/memory-work-researchguidei7.pdf.

7 The INTO Learning Unit also runs the INTO Learning Programme of Trade Union Training as well as the INTO Learning Programme for School Leaders and Retirement Planning Seminars. The INTO Learning Unit has its own committee which meets bi-monthly and oversees the INTO's professional development and trade union training programme (INTO CEC report, 2016–2017).

8 The transcript of this interview was accessed 1 April 2017, from 'Voice for Teachers' online, which noted its contact details: @VoiceForTeachers; voiceforteachers@yahoo.ie and a Facebook page, said to have been 'established as a facility to inform and update teachers from both the Primary and Secondary Educational sectors'; see www.facebook.com/VoiceForTeachers/.

9 The *Irish Teachers' Journal* is a peer-reviewed journal re-established by the INTO in 2013. The journal is distributed to all primary schools in the Republic of Ireland and all post primary schools in Northern Ireland. It is intended to provide an outlet for teachers to bring their research findings to a broader audience and to stimulate thinking and reflection on current educational issues. This compliments the INTO's *InTouch* magazine distributed to members and educational institutions. Ten editions have been published annually since 1999 when it replaced Tuarascáil, which was then the INTO monthly magazine. Each edition features an editorial from the General Secretary, trade union news, advice to members on teaching and educational matters including, curricular, health related and pedagogical information. It is the most widely circulated education magazine in Ireland. Articles published in *InTouch* are also available on the INTO website www.into.ie.

10 The International Financial Services situated at the edge of Dublin's docklands was established by the Haughey Fianna Fail Government in 1982, and it has developed into one of the leading hedge fund service centres in Europe. It attracts many of the world's main financial institutions, which have a presence in Dublin and in other parts of the island of Ireland.

11 In her response to Lynch, Leitch was drawing on research, notably the work of Bourdieu (1977), who described how neoliberalism establishes itself as a *doxa* – an unquestionable orthodoxy that operates as if it were the objective truth – across social space in its entirety, from the practices and perceptions of individuals to the practices and perceptions of the state and social groups.

12 It was timely given a need to simulate the local and national economies, and a first task was to seek funding for the study of Vere Foster's local assisted emigration records, located in scattered places such as Drogheda, the Louth Archeological and Historical Association, and Public Records Office of Northern Ireland. This was considered critically important foundational work to begin the task of connecting the fragmented resources available for Diaspora study. It also showed an obligation to the people of Ireland, north and south, and to the émigré communities abroad.

Afterword The politics of teacher unions and archives

Bob Lingard School of Education, the University of Queensland

Introduction

In this afterword, I reflect on what was provoked in me by engagement with John Carr and Lori Beckett's text, *Teachers and Teacher Unions in a Globalised World*. In my view, there is not enough research about teachers and their work, and about teacher unions and what they do today, nor sufficient research about the relationships between these. We need to know more about teacher unions' actual and desired place in a progressive contemporary education politics and policy. I hope *Teachers and Teacher Unions in a Globalised World* encourages more such research work.

My engagement also stems from acknowledgement of the importance of teacher unions as the collective professional and industrial voice of teachers and to a progressive rethinking of educational policy and for effective opposition to contemporary neoliberal policy developments in education. I have conducted research for the teacher unions (Lingard et al., 2017), have worked with them on policy matters, spoken at union conferences, been involved in campaigns and engaged with the leadership of the teacher unions. I have worked with teacher unions at state and national level in Australia and with Education International (EI), the international federation of teacher unions, headquartered in Brussels and with more than 30 million affiliate members.

Given the global character of corporate and neoliberal reform agendas in schooling, in my view the work of EI takes on even greater salience today. This is Carr and Beckett's 'globalised world'. In this respect, I note here the significant political strategising and research work of EI in respect of the privatisation and commercialisation agendas in contemporary schooling in both the Global North, but particularly in the Global South, which has witnessed the creation of low fee for profit schools in a challenge to quality public provision. The political agendas framing much contemporary education reform are global in reach and aspiration, while policy agendas are also generated within the global education policy field and network governance sees political networks reaching across national borders. This means effective opposition and resistance must also have global reach and understanding. All politics today is a melange of the local, national and global and this carries implications for the work of the teacher unions, including national ones such as the INTO and their relationships with other national unions and particularly with EI. There is necessarily a new politics needed here.

Research

Research is central to the effective work of teacher unions. I note here with elation that the INTO has a director of research. There are actual and desired relationships between teacher unions and research. Lori Beckett has been a passionate and committed advocate of a professional model of teacher as researcher and the importance of academic researchers working in partnerships with teachers around improvement agendas (see, for example, Beckett, 2016). She sees such a model of teacher professionalism as one that ought to be supported and sponsored by teacher unions. She would also see the very production of *Teachers and Teacher Unions* as a manifestation of such a productive teacher/academic partnership. I agree with Lori's stance and accept the necessity of a 'researchly disposition' to teacher professionalism. Nevertheless, I suggest this is only one of the multiple relationships between teacher unions and research. And, of course, the broader field of educational research in all of its contested complexity ought to frame teacher education and teachers' work, as well as that of teacher unions. I am not advocating here for evidence-based practice, but rather research-informed professional practice for teachers. Values and professional judgements are also important component parts of professional practice, and indeed of educational policy, along with research evidence. The teacher unions need to support research-informed policy and practice and enact it in their own work. Here it is my view that they should commit as well to support funding and opportunities for independent, high quality education research of a critical kind to be conducted in the universities.

Young (2011), writing in the US context, has argued that there are five sets of resources that relate to teacher unions in their political and advocacy work. He lists these as membership, benefits, proposed government initiatives, finances and access to policy processes. I would argue that another important resource for the teacher unions in all aspects of their work, industrial, political, professional, advocacy is research. Here I include research conducted by the teacher unions, as well as research commissioned by them. Also important here is the union usage of other research from the broader field of educational research. Relationships between critical academic researchers and teacher unions are also very important here. This is very evident in the contemporary work of EI. I would agree unequivocally with Verger and colleagues (2016) that research in the context of privatisation, commercialisation and the broader neoliberal and corporate agenda on a global scale that challenges the democratic and social justice purposes of public schooling demands a research and knowledge production response as one important defence in teacher union political strategies. Such research can validate union policy claims and union challenges to regressive educational policy reforms. Teacher unions must be in the business of knowledge production. Carr and Beckett's book confirms such a position and the additional point that teachers as professionals should also be knowledge producers. This is Beckett's teacher as researcher model.

Teachers

Teachers are the professionals who constitute what we know as schooling. This is the case be they early years teachers, special needs teachers, primary or secondary teachers, specialist teachers, heads of department, deputy principals or principals. The most important collective organisation for teachers is their teacher union. The more powerful teacher unions globally tend to have the entire spectrum of teachers from classroom practitioners through principals in their membership and thus have a strong voice in industrial matters of collective bargaining around pay and work conditions. Such strength also has financial implications that enable the 'mobilization capacity and political influence' of the teacher unions (Verger, Fontdevila and Zancajo, 2016, p. 167). The teacher unions came into existence paralleling the creation of mass schooling in the late nineteenth century in the so-called advanced nations; in 1868, for example, in Ireland. Teachers often belong to other professional associations; for example, history teachers association, primary teachers, special needs teachers and so on. However, it is the teacher unions in the most advanced nations, which have been the strongest professional and industrial voice for teachers. In some ways, this teacher union strength and industrial/professional tensions represent the idiosyncratic nature of teaching as a profession. This is very evident throughout Carr and Beckett's argument. Their account documents how these tensions have played out in different historical eras.

The balance and imbrications between the professional and the industrial in teacher union work are very important and a source of ongoing tensions (McCollow, 2017). The industrial gives focus to pay and working conditions and teachers as employees and as a collectivity, while the professional focuses more on improving teacher professional knowledges and practices towards improving student learning. While teacher collective interests and student interests are not necessarily one, good working conditions in schools, attractive pay and high teacher morale will have positive indirect effects on student learning. Carr and Beckett document and comment on this ongoing tension in the work of the INTO. Neoliberals, of course, see teachers and their unions as simply vested interests inhibiting change. There are significant strategic and political issues here for teacher unions, as Carr and Beckett illustrate in respect of the INTO and the current emergent Irish policy settlement in education.

Unlike the traditional professions of say law and medicine, teaching is a mass profession and a state-managed one. A common sociological approach to the study of professions was what is called the 'trait model'. This model suggested certain traits which an occupation had to exhibit to be classified as a profession. These traits were drawn from the characteristics of the traditional professions. They include a long period of specialist training, possession of expert esoteric knowledge, self-governance of the occupation, a code of ethics, priority granted to the needs of clients in professional practice and so on. Sometimes, when set against these traits, teachers (and nurses) were classified as semi-professionals. Nonetheless, teachers exhibit many of these broad professional characteristics. The distinguishing feature, though, of teaching as a job is its mass and state-managed character, when compared with the traditional professions.

In a sense, teaching and the whole enterprise of schooling are too significant to leave to individual professional judgement. Schools and their curricular and extra-curricular work are central to the creation of citizens and the imagined community that is the nation; they are central to social cohesion; they are central to social and cultural reproduction; they are central to meritocracy and the provision of equal opportunities; they are central to the future prosperity of the nation and to embedding the values aspired to by the people. In this way, and for these reasons, the state is heavily involved in framing teachers' work in respect of what Bernstein (1971) called the three message systems of schooling, notably, curriculum, pedagogy and evaluation. In the immediate post–World War II years of Keynesianism, teachers had considerable pedagogical autonomy. Central to their professional identity for me was 'pedagogical content knowledge' and this remains so. However the neoliberal policy frames of contemporary schooling systems, as in Ireland with the current Minister's *Action Plan for Education*, implicitly tighten control over pedagogies, as these systems are increasingly steered by high stakes standardised testing and test-based accountability linked to student performance. There has thus been an implicit standardising of teacher pedagogical work. Interestingly, Carr and Beckett show how the founders of the INTO argued for full professional standing for teachers because of the great significance of their work to the nation and for the future. Paradoxically, it is this significance that frames teaching as a state-managed profession.

There is not the same extent of state involvement in the work of doctors and lawyers, nor pressures for the standardisation of their work. Unlike the traditional professions, teachers also serve multiple 'clients' at any one time (25 students in a class) and also serve many 'masters': the system, the school, the principal, parents, communities and students. Furthermore, because teaching is a mass profession with salaries by and large paid for by the public purse, teacher salaries have never matched those of the traditional professions and perhaps never will. Teacher salaries constitute a very high proportion of the recurrent budget of schooling system expenditure and thus teacher pay is very directly affected by the budget philosophy of any given government. This is very evident in the context of contemporary post global financial crisis austerity politics; a politics with debilitating impact in Ireland.

These unique features of teaching see a particular playing out of the industrial and professional foci in the work of teacher unions. In the USA, for example, there are two national federated bodies of teacher unions, the National Education Association and the American Federation of Teachers, with the former more professionally focussed and the latter more industrial in orientation. This professional/industrial tension is very evident in the analyses and documents provided by Carr and Beckett in respect to the INTO.

This concept of a state-managed profession is explicit in respect of all the struggles around the creation of self-governance for the teaching profession. Carr and

Beckett analyse this in relation to the creation of the Teaching Council to regulate the profession in Ireland in 2001 and the significant advocacy work of the INTO in achieving this. Yet Carr and Beckett show how this is under threat in the current political moment. This is reflective of the nature of the teaching profession documented earlier.

An Australian case well exemplifies this professional/industrial binary. Reforming federal Labour governments in Australia (2007–2013) created for the first time a national curriculum and national census testing in literacy and numeracy, as well as establishing the Australian Institute for Teachers and School Leaders (AITSL). Under Labour governments, the teacher unions had representation on the governing body of AITSL. AITSL in conjunction with state level teacher registration authorities, regulates the profession and sets criteria for career progression and also sets out mandatory requirements for teacher education programs run by universities. When the conservatives returned to power in Canberra in 2013, they set about reducing the size of the governing body of AITSL in line with what they argued was best private sector practice in governance and removed all teacher union representation from it. Subsequently, the teacher unions in Australia have refused to work and cooperate with AITSL. We see here a particular politics at work, but also a manifestation of teaching as a state-managed profession; board members are system leaders and academics aligned with the government agenda. In stark contrast, teacher union partnerships (an accord) with government in Australia during the period of Hawke-Keating Labour governments (1983–1996) demonstrated the effectiveness of such a collaborative strategy for progressive educational reform.

This regressive stance by the Abbott and Turnbull conservative government since 2013 links to broader neoliberal policy frames, which see teachers as having a vested interest and as such, holding back necessary reform of schools and schooling systems. Hursh (2016) has unequivocally demonstrated such a political strategy in the US context in the corporate reform agenda of schooling. This agenda, Hursh shows, first critiques public schooling as failing and then seeks to weaken the policy influence of the teacher unions. Teacher union representation of teachers has been a collective activity, while contemporary neoliberal reforms attempt to weaken teacher unions' collective voice and hold individual teachers solely responsible for their students' learning, without any consideration of the effects on this learning of varying socio-economic contexts. Carr and Beckett appear to suggest there are some echoes of this in contemporary Ireland. There is important political work for the teacher unions here, both in Ireland and globally, as the neoliberal and corporate reform agenda is a global one. There are also implications regarding the multiple spatial foci for strategy.

Archive

In *Teachers and Teacher Unions in a Globalised World,* John Carr and Lori Beckett have created an interesting and particular archive or annals of the history and politics of the INTO. This consists of two data sets, as it were. The first is constituted by actual primary documents, the second the memory work of John. It is important to think reflexively here about the archive more generally and its work in historiography. I see this book as a curated archive produced for teachers, the INTO, INTO members, future historians and educational researchers and at the same time serving to celebrate the sesquicentenary of the establishment of the INTO in 1868. It also contributes to the body of research on teacher unions.

Regarding archives generally, there is a tendency to consider such compendiums of historical primary documents as (re)presenting an unsullied version of the past: one without the finger prints of human intervention upon them, as it were, leaving no forensic evidence other than the text. We need to stop and think about this conceptualisation for a moment. Derrida, the French deconstructionist philosopher, is most helpful here. In his most interesting short Freudian influenced book, *Archive Fever* (1998), he rejects any conception of the unsullied nature of primary source archives. He makes a number of points most salient to consideration of the work of archives and for reflection on Carr and Beckett's book. The first is picked up in his observation, 'The archivization produces as much as it records the event' (p. 17). We might conceptualise this as the constitutive aspect of the archive. I would suggest there is another step in this constitutive work of the archive; in respect of this book, Carr and Beckett have chosen the source materials to include. This selectivity also contributes to the constitutive work of the archive and is linked to the political narrative of the work of the INTO over its history that they seek to represent. Furthermore, Derrida argues that the technical structure of the archive (written, material, spoken) described as an 'inscription artefact' also helps constitute the event that the document is taken to represent, given the possibilities and limitations of for example the written word. The same of course is the case with the spoken word, say in an historical interview and I dare say also of memory work. It is interesting in respect of types of inscription of historical artefacts to contemplate the effect on future archives of the current moment of digitalisation and deep mediatisation (Hepp Breiter, and Hasebrink, 2018). Finally, the selectivity and the technical framing of the document, Derrida argues, in a Freudian sense kills the past in constructing it in particular ways and is also importantly as much about imagining a particular future. Foucault in *The Archaeology of Knowledge* has similar things to say about archives and historical traces of various kinds in relation to a particular episteme or truth regime. I am also reminded of the concept of a 'history of the present in respect of the archive'. In a way, Carr and Beckett's book might be seen as providing a history of the present of the INTO.

Politics

Now, none of this reflection on archives is meant as a critique of this book. Rather and very much to the contrary, it is proffered to make us think of the narrative Carr and Beckett are constructing and the ways they think contemporary educational politics ought to work (the desired as opposed to the actual, ought as opposed to is). Rightly in my view, they wish to see a more substantial professional role for teachers in policy production processes; more teachers' voices need to be encouraged and listened to by policymakers and politicians. This would also enhance policy enactment. I note, though, the need to consider the appropriate role of teacher unions here within a democracy with other legitimate interests such as parents and students. This has implications for thinking about teaching as a profession and I would suggest means teaching should not simply take the exclusionary model of the traditional professions as the model. There is intellectual work to be done in this respect.

Carr and Beckett also want more professional trust to be placed in the work of teachers, and again rightly so, rather than the mistrust evident in contemporary manifestations of accountability framed by standardised tests of a census kind (Lingard et al., 2016; Lingard and Lewis, 2016). More importantly, though, they want to see different policy content: policy content that grants more emphasis to the democratic citizenship work of schools, which gives more emphasis to the social justice purposes of schooling linked to the amelioration of poverty and disadvantage, all intimately connected to the constitution of a better nation. I am reminded here of the exhortation of the Scottish poet and artist Alasdair Gray expressed on the exterior walls of the Scottish parliament, 'Work as if you live in the early days of a better nation'. Carr and Beckett's archive is constructed and the text written, as if we are in the early days of a better Ireland, a better Europe, a better schooling system and a better teachers' union. This is a good thing, as without such aspirations, we are condemned to repeat the atrocities, big and small, of the past and of the contemporary present; all to the detriment of young people, the society, its prosperity and cohesion and Ireland's future.

Yet the achievement of such aspirations will have to confront the contemporary politics of austerity and vernacularised version of neoliberal hegemony, as they are played out broadly and specifically within education, and in 'path dependent' ways in Ireland. That will be difficult. Carter, Stevenson and Passy (2010) have argued there have been three ways to date through which the teacher unions across the globe have responded to the current policy moment. They describe these as *rapprochement*, a pragmatic approach that seeks to maximise benefits for members from the changes that are not necessarily supported; *renewal*, use of neoliberal frames, for example, devolution and school autonomy, to strengthen rank and file political involvement and local activism; and *resistance* of varying kinds from confrontation, strike action, through legal challenges to legislation, to less visible mediations of the worst depredations of neoliberal in education in the quotidian everyday of schooling. It seems to me, and this is implicit in Carr and Beckett's argument and archive, there is a necessary additional strategy. I would see this as an aspirational alternative set of policies and politics, one that not only critiques the contemporary hegemonic neoliberal policies and resists them, but also constructs alternative policies towards a more progressive future. This seems to me to be a pressing necessity for contemporary teacher unions around the globe, including for the INTO. This might be seen as strategic as opposed to tactical work and proactive as opposed to reactive. Verger and colleagues (2016) have suggested that teacher union roles are usually reactive with limited teacher union role in agenda setting. Donations by the teacher unions to political parties are one element of a strategy to impact policy and political agendas in education. Research is another.

Let me give an example. No teachers or teacher unions would reject the necessity of accountability in education. Contemporary union resistance and opposition to accountability are to the current anti-educational, managerialist, top-down, test-based construction of accountability (Ranson, 2003; Lingard and Lewis, 2016; Lingard, Sellar and Lewis, 2017). The question rather is how we conceptualise an educative and progressive concept of educational accountability, including considerations about what the role of teachers and their collective voice expressed through their union ought to be in all of this, and what types of accountability might have the most positive impact mediated by teacher professionalism on student learning, including the learning of the most disadvantaged students. In such a mode of accountability there needs to be opportunity for the profession and school communities more broadly to hold policymakers and politicians to account as well, what has been referred to as the demand for the provision of 'opportunity to learn' standards for all.

So it seems to me there is a real need here for a positive thesis in teacher unions' political resistance to contemporary policies. The immediate issues and struggles that teachers and teacher unions face often takes the focus away from developing such positive thesis about the whole gamut of education policies, including importantly funding. My criticism is not only directed to teacher unions here, but also to my academic colleagues in my fields of sociology of education and policy sociology in education, the fields in which Carr and Beckett's text is situated. Both fields fit within a modernist redemptive political project, but at the same time have (over)emphasised the critical and the negative as opposed to the aspirational and positive.

Conclusion

John Carr and Lori Beckett's *Teachers and Teacher Unions in a Globalised World* contributes to the extant research and scholarship on teacher unions. I hope it provokes more such research. Teacher unions have been a significant source of opposition and resistance to the contemporary neoliberal education policy settlement. In my view, they also need to be central players in the construction of alternative policies towards a more socially just future. Contemporary global neoliberalism has exacerbated inequalities, indeed produced and legitimated them through schooling. Research and data evidencing this must be another element in the broader oppositional strategies of the teacher unions. Carr and Beckett's text also importantly demonstrates how the INTO has been able to adapt quite adroitly to changing political contexts since its inception in 1868. This is why their book, their archive, is celebrating the sesquicentenary of the INTO. They also show how the industrial/professional tension has played out in different ways since 1868. What is new today is the global reach of educational reform movements and the involvement of new policy actors, including international and supranational organisations, edu-businesses and philanthro-capitalists. This demands new political strategies. The teacher unions are now more important than ever in the broader union movement and as such need to take a leadership role in opposing the neoliberal, but also in imaging progressive alternatives and a more socially just schooling for a more desirable future.

References

Beckett, L. (2016) *Teachers and Academic Partners in Urban Schools: Threats to Professional Practice*. London: Routledge.

Bernstein, B. (1971) On the classification and framing of educational knowledge. In M.F.D. Young (ed.), *Knowledge and Control: Towards a New Sociology of Education*. London: Collier-MacMillan.

Carter, B., Stevenson, H., and Passy, R. (2010) *Industrial Relations in Education*. New York: Routledge.

Derrida, J. (1998) *Archive Fever: A Freudian Impression*. Chicago: Chicago University Press.

Hepp, A., Breiter, A., and Hasebrink, U. (eds.). (2018) *Communicative Figurations: Transforming Communications in Times of Deep Mediatization*. London: Palgrave MacMillan.

Hursh, D. (2016) *The End of Public Schools: The Corporate Reform Agenda to Privatize Public Education*. New York: Routledge.

Lingard, B., and Lewis, S. (2016) Globalization of the Anglo-American approach to top-down, test-based educational accountability. In G.T. Brown and L.R. Harris (eds.), *Handbook of Human and Social Conditions in Assessment*. New York: Routledge, pp. 387–403.

Lingard, B., Martino, W., Rezai-Rashti, G., and Sellar, S. (2016) *Globalizing Educational Accountabilities*. New York: Routledge.

Lingard, B., Sellar, S., Hogan, A., and Thompson, G. (2017) *Commercialisation in Public Schooling*. Sydney: The New South Wales Teachers Federation.

Lingard, B., Sellar, S., and Lewis, S. (2017) Accountabilities in schools and school systems. In G.W. Noblit (ed.), *Oxford Research Encyclopaedia of Education*. New York: Oxford University Press.

McCollow, J. (2017) Teacher unions. In G.W. Noblit (ed.), *Oxford Research Encyclopaedia of Education*. New York: Oxford University Press.

Ranson, S. (2003) Public accountability in the age of neo-liberal governance. *Journal of Education Policy*, 18(5): 459–480.

Verger, A., Fontdevila, C., and Zancajo, A. (2016) *The Privatization of Education: A Political Economy of Global Education Reform*. New York: Teachers College Press.

Young, T. (2011) Teacher unions in turbulent times: Maintaining their niche. *Peabody Journal of Education*, 86(3): 338–351.

Bibliography

Addey, C., Sellar, S., Steiner-Khamsi, G., Lingard, B., and Verger, A. (2017) The rise of international large-scale assessments and rationales for participation. *Compare: A Journal of Comparative and International Education.* doi:10.1080/03057925.2017.1301399

Adelman, C., and Alexander, R.J. (1982) *The Self-Evaluating Institution: Practice and Principles in the Management of Educational Change.* London: Methuen.

Agasisti, T., Catalano, G., and Sibiano, P. (2013) Can schools be autonomous in a centralised educational system? On formal and actual school autonomy in the Italian context. *International Journal of Educational Management*, 27(3): 292–310. www.emeraldinsight.com/journals.htm?articleid=17084616&show=abstract

Akenson, D.H. (1970) *The Irish Educational Experiment: The National System of Education in the Nineteenth Century.* London: Routledge & Kegan Paul.

Antoniades, A. (2010) *Producing Globalisation: Politics of Discourse and Institutions in Greece and Ireland.* Manchester: Manchester University Press.

Apple, M. (1982) *Education and Power.* London and New York: Routledge.

Arcia, G., and Macdonald, K. (2011) School autonomy and accountability. *System Assessment and Benchmarking for Education Results (SABER) Paper*, April. http://siteresources.worldbank.org/EDUCATION/Resources/278200-1290520949227/School_Autonomy_Accountability_Framework.pdf (accessed 30 January 2014).

Ball, S.J. (2003) The teachers' soul and the terrors of performativity. *Journal of Educational Policy*, 18(2): 215–228.

Ball, S.J. (2013a) Neoliberal education? Confronting the slouching beast. Vere Foster Public Lecture, National Gallery of Ireland, Dublin, 26 February.

Ball, S.J. (2013b) *The Education Debate*, 2nd ed. Bristol: Policy Press.

Ball, S.J. (2013c) *Education, Justice and Democracy: The struggle over ignorance and opportunity.* Policy Paper for the Centre for Labour and Social Studies (CLASS). http://classonline.org.uk/docs/2013_Policy_Paper_-_Education,_justice_and_democracy_(Stephen_Ball).pdf

Barrington, T.J. (1980) *The Irish Administrative System.* Dublin: Institute of Public Administration.

Bascia, N. (1994) *Unions in Teachers' Professional Lives: Social, Intellectual and Practical Contexts.* New York: Teachers' College Press.

Bascia, N. (2008) What teachers want from their unions: What the literature tells us. In M. Compton and L. Weiner (eds.), *The Global Assault on Teaching, Teachers, and Their Unions.* New York: Palgrave Macmillan.

Bascia, N. (2009) Pushing on the paradigm: Research on teachers' organizations as policy actors. In G. Sykes, B. Schneider, and D. Plank (eds.), *Handbook on Educational Policy Research*. London and New York: Routledge.

Bascia, N. (2015) *Teacher Unions in Public Education*. New York: Palgrave Macmillan.

Bascia, N., and Osmond, P. (2012) *Teacher Unions and Educational Reform: A Research Review*. Washington, DC: National Education Association Research.

Beckett, L. (1996) The radical conservative experiment in New South Wales education. Unpublished Ph.D. thesis. Geelong: Deakin University Library.

Beckett, L. (ed.). (2013) *Teacher Education Through Active Engagement: Raising the Professional Voice*. London and New York: Routledge.

Beckett, L. (2014) Editorial: 'Raising teachers' voice on achievement in urban schools in England. *Urban Review*, 46(5): 783–799.

Beckett, L. (2016) *Teachers and Academic Partners in Urban Schools: Threats to Professional Practice*. London and New York: Routledge.

Beckett, L. and Nuttall, A. (2017) A 'usable past' of teacher education in England: history in JET's anniversary issue. *Journal of Education for Teaching*, 43(5): 616–627, DOI: 10.1080/02607476.2017.1370479.

Beckett, L. (2018) Beyond 'naïve possibilitarianism' in urban schools in England. In S. Gannon, R. Hattam, and W. Sawyer (eds.), *Resisting Educational Inequality Reframing Policy and Practice in Schools Serving Vulnerable Communities*, Chapter 3. London and New York: Routledge.

Begg, D. (2016) *Ireland, Small Open Economics and European Integration*. London: Palgrave MacMillan.

BERA – RSA. (2014) The role of research in teacher education – reviewing the evidence. *Interim Report of the BERA – RSA Inquiry*, January. London: BERA. www.bera.ac.uk/wp-content/uploads/2014/02/BERA-RSA-Interim-Report.pdf (accessed 3 September 2016).

Berberoglu, B. (2005) *An Introduction to Classical and Contemporary Classical Social Theory: A Critical Perspective*. Maryland: Rowman & Littlefield.

Bergen, B.H. (1988) Only a schoolmaster: Gender, class and effort to professionalise elementary teaching in England 1870–1910. In J. Ozga (ed.), *Schoolwork: Approaches to the Labour Process of Teaching*. Milton Keynes: Open University Press, pp. 39–60.

Beveridge, W., (1942) *The Beveridge Report: The Way to Freedom From Want*. http://filestore.nationalarchives.gov.uk/pdfs/small/cab-66-31-wp-42-547-27.pdf

Beveridge, S., Groundwater-Smith, S., Kemmis, S., and Wasson, D. (2005) 'Professional Learning that makes a difference': Successful strategies implemented by priority action schools in New South Wales. *Journal of In-Service Education*, 31(4).

Biagini, E., and Mulhall, D. (eds.). (2016) *The Shaping of Modern Ireland: A Centenary Assessment*. Dublin: Irish Academic Press.

Bibby, T., Lupton, R., and Raffo, C. (2017) *Responding to Poverty and Disadvantage in Schools: A Reader for Teachers*. London: Palgrave Macmillan.

Bourdieu, P. (1977) *Outline of a Theory of Practice*. Cambridge: Cambridge University Press.

Brady, C. (ed.). (1994) *Interpreting Irish History: The Debate on Historical Revisionism 1938–1994*. Newbridge: Irish Academic Press.

Braithwaite, J., Makai, T., and Braithwaite, V. (2007) *Regulating Aged Care: Ritualism and the New Pyramid*. Cheltenham: Elgar.

British Educational Research Association (BERA). (2013) *Why Educational Research Matters: A Briefing to Inform Future Funding Decisions [pamphlet]*. London: BERA.

Brock, P., Baxter, D., and Sawyer, W. (2007) *Exceptional Outcomes in ESL/Literacy Achievement*. AESOP Series. Armidale, New South Wales: University of New England.

Brown, T. (1981) *Ireland: A Social and Cultural History 1922–1979*. London: Fontana.

Bruton, R. (1999) Quality – the key debate in education. In N. Ward and T. Dooney (eds.), *Irish Education in the 21st Century*, Chapter 3. Michigan: Oak Tree Press.

Carr, J. (1991a) *A Teacher's Perspective on Professionalism*. Mimeo. Dublin: Irish National Teachers Organisation.

Carr, J. (1991b) Issues of provision, access, participation and incentives: The professional response. In D. Swan (ed.), *Teachers as Learners*, Chapter 5. Dublin: Irish National Teachers Organisation.

Carr, J., and Beckett, L. (2016) Analysing the present: Drawing on the legacy of Vere Foster in public policy debate on futures of schools. Article first published online: *Policy Futures*, 13 December 2016, Issue published, 1 November 2016. https://doi.org/10.1177/1478210316663755

Carr, W. (1989) *Quality in Teaching: Arguments for a Reflective Profession*. London and New York: RoutledgeFalmer.

Carter, B., Stevenson, H., and Passy, R. (2010) *Industrial Relations in Education*. London and New York: Routledge.

Children and their Primary Schools A Report of the Central Advisory Council for Education (England) London: Her Majesty's Stationery Office 1967

Cochran-Smith, M., and Lytle, S.L. (2009) *Inquiry as Stance: Practitioner Research for the Next Generation*. New York: Teachers' College Press.

Cochran-Smith, M., Piazza, P., and Power, C. (2013) The politics of accountability: Assessing teacher education in the United States. *The Educational Forum*, 77(1): 6–27.

Colgan, B. (2001) *Vere Foster: English Gentleman, Irish Champion, 1819–1900*. Rochester, MI: Fountain Publishing.

Compton, M., and Weiner, L. (2008) *The Global Assault on Teaching, Teachers and Their Unions: Stories for Resistance*. New York: Palgrave Macmillan.

Conway, P.F. (2012) Cultural flashpoint: The politics of teacher education reform in Ireland. *The Educational Forum*, 77(1): 51–72.

Conway, P.F., and Murphy, R. (2013) A rising tide meets a perfect storm: New accountabilities in teaching and teacher education in Ireland. *The Educational Forum*, 32(1): 11–36.

Coogan, T.P. (1993a) *Eamon de Valera: The Man who was Ireland*. St Louis: Harper-Collins.

Coogan, T.P. (1993b) *Long Fellow, Long Shadow*. London: Hutchinson.

Coogan, T.P. (1996) *The Troubles: Ireland's Ordeal 1966–1996 and the Search for Peace*. London: Arrow.

Coogan, T.P. (2015) *1916 The Morning After: from the Court Martials to the Troubles*. London: Head of Zeus.

Coolahan, J. (1981) *Irish Education: History and Structure*. Dublin: Institute of Public Administration.

Coolahan, J. (1984) *The ASTI and Post-Primary Education in Ireland, 1909–1984.* Dublin: Association of Secondary Teachers, Ireland.

Coolahan, J. (1987) The changing context for the exercise of professionalism in teaching. article. In P. Hogan (ed.), *Willingly to School? Perspectives on Teaching as a Profession in Ireland in the Eighties.* Dublin: Educational Studies Association of Ireland.

Coolahan, J. (ed.) (1994) *Report on the National Education Convention.* Dublin: National Education Convention Secretariat.

Coolahan, J. (2017) *Towards The Era of Lifelong Learning A History of Education 1800–2016.* Dublin: Institute of Public Administration.

Chuinneagáin, S. (1997) The politics of equality: Catherine Mahon and the Irish National teachers' organisation, 1905–1916. *Women's History Review,* 6(4): 337–346.

Chuinneagáin, S. (1998) *Catherine Mahon: The First Woman President of the INTO.* Dublin: Irish National Teachers Organisation.

Curriculum and Examinations Board. (1985) *Primary Education: A Curriculum and Examinations Board Discussion Paper.* Dublin: author.

Curriculum and Examinations Board. (1985) *Discussion Paper on Primary Education.* Dublin: author.

Darling-Hammond, L. (2000) How teacher education matters. *Journal of Teacher Education,* 51(3): 166–173.

Darling-Hammond, L. (2006) *Powerful Teacher Education: Lessons from Exemplary Programs.* San Francisco, CA: Jossey-Bass.

De Buitléir, S. (1985) Towards a general theory of curriculum and evaluation. Unpublished paper presented to INTO General Secretary, Gerry Quigley on 15 November 1990.

Department of Education. (1951) *An Naí-Scoil.* Dublin: Stationery Office.

Department of Education. (1967) *Report of the Commission on Higher Education 1960–1967.* Dublin: Stationery Office.

Department of Education. (1970) *Higher Education Authority Report on Teacher Education.* Dublin: Stationery Office.

Department of Education. (1971) *Curaclam na Bunscoile-Primary School Curriculum-Teachers' Handbooks, Parts 1 and 2.* Dublin: Browne and Nolan.

Department of Education. (1990) *Report of the Review Body on the Primary Curriculum.* Dublin: Stationery Office.

Department of Education and Skills. (2005) DEIS: Delivering equality of opportunity in schools: An action plan for educational inclusion. www.education.ie/en/Publications/Policy-Reports/deis_action_plan_on_educational_inclusion.pdf (accessed 3 September 2016).

Department of Education and Skills. (2011) An evaluation of the planning processes in DEIS primary schools. www.education.ie/en/Publications/Inspection-Reports-Publications/Evaluation-Reports-Guidelines/insp_deis_primary_2011.pdf (accessed 3 September 2016).

Department of Education and Skills (2015a) Advancing school autonomy in the Irish school system. Consultation Paper issued by Department of Education and Skills Dublin: DES.

Department of Education (2015b) Advancing school autonomy in the Irish school system. Research Paper. Dublin: author.

Department of Education and Skills (2016a) Minister's briefing overview. https://www.education.ie/en/Publications/Ministers-Brief-/Ministers-Brief-2016-Overview-.pdf

Department of Education and Skills. (2016b) Looking at our school 2016: A quality framework for primary schools. https://www.education.ie/en/Press-Events/Press-Releases/2016-Press-Releases/PR2016-09-15.html

Department of Education and Skills. (2016c) Action plan for education, 2016–2019. Dublin. www.education.ie/en/Publications/Corporate-Reports/Strategy-Statement/Department-of-Education-and-Skills-Strategy-Statement-2016-2019.pdf

Department of Education and Skills. (2016d) School self-evaluation guidelines 2016–2020. www.education.ie/en/Publications/Inspection-Reports-Publications/Evaluation-Reports-Guidelines/School-Self-Evaluation-Guidelines-2016-2020-Primary.pdf

Department of Education and Science (2016e) Looking at our school 2016: A quality framework for primary-schools. https://www.education.ie/en/Publications/Inspection-Reports-Publications/Evaluation-Reports-Guidelines/Looking-at-Our-School-2016-A-Quality-Framework-for-Primary-Schools.pdf

Department of Education and Skills. (2017) Action plan for education 2017. www.education.ie/en/Publications/Corporate-Reports/Strategy-Statement/Action-Plan-for-Education-2017.pdf

Department of Education and Skills (2018) Action plan for education. https://www.education.ie/en/Publications/Corporate-Reports/Strategy-Statement/action-plan-for-education-2018.pdf

Dewey, J. (1938) *Experience and Education*. New York: Palgrave MacMillan.

Dolton, P., McIntosh, S., and Chevalier A. (2003) *Teachers Pay and Performance*. London: Institute of Education, University of London.

Doyle, M. (1914) *A Glance at the Past: The Central Educational Annual*. Dublin: Dublin Central Teachers' Association.

Dudnik, S., Hagemann, K., and Tosh, J. (eds.). (2004) *Masculinities in Politics and War: Gendered Modern History*. Manchester: Manchester University Press.

Elliot, J. (1995) Self-evaluation and teacher competence. *Irish Educational Studies*, 14: 1–12.

Etzioni, T. (ed.) (1969) *The Semi-Professionals and Their Organization: Teachers, Nurses and Social Workers*. New York: The Free Press.

European Council Directive 89/48/EEC of 21 December 1988 on a general system for the recognition of higher-education diplomas awarded on completion of professional education and training of at least three years' duration. http://eurlex.europa.eu/LexUriServ/LexUriServ.do?uri=CELEX:31989L0048:en:HTML

Evers, J., and Kneyber, R. (ed.). (2016) *Flip the System: Changing Education from the Ground Up*. London and New York: Routledge. www.flippingthesystem.co.uk.

Fanning, R. (2015) *Eamon de Valera: A Will to Power*. Cambridge, MA: Harvard University Press.

Fanning, R. (2016) *Eamonn de Valera: A Will to Power*. London: Faber and Faber.

Farrell, M., Knirck, J., and Meehan, C. (eds.). (2015) *A Formative decade: Ireland in the 1920s*. Newbridge: Irish Academic Press – Merrion Press.

Fennell, D. (1983) *State of the Nation: Ireland since the Sixties*. Ward River.

Fennell, D. (1984) *Irish Catholics and Freedom since 1916* (A Doctrine & life special). Dublin: Dominican Publications.

Fennell, D. (1993) *Heresy: The Battle of Ideas in Modern Ireland*. Belfast: Blackstaff Press.
Fennell, D. (2016) In defence of populism. *The Irish Times*, 23 December.
Ferriter, D. (2015) *A Nation and Not a Rabble: The Irish Revolution 1913–1923*. London: Profile Books.
Ferriter, D. (2016a) Keynote address to Irish national teachers organisation annual congress. Dublin. www.into.ie/ROI/NewsEvents/Conferences/AnnualCongress/AnnualCongress2016/WebcastArchive/Tuesday29March/
Ferriter, D. (2016b) After commemoration comes the hard part. *The Irish Times*, 2 April. www.irishtimes.com/opinion/diarmaid-ferriter-after-commemoration-comes-the-hard-part-1.2595340
Flanagan, F. (1994) Patrick Pearse. Paper for Programme 8 of the Great Educators First series broadcast by RTE Radio 1 May 16 1994: http://www.minerva.mic.ul.ie/vol1/pearse.html
Follet, M.P. (1957) *Dynamic Administration: The collected papers of Mary Parker Follett*. London: Pitman.
Foley, M (2014) *The Bloodied Field*. Dublin: The O'Brien Press.
Foster, R.F. (1983) History and the Irish question. *Transactions of the Royal Historical Society*, 33: 169–192.
Foster, R.F. (1989/2012) *Modern Ireland: 1600–1972*. London: Penguin.
Gale, T., and Densmore, K. (2000) *Just Schooling: Explorations in the Cultural Politics of Teaching*. Buckingham and Philadelphia: Open University Press.
Gallagher, C. (2017) Quality in education-GERM theory and professional vaccination. In Irish National Teachers Organisation (ed.), *Quality in Education: Accountability and Responsibility*. Dublin: Irish National Teachers Organisation.
Galvin, C. (2008) The licensed teacher scheme in England and Wales: Its significance within the wider context of initial teacher preparation. *Irish Educational Studies*, 13(1): 130-144, DOI: 10.1080/0332331940130113
Garvin, T. (1981) The growth of faction in the Fianna fail party, 1966–80. *Parliamentary Affairs*, XXIV: 110–123.
Garvin, T. (2004) *Preventing the Future: Why Was Ireland So Poor for So Long?* Dublin: Gill and MacMillan.Ghale, B., and Beckett, L. (2013) Teachers' politicisation. In L. Beckett (ed.), *Teacher Education through Active Engagement: Raising the Professional Voice*, Chapter 13. London and New York: Routledge.
Gillis, L. (2016) *Women of the Irish Revolution*. Cork: Mercier Press.
Girvin, B. (2006) *The Emergency: Neutral Ireland, 1939–1945*. London: Palgrave Macmillan.
Gleeson, J. (2010) *Curriculum Context: Partnership, Power and Praxis in Ireland*. Oxford: Peter Lang.
Gleeson, J. (2012) The professional knowledge base and practice of Irish post-primary teachers: What is the research evidence telling us? *Irish Educational Studies*, 31(1): 1–17.
Gleeson, J., and Ó'Donnabháin, D. (2009) Strategic planning and accountability in Irish Education. *Irish Educational Studies*, 28(1): 27–46.
Glynn,P. (1869) *The Irish National Teachers: Case Stated*. Dublin: Robert M.Chamney opac.oireachtas.ie/Data/Library3/Library3/DCT109001.pdf
Goodson, I.F. (ed.). (1985) *Social Histories of the Secondary Curriculum: Subjects for Study*. London, New York and Philadelphia: Falmer Press.

Goodson, I.F., and Ball, S. (eds.). (1984) *Defining the Curriculum: Histories and Ethnographies*. London, New York and Philadelphia: Falmer Press.

Goodway, D. (1996) *Anarchist Seeds beneath the Snow: Libertarian Thought and British Writers*. Liverpool: Liverpool University Press.

Gorton, J., Williams, M., and Wrigley, T. (2014) Inspection judgements on urban schools: A case for the defence. *Urban Review*, 46 (5).

Government of Ireland. (1958) *Programme for Economic Expansion*. Dublin: Stationery Office. http://opac.oireachtas.ie/AWData/Library3/Library2/DL006590.pdf

Government of Ireland. (1963) *Second Programme for Economic Expansion*. Dublin: Stationery Office. http://opac.oireachtas.ie/AWData/Library3/Library2/DL013474.pdf

Government of Ireland. (1968) *Tribunal on Teachers' Salaries: Report Presented to the Minister for Education*. Dublin: Stationery Office. http://opac.oireachtas.ie/AWData/Library3/Library2/DL022089.pdf

Government of Ireland. (1991) *Programme for Economic and Social Progress*. Dublin: Stationery Office. www.taoiseach.gov.ie/eng/Publications/Publications_Archive/Publications_pre_1997/ProgramForEconomicandSocialProgress.pdf

Government of Ireland. (1992) *Education for a Changing World: Green Paper on Education*. Dublin: Stationery Office. www.education.ie/en/Publications/Policy-Reports/Education-for-a-Changing-World-Green-Paper.pdf

Government of Ireland. (1995) *Charting Our Education Future*. Dublin: Stationery Office. www.education.ie/en/Publications/Policy-Reports/Charting-Our-Education-Future-White-Paper-On-Education-Launch-Copy-1995-.pdf

Government of Ireland. (1998) Education Act 1998. www.irishstatutebook.ie/eli/1998/act/51/enacted/en/html

Government of Ireland. (2011–2016) Programme for government 2011–2016. www.taoiseach.gov.ie/eng/Work_Of_The_Department/Programme_for_Government/Programme_for_Government_2011-2016.pdf

Granville, G. (2012) *Dublin in 1913: Lockout and Legacy*. Dublin: O'Brien Press.

Groundwater-Smith, S., and Campbell, A. (2007) *An Ethical Approach to Practitioner Research*. London and New York: Routledge.

Groundwater-Smith, S., and Kemmis, S. (2005) *Knowledge-Building Schools: Educational Development for All: Companion Paper 4 in New South Wales Department of Education and Training*. Report of the consultation on the future directions of education and training. Sydney: NSW Department of Education and Training. www.det.nsw.edu.au/reviews/futuresproject/ index.htm (accessed 31 August 2010).

Groundwater-Smith, S., Le Cornu, R., and Ewing, R. (2006) *Teaching: Challenges and Dilemmas*. Southbank, VIC: Thomson Learning.

Groundwater-Smith, S., Mitchell, J., and Mockler, N. (2007) *Learning in the Middle Years: More than a Transition*. Melbourne: Thomson.

Groundwater-Smith, S., and Mockler, N. (2007) Ethics in practitioner research: An issue of quality. *Research Papers in Education*, 22(2): 199–211. www.tandfonline.com/doi/abs/10.1080/02671520701296171#.U7v4yZRdWSo

Grummell, B., and Lynch, K. (2016) Rethinking the Irish Welfare State: Challenges and Change? In F. Dukelow and M.P. Murphy (eds.), *New Managerialism as a Political Project in Irish Education*, Chapter 10. Basingstoke: Palgrave Macmillan.

Gunningham, N., Grabosky, P.N. (1998) *Smart Regulation: Designing Environmental Policy*. Oxford: Clarendon Press.

Gunter, H.M. (2016). *An Intellectual History of School Leadership Practice and Research*. London: Bloomsbury Academic.

Hall, S., Massey, D., and Rustin, M. (2015) *After Neoliberalism? The Kilburn Manifesto*. https://www.lwbooks.co.uk/sites/default/files/freebook/after_neoliberalism_complete_0.pdf

Hardiman, M. (2012) *The Brain-Targeted Teaching Model for 21st Century Schools*. London: Sage Publications.

Hardiman, N. (ed.). (2012) *Irish Governance in Crises*. Manchester and New York: Manchester University Press.

Hegarty, S., and O'Toole, F. (2006) *Irish Times Book of 1916 Rising*. Dublin: Gill & Macmillan.

Held, D. (2006) *Models of Democracy*. Cambridge: Polity Press.

Henry, M., Knight, J., Lingard, R., & Taylor, S. (1988) *Understanding Schooling: An Introductory Sociology of Australian Education*. London: Routledge.

Hislop, H. (2012) The professor seamas Ó Súilleabháin memorial lecture: The quality assurance of Irish schools and the role of evaluation: Current and future trends. National University of Ireland – Maynooth, 2 May. www.education.ie/en/Publications/Inspection-Reports-Publications/Evaluation-Reports-Guidelines/The-Quality-Assurance-of-Irish-Schools-and-the-Role-of-Evaluation-Current-and-Future-Trends.pdf

Hislop, H. (2013) Applying an evaluation and assessment framework: An Irish perspective. EU Presidency Conference: Better Assessment and Evaluation to Improve Teaching and Learning, Dublin, 19–20 March (delivered During the Irish Presidency of the European Union). www.eu2013.ie/media/eupresidency/content/documents/Applying-an-Evaluation-and-Assessment-Framework-An-Irish-Perspective-(Dr-Harold-Hislop).pdf (accessed 28 July 2016).

Hislop, H. (2017) A co-professional approach to inspection for accountability and improvement: Progress and prospects in the Irish context, inaugural public lecture to mark the incorporation of the centre for evaluation, quality and inspection within the DCU Institute of Education, Dublin City University, St Patrick's Campus Thursday, 11 May. www.education.ie/en/Publications/Inspection-Reports-Publications/Evaluation-Reports-Guidelines/A-Co-professional-Approach-to-Inspection-for-Accountability-Improvement.pdf

Hogan, P. (1985) Progressivism and the primary school curriculum 1. *Studies in Education: A Journal of Educational Research*, 3(1): 42–45. Dublin: Trinity College.

Hogan, P. (1986) 'Progressivism' and the Primary School Curriculum, in Oideas 29. Dublin: Government Publications Office, pp. 25–40.

Honohan, P. (2009) What went wrong in Ireland? Paper prepared for the World Bank, May. Paris: Organisation for Economic Cooperation and Development (OECD) Publishing.

Hursh, D. (2008) *High Stakes Testing and the Decline of Education: The Real Crisis in Education*. Lanham, MD: Rowman & Littlefield.

Hursh, D. (2015) Even more of the same: How free market capitalism dominates education. In P. Carr and B. Porfilio (eds.), *The Phenomenon of Obama and the Agenda for Education: Can Hope Audaciously Trump Neoliberalism?* 2nd ed. Charlotte, NC: Information Publishing.

Irish National Teachers' Organisation. (1941) Report of the Committee of Inquiry into the Use of Irish as a Teaching Medium to Children whose Home Language is English. Dublin: author.

Irish National Teachers' Organisation. (1947) *A Plan for Education*. Dublin: author.
Irish National Teachers' Organisation (1948) *80 Years of Progress*. Dublin: author.
Irish National Teachers' Organisation. (1980) *A Proposal for Growth: The Administration of National Schools*. Report by Special committee. Dublin: author.
Irish National Teachers' Organisation. (1988) *Primary Curriculum and Related Matters*. Dublin: author.
Irish National Teachers' Organisation. (1992) *Professionalism in the 1990s*. Dublin: author.
Irish National Teachers' Organisation. (1994) *Comhairle Múinteoireachta: A Teaching Council: Accessible, Accountable and Autonomous*. Dublin: author.
Irish National Teachers' Organisation Central Executive Annual Reports 1963–1964; 1967–1968; 1975–1976; 1985–1986; 1989–1990; 1990–1991; 1994–1995 and 2016–2017. Dublin: author.
Irish National Teachers' Organisation. Evidence of the Irish national teachers' association in reply to queries addressed by the commissioners to Vere Foster, Esq., and submitted by him for their consideration. Dublin: author. http://opac.oireachtas.ie/Data/Library3/Library3/DCT109002.pdf
Johnson, T.J. (1972) *Professions and Power*. London: Palgrave Macmillan.
Jones, K. and O'Brien, J. (2014) *European Perspectives on Professional Development in Teacher Education*. London and New York: Routledge.
Knirck, J. (2013) *Afterimage of the Revolution: Cumann na nGaedheal and Irish Politics, 1922–1932 (History of Ireland and the Irish Diaspora)*. Madison: University of Wisconsin Press.
Kauffman, L.A. (2017) *Direct Action Protest and the Reinvention of American Radicalism*. New York: Verso.
Kelly, A. (2002) *Compulsory Irish: Irish Language and Education in Ireland 1870s-1970s*. Dublin: Irish Academic Press.
Kemmis, S., and Stake, R. (1988) *Evaluating Curriculum*. Sydney: UNSW Press.
Larson, M.S. (1977) *The Rise of Professionalism: A Sociological Analysis*. Berkeley: University of California Press.
Leahy, P. (2013) *The Price of Power, Inside Ireland's Crises Coalition*. London: Penguin Ireland.
Lee, J.J. (1980) Worker and society in modern Ireland. In D. Nevin (ed.), *Trade Unions and Change in Irish Society*. Cork: Mercier Press.
Lee, J.J. (1989) *Ireland 1912–1985: Politics and Society*. Cambridge: Cambridge University Press.
Lee, J.J (2008) *The Modernisation of Irish Society 1848–1918*. Dublin: Gill and Macmillan.
Leitch, R. (2013) *Living in a Professional 'Hall of Mirrors': Caring, Sharing and Researching in Education in Ireland, North and South*. A Response to Kathleen Lynch. Belfast: Queens University Mimeo.
Lieberman, A., and Miller, L. (2008). *Teachers in Professional Communities: Improving Teaching and Learning*. New York: Teachers College Press.
Limond, D. (2007) Education, neo-liberalism and contemporary Ireland. *Studies: An Irish Quarterly Review*, 96(382): 169–178.
Lingard, B. (2009) *Testing Times: The Need for New Intelligent Accountabilities for Schooling*. Brisbane: Queensland Teachers' Union. www.qtu.asn.au/files/9113/2780/3358/29-01-2012_1315_170.pdf
Lingard, B. (2011) Policy as numbers: AC/counting for educational research. *Australian Educational Researcher*, 38: 355–382.

Lingard, B. (2012) Schooling and pupil progress: What needs to be done in policy, schools and classrooms? Vere Foster Public Lecture. Dublin: Royal Irish Academy, 10 September.

Lingard, B. (2013) Historicizing and contextualizing global policy discourses: Test- and standards-based accountabilities in education. *The International Education Journal: Comparative Perspectives*, 12(2): 122–132.

Lingard, B., and Grek, S. (2007) *The OECD, Indicators and PISA: An Exploration of Events and Theoretical Perspectives*. Edinburgh: ESRC/ESP Research Project.

Lingard, B., and Ozga, J. (2007) Introduction: Reading education policy and politics. In B. Lingard and J. Ozga (eds.), *The Routledge Falmer Reader in Education Policy and Politics*. London and New York: Routledge, pp. 1–8.

Lingard, B., and Renshaw, P. (2010) Teaching as a research-informed profession. In A. Campbell and S. Groundwater-Smith (eds.), *Connecting Inquiry and Professional Learning in Education: International Perspectives and Practical Solutions*, Chapter 3. London and New York: Routledge.Lingard, B., and Sellar, S. (2012) A policy sociology reflection on school reform in England: From the Third Way to the Big Society. *Journal of Educational Administration and History*, 44(1): 43–63.

Little, G. (ed.) (2015) *Global Education 'Reform': Building Resistance and Solidarity*. London: Manifesto Press. http://manifestopress.org.uk/index.php/publications2/38-global-education

Littler, J. (2017) *Against Meritocracy: Culture, Power and Myths of Mobility*. London and New York: Routledge.

Looney, A. (2014) Curriculum politics and practice: From implementation to agency. *Irish Teachers' Journal*, 2(1): 7–14.

Lukacs, J. (2005) *Remembered Past: John Lukacs on History, Historians and Historical Knowledge*. A reader. In John Lukacs (ed.), with an Introduction by Malvasi, M.G and Nelson, J. O. 1st ed Wilmington, Delaware: ISI Books

Lupton, R. (2004) Understanding local contexts for schooling and their implications for school processes and quality. *Research Intelligence* (BERA Newsletter) 89.

Lupton, R. (2006) Schools in disadvantaged areas: Low attainment and a contextualised policy response. In L. Lauder, P. Brown, J. Dillabough, and A.H. Halsey (eds.), *Education, Globalisation and Social Change*, Chapter 45. Oxford: Oxford University Press.

Lynch, K. (2013) New managerialism in education. Vere Foster Public Lecture. Belfast: Queen's University, 27 September.

Lynch, K., Grummell, B., and Devine, D. (2012) *New Managerialism in Education, Commercialization, Carelessness and Gender*. Basingstoke: Palgrave MacMillan.

Lynch, K., Grummell, B., and Devine, D. (2015) *New Managerialism in Education: Commercialization, Carelessness and Gender*, 2nd ed. Basingstoke: Palgrave Macmillan.

MacBeath, J. (1999) *School Must Speak for Themselves: The Case for School Self-Evaluation*. London and New York: Routledge.

MacLean, N. (2017) *Democracy in Chains: The Deep History of the Radical Right's Stealth Plan for America*. New York: Viking Press Inc.

Mahon, C. (1914) *University Education and Training of Teachers in the Central Educational Annual, 1914*. Dublin: Dublin Central Teachers Association

Mahon, C., Mills, D., and Morton, M. (2013) *Ethnography in Education*. London: Sage Books.

Mansergh, M. (2016) Was it for this? The state of the nation. First published in *The Irish Times*, Saturday 20 November, 2010. Reproduced in R. Mc Greevy (ed.),

Was It for This? Reflections on the Easter Rising and What It Means to Us Now 1916–2016. Dublin: The Irish Times.
Marwick, A. (1981) *The Nature of History*. London: Palgrave Macmillan.
McAullife, M., and Gillis, L. (2016) *Richmond Barracks 1916, 'We Were There' 77 Women of the Easter Rising*. Dublin: Four Courts Press.
McCarthy, D. (2007) Teaching self-advocacy to students with disability. *About Campus*, November/December.
McCormick, E. (1996) *The INTO and the 1946 Teachers' Strike*. Dublin: Irish National Teachers Organisation.
McCulloch, G. (2004) *Documentary Research in Education, History and Social Sciences*. London and New York: RoutledgeFalmer.
McCulloch, G. (2011) *The Struggle for the History of Education*. London and New York: Routledge.
McCulloch, G., and Richardson, W. (2000) *Historical Research in Historical Settings: Doing Qualitative Research in Educational Settings*. Milton Keynes: Open University.
McCune Reid, H.F. (1956) *A Short Biographical Study of Vere Foster: First President*. Dublin: Irish National Teachers Organisation.
McDonnell, L.M., and Pascal, A. (1988) *Teacher Unions and Educational Reform*. Rand Corporation and Center for Policy Research in Education: Rutgers University and University of Wisconsin Madison.
McGreevy, R. (ed.) (2016) *Was It for This? Reflections on the Easter Rising and What It Means to Us Now, 1916–2016*. Dublin: The Irish Times.
McKinsey and Co. (1997) War for talent. Survey. https://invosights.wordpress.com/2011/11/23/war-for-talent-the-mckinsey-survey/
McNamara, G., and O'Hara, J. (2006) Workable compromise or pointless exercise? School-based evaluation in the Irish context. *Education Management and Administration and Leadership*, 34(4): 134–145.
McNamara, G., and O'Hara, J. (2008a) The importance of the concept of self-evaluation in the changing landscape of education policy. *Educational Evaluation*, 34: 173–179.
McNamara, G., and O'Hara, J. (2008b) *Trusting Schools and Teachers: Developing Educational Professionalism through Self-Evaluation*. New York: Peter Lang.
McNamara, G., and O'Hara, J. (2012) From looking at our schools (LAOS) to whole school evaluation – management, leadership and learning (WSE-MLL): The evolution of inspection in Irish schools over the past decade. *Educational Assessment, Evaluation and Accountability*, May, 24(2): 79–97.
McNeill, M. (1971) *Vere Foster 1819–1900: An Irish Benefactor*. Belfast: Institute of Irish Studies, Queen's University Belfast.
Michaels, E., Hansfield-Jones, H., and Axelrod, B.(2001) *The War for Talent*. Cambridge, MA: Harvard Business Press.
Mills, D., and Morton, M. (2013) *Ethnography in Education* (BERA/SAGE Research Methods in Education). London: Sage publications.
Mills, M. (2013) Challenging the 'Tyranny of no alternative': Teachers and students working towards socially just schooling. Vere Foster Public Lecture, National Gallery of Ireland, Dublin, 7 November.
Mooney Simmie, G. (2012) The pied piper of neo liberalism calls the tune in the Republic of Ireland: An analysis of education policy text from 2000–2012. *Journal for Critical Education Policy Studies*, 10(2): 485–514. www.jceps.com/wp-content/uploads/PDFs/10-2-18.pdf (accessed 3 September 2016).

Moroney, M. (2007) *National Teachers' Salaries and Pensions 1831–2000-A Historical Chronology and Review of the Role of the INTO*. Dublin: Institute of Public Administration.

Mortimore, P. (2014) *Education under Siege: Why There Is A Better Alternative*. Bristol: Policy Press.

Mortimore, P., and Whitty, G. (1997/2000) *Can School Improvement Overcome the Effects of Disadvantage?* London: Institute of Education (Perspectives on Education Policy; 9).

Mortimore, P., and Whitty, G. (2000) Can school improvement overcome the effects of educational disadvantage? In T. Cox (ed.), *Combating Educational Disadvantage: Meeting the Needs of Vulnerable Children*. London: Falmer Press.

Mourshed, M., Chikioke, C., and Barber, M. (2010) *How the World's Most Improved School Systems Keep Getting Better*. McKinsey and Company. http://mckinseyonsociety.com/how-the-worlds-most-improved-school-systems-keep-getting-better/

Mulcahy, D.J., and O'Sullivan, D. (eds.). (1989) *Irish Educational Policy: Process & Substance*. Dublin. Institute of Public Administration.

Munck, R. (1985) *Ireland: Nation, State, and Class Conflict*. Boulder, CO: Westview Press.

Munn, P. (2014) Taking research-informed teaching seriously: From aspiration to reality. Vere Foster Trust lecture, National Gallery of Ireland, Dublin, 11 September.

Murphy, D. (1984) The dilemmas of primary curriculum reform. *Studies in Education: A Journal of Educational Research*, 2(1): 7–21.

Murphy, D. (1985) Progressivism and the primary school curriculum 1. *Studies in Education: A Journal of Educational Research*, 3(1): 56–63.

Murphy, D. (1986) The dilemmas of primary curriculum reform. *Oideas*, 29: 7–24. Dublin: Department of Education.

Murphy, M. (1990) *Blackboard Unions: The AFT and the NEA, 1900–1980*. Ithaca, NY: Cornell University Press.

National Council for Special Education. (2011) *The Future Role of Special Schools and Classes in Ireland – Policy Advice*. Dublin: National Council for Special Education.

National Economic and Social Council (2011), Quality and standards in human services in Ireland: Overview of concepts and practice, Report No. 124, December 2011, Dublin: National Economic and Social Council. Quoted in National Economic and Social Council (2012). *Quality and Standards in Human Services in Ireland: The School System*. Dublin: author. http://files.nesc.ie/nesc_reports/en/NESC_129_main_report.pdf

National Economic and Social Council. (2012) *Quality and Standards in Human Services in Ireland: The School System*. Dublin: author. http://files.nesc.ie/nesc_reports/en/NESC_129_main_report.pdf

National Programme Conference. (1922) *National Programme of Primary Instruction*. Dublin: National Programme Conference/Educational Company.

National Programme Conference. (1926) *Report and Programme Presented by the National Programme Conference to the Minister for Education*. Dublin: Stationery Office.

Nevo, D. (ed.). (2002) *School-Based Evaluation: An International Perspective*. Oxford: Elsevier Science.

Nicholas, T. (1999). *The Myth of Meritocracy: An Inquiry into the Social Origins of Britain's Business Leaders since 1850*. [online] Available at: http://eprints.lse.ac.uk/22385/1/wp53.pdf [Accessed 24 Oct. 2016].

Ó'Buachalla, S. (1988) *Education Policy in Twentieth Century Ireland*. Dublin: Wolfhound Press.

O'Connell, T.J. (1968) *100 Years of Progress: The Story of the Irish National Teachers' Organisation, 1868–1968*. Dublin: Irish National Teachers Organisation.

O'Connor, S. (1986) *A Troubled Sky. Reflections on the Irish Educational Scene 1957–1968*. Dublin: St Patrick's College Educational Research Centre.

O'Donnell, M. (2017) Quality education: Teacher responsibility and accountability. In INTO (ed.), *Quality in Education: Accountability and Responsibility*. Dublin: Irish National Teachers Organisation.

O'Donoghue, T., and Harford, J. (2012) Contesting the Limond thesis on British influence in Irish education since 1922: A comparative perspective. *Comparative Education*, 48(3): 337–246.

O'Donoghue, T., and Harford, J. (2016) *Secondary School Education in Ireland History, Memories and Life Stories, 1922–1967*. London: Palgrave Macmillan.

O'Neill, O. (2002) *A Question of Trust*. Cambridge: Cambridge University Press.

O'Riain, S. (2016) *The Rise and Fall of Ireland's Celtic Tiger: Liberalism, Boom and Bust*. New York: Cambridge University Press.

O'Riordan, B. (1977) The documentation of the Irish labour party in education. *Studies: An Irish Quarterly Review*, 66: 262–263, 122–134.

O'Sullivan, D. (2005) *Cultural Politics and Irish Education since the 1950s*. Dublin: Institute of Public Administration.

O'Toole, F. (2009) *Ship of Fools: How Stupidity and Corruption Sank the Celtic Tiger*. London: Faber and Faber.

O'Toole, F. (1994) Why social partnership needs to be revived. *The Irish Times*, Tuesday, 1 November. www.irishtimes.com/opinion/fintan-o-toole-why-social-partnership-needs-to-be-revived-1.2848959

Organisation for Economic Cooperation and Development (OECD). (1965) *Survey Team, Investment in Education*. Paris: OECD Publishing.

Organisation for Economic Cooperation and Development (OECD). (1991) *Review of National Policies for Education: Ireland 1992*. Paris: OECD Publishing.

Organisation of Economic Cooperation and Development (OECD). (2012) *Equity and Quality in Education: Supporting Disadvantaged Students and Schools*. OECD Publishing. http://dx.doi.org/10.1787/9789264130852-en

Owens, R.C. (2005) *A Social History of Women in Ireland 1870–1970*. Dublin: Gill and Macmillan.

Pearse, P.H. (1916; 1976, reprint ed.) *The Murder Machine and Other Essays*. Cork: Mercier Press.

Pelling, H. (1963) *A History of British Trade Unionism*. Harmondsworth: Penguin Books.

Peters, R.S. (ed.) (1969) *Perspectives on Plowden*. London: Routledge & Kegan Paul.

Philpott, C. (2014) *Theories of Professional Learning: A Critical Guide for Teacher Educators*. Northwich: Critical Publishing.

Plowden. (1967) The Plowden Report (1967)

Poole, W. (2015) Defending Teachers' Rights and Promoting Public Education: Evolving and Emerging Union Strategies within a Globalised Neoliberal Context. In Bascia, N. (Ed), *Teacher Unions in Public Education. Politics, History, and the Future*, Chapter 3. New York: Palgrave Macmillan.

Puirséil, N. (2017) *Kindling the Flame-150 Years of the Irish National Teachers' Organisation*. Dublin: Gill Books.

Punch, K.F. (2009) *Introduction to Research Methods in Education*. London: Sage Publications.
Purvis, J. (1985) Reflections upon doing historical documentary research from a feminist perspective. In R. Burgess (ed.), *Strategies of Educational Research: Qualitative Methods*, Chapter 7. London: Falmer Press.
Putnam RD. (2000) *Bowling Alone: The Collapse and Revival of American Community*. New York: Simon & Schuster.
Quinn, R. (2012) The future development of education in Ireland. *Studies: An Irish Quarterly Review*, 101(402): 123–138.
Quinn, R. (2014) Reforming education: Building a better future. www.education.ie/en/Press-Events/Speeches/2014-Speeches/SP14-03-05.html (accessed 3 September 2016).
Raworth, K. (2017) *Doughnut Economics Seven Ways to Think Like a 21st-Century Economist*. New York: Cornerstone.
Rizvi, F., and Lingard, B. (2010) *Globalising Education Policy*. London and New York: Routledge.
Rooney, M. (2016) *Margaret Skinnider, 1916 Heroine: The Monaghan Connection*. Monaghan: The Margaret Skinnider Appreciation Society.
Rosen, B.C. (1998) *Winners and Losers of the Information Revolution: Psychosocial Change and Its Discontents*. Westport, CT: Praeger.
Roy, W. (1983) *Teaching under Attack*. London and New York: Routledge.
Rudduck, J., and Hopkins, D. (1985) *Research as a Basis for Teaching: Readings from the Work of Lawrence Stenhouse*. London: Heinemann Educational Books.
Sachs, J. (2003a) *The Activist Teaching Profession*. Milton Keynes: Open University Press.
Sachs, J. (2003b) Teacher activism: Mobilising the profession. Keynote address to the British Educational Research Association Conference, Edinburgh.
Sahlberg, P. (2011) Paradoxes of educational improvement: The Finnish experience. *Scottish Educational Review*, 43(1): 3–23.
Sahlberg, P. (2012) The most wanted: Teachers and teacher education in Finland. In L. Darling-Hammond and A. Lieberman (eds.), *Teacher Education around the World*. New York: Taylor and Francis, p. 1721.
Sahlberg, P., Furlong, J., and Munn, P. (2012) *Report of the International Review Panel on the Structure of Initial Teacher Education Provision in Ireland*. Dublin: Department of Education and Skills. www.education.ie/en/Press-Events/Press-Releases/2012-Press-Releases/Report-of-the-International-Review-Panel-on-the-Structure-of-Initial-Teacher-Education-Provision-in-Ireland.pdf
Saunders, L. (2007) *Educational Research and Policy-making: Exploring the Border Country between Research and Policy*. London and New York: Routledge.
Schleicher, A. (2008) *Education at a Glance 2008 OECD Indicators*. Paris: Organisation for Economic Cooperation and Development (OECD) Publishing.
Schmidt, V.A. (2006) *Democracy in Europe: The EU and National Politics*. Oxford: University Press.
Seddon, T. (1994) *Context and Beyond: Reframing Theory and Practice in Education*. London: Falmer Press.
Seddon, T. (2008) Youth, heroin, crack: A review of recent British trends. *Health Education*, 108(3): 237–246. https://doi.org/10.1108/09654280810867105
Seddon, T., Billett, S., and Clemans, A. (2004) The Politics of Social Partnerships. In B. Lingard and J. Ozga (eds.), *Education Policy and Politics*, Chapter 14. London and New York: Routledge.

Seddon. T., Billet, S., and Clemans, A. (2007) The Politics of Social Partnerships: A framework for theorizing. In Lingard, B. and Ozga, J. (eds.) *The Routledge-Falmer Reader in Education Policy and Politics*, Chapter 14. London and New York: Routledge.

Sellar, S., and Lingard, B. (2013) The OECD and the expansion of PISA: New global modes of governance in education. *British Educational Research Journal*, First published, 6 August.

Sharma, R. (2016) Globalisation as we know it is over – and Brexit is the biggest sign yet. *The Guardian*, 28 July. www.theguardian.com/commentisfree/2016/jul/28/era-globalisation-brexit-eu-britain-economic-frustration

Sheehan, B. (2008) Deputy opposition leader calls for reform of social partnership system in EuroWork European Observatory of Working life. https://www.eurofound.europa.eu/observatories/eurwork/articles/deputy-opposition-leader-calls-for-reform-of-social-partnership-system

Sheehan, B. (2015) Ireland call to revive a 'sensible' social partnership article in EuroWork European Observatory of Working life. https://www.eurofound.europa.eu/observatories/eurwork/articles/industrial-relations/ireland-call-to-revive-a-sensible-social-partnership

Simon, B. (1974) *The Politics of Educational Reform 1920–1940*. Dagenham: Lawrence & Wishart.

Skinnider, M. (1917) *Doing My Bit for Ireland: A First-Hand Account of the Easter Rising*. New York: Century.

Skinnider, M. (1957) *Doing My Bit for Ireland*. New York: The Century Company.

Smith, N., and Hay, C. (2008) Mapping the discourse of globalisation and European integration in the United Kingdom and Ireland empirically. *European Journal of Political Research*, 47: 359–382.

Smyth, J., and Wrigley, T. (2013) *Living on the Edge: Re-thinking Poverty, Class and Schooling*. New York: Peter Lang Publishing.

Somekh, B., and Lewin, C. (eds.). (2005) *Research Methods in the Social Sciences*. London: Sage Books.

Spencer, T. (2001) *Soldier-Teacher War Memorials: World War I, World War II, Post World War II*. Sydney: [jointly published by] NSW Department of Education, NSW Teachers Federation, Teachers Sub-Branch, RSL.

Stenhouse, L. (1975) *An Introduction to Curriculum Research and Development*. London: Heinemann.

Stenhouse, L. (1976) Teacher development and curriculum design. Centre for Applied Research in Education, University of East Anglia. https://www.uea.ac.uk/documents/4059364/4994243/Stenhouse-1976-Teacher+Development+and+Curriculum+Design.pdf/7c8ec464-fce2-4921-bed8-141e03fe4f17

Stevenson, H. (2014) *INTO Members' Views about Their Work and Their Union: Republic of Ireland*. Dublin: Irish National Teachers' Organisation.

Stevenson, H. (2015) Teacher unionism in changing times: Is this the real 'new unionism'? *Journal of School Choice*, 9(4): 604–625.

Stevenson, H. and Gilliland, A. (2016) In Evers, J. and Kneyber, R. (eds.) *Flip the System: Changing Education from the Ground Up*, Chapter 8. London and New York: Routledge.

Sugrue, C. (1997) *Complexities of Teaching: Child-Centred Perspectives*. London: Falmer Press.

Sugrue, C. (2009a) Performativity and professionalism: Irish primary principals' experience of building leadership capacity. *European Educational Research Journal*, 8(3).

Sugrue, C. (2009b) From heroes and heroines to hermaphrodites: Emancipation or emasculation of school leaders and leadership? *School Leadership and Management*, 29(4): 361–372.

Sugrue, C. (2013) Regimes of control and teacher educators' Janus face? In L. Beckett (ed.), *Teacher Education through Active Engagement: Raising the Professional Voice*, Chapter 10. London and New York: Routledge.

Sugrue, C., and Solbrekke, T. (eds.). (2011) *Professional Responsibility: New Horizons of Praxis*. London and New York: Routledge.

Sylvester, D.W. (1974) *Robert Lowe and Education*. Cambridge: CUP.

Taylor, S., Rizvi, F., Lingard, B., and Henry, M. (1997) *Educational Policy and the Politics of Change*. Abingdon, Oxon: Routledge.

Thompson, D. (2001) *The Essential E.P.Thompson*. New York: The New Press.

Thompson, D'Arcy. (1867) What are the best means for improving the status of teachers, and for securing for the public sufficient guarantees for the efficiency of their teaching? In *Proceedings of the Education Department of National Association for the Promotion of Social Science, Belfast Meeting*, in the section dealing with the Irish Education Question.

Thompson, E. (1966) History from below. First published in *The Times Literary Supplement*, 7 April. Reproduced In D. Thompson (ed.), *The Essential E.P.Thompson*. New York: The New Press.

Thrupp, M. (1999) *Schools Making a Difference: Let's be Realistic! School Mix, School Effectiveness and the Social Limits of Reform*. Buckingham: Open University Press.

Thrupp, M. (2005) *School Improvement: An Unofficial Approach*. London and New York: Continuum.

Tosh, J. (1999) *A Man's Place: Masculinity and Middle-Class Homes in Victorian England*. London: Yale University Press.

Tosh, J. (2002) *The Pursuit of History: Aims, Methods and New Directions in the Study of Modern History*. London: Longman.

Tosh, J. (2003) *The Making of Manhood and the Uses of History*. Surrey: Research Office, University of Surrey.

Verger, A., Altinyelken, H., and de Koning, M. (eds.). (2013) *Global Managerial Education Reforms and Teachers: Emerging Policies, Controversies and Issues in Developing Contexts*. Brussels: Education International.

Wall, E. (2017) De-testing accountability. In INTO (ed.), *Quality in Education: Accountability and Responsibility*. Dublin: Irish National Teachers Organisation.

Wall, P. (1986) The discussion documents of the curriculum and examinations board: Primary education. *Studies in Education: A Journal of Educational Research*, 4(1): 49–51.

Walsh, T. (2012) *Primary Education in Ireland, 1897–1990: Curriculum and Context*. Bern: Peter Lang Academic Publishers.

Ward, N., and Dooney, T. (eds.). (1999) *Irish Education in the 21st Century*. Michigan: Oak Tree Press.

Weale, S. (2017) Married Head and Deputy Condemn Education Policy in Resignation Letter. *The Guardian*, Saturday 29 April.

Whelan, K. (2013) Ireland's economic crisis: The good, the bad and the ugly. Paper presented at Bank of Greece conference on the Euro Crisis, Athens, 24 May.

Whitty, G. (1985) *Sociology and School Knowledge: Curriculum Theory, Research and Politics*. London: Methuen.

Whitty, G. (1998) New labour, education and disadvantage. *Education and Social Justice*, 1(1).

Whitty, G. (2002) *Making Sense of Education Policy: Studies in the Sociology and Politics of Education*. London: Sage Publications.

Whitty, G. (2008) Changing modes of teacher professionalism: Traditional, managerial, collaborative and democratic. In B. Cunningham (ed.), *Exploring Professionalism: The Bedford Papers*. London: Institute of Education.

Whitty, G., and Young, M. (1976) *Explorations in the Politics of School Knowledge*. Driffield: Nafferton Books.

Wrigley, T., Thompson, P., and Lingard, B. (2012) *Changing Schools: An Alternative Way to Make a World of Difference*. London and New York: Routledge.

Yeatman, A. (ed.). (1998) *Activism and the Policy Process*. Sydney: Allen and Unwin.

Young, M.F.D. (1971) *Knowledge and Control*. London: Collier Macmillan.

Young, M.F.D. (1998) *The Curriculum of the Future: From the 'New Sociology of Education' to a Critical Theory of Learning*. Lewes: Falmer Press.

Young, M.F.D., and Whitty, T. (eds.). (1977) Introduction. In *Society, State and Schooling: Readings on the Possibilities of Radical Education*. London: Falmer Press.

Index

Page numbers in italic indicate a figure on the corresponding page

Action Plan for Education (Bruton) 2–3, 4, 8, 12, 15, 24, 41–44, *42*, 76, 115, 167; components of 153–155; Cosán, development of 161–162; Droichead policy, action 65 of 158–161; school-based evaluation, Action 69 of 155–162
Action Plan for Jobs (Bruton) 43
activist teachers, INTO and 75–90; introduction to 75–77; Irish language question, INTO inquiry into, 1941 86–89; Mahon, Catherine, women's struggles and 80–82; *Murder Machine, The* (1916 Pearse pamphlet) 77–80; national programme of primary instruction, 1922 82–86
Activist Teaching Profession, The (Sachs) 71
Adelman, C. 46
Advancing School Autonomy in the Irish School System (Department of Education and Skills) 143
After Neoliberalism? The Kilburn Manifesto 27
Ahern Fianna Fáil and Progressive Democrats Coalition 11
Ahern-Harney Fianna Fáil and Progressive Democrats Coalition 9, 11
Aiken, F. 101
Akenson, D. H. 39–40, 50–51
Alexander, R. J. 46
American Federation of Teachers 189
An Comhairle Mhúinteoireachta. A Teaching Council (INTO booklet) 9, 115, 133, 142, 182; 1990 letter on 144–153, *148*
An Foras Oideachais (Education Foundation) 126–127
Apple, M. 149
'Applying an Evaluation and Assessment Framework: An Irish Perspective' (Hislop) 27
Archaeology of Knowledge, The (Foucault) 191
Archive Fever (Derrida) 191
Association of Protestant Managers for the Church of Ireland, Methodists and Presbyterians 111
Association of Secondary Teachers of Ireland (ASTI) 121, 122
Australian Institute for Teachers and School Leaders (AITSL) 190

Ball, S. J. 7, 11, 27, 100, 119, 174, 175–176, 180
Barrington, T. 131
Bascia, N. 2, 9, 10, 15–16, 23, 28, 30, 31, 171, 172
battles of ideas 167–168
Beckett, L. 11, 13, 27, 46, 187
Behan, V. 7
Belfast Education Journal 64
Bereford, M. 100
Bernstein, B. 189
Beveridge, W. 57
Billett, S. 10
Blyth, E. 101
Brady, C. 6, 80, 173
Breathnach, N. 147
Brosnahan, S. 110, 120

Bruton, R. 2–3, 4, 9, 10, 14, 32; *Action Plan for Education* 41–44, 153–155
Burke, M. 7
Burke, R. 128
Burnham Committee 121
Byrne, C. 170

Cameron-Clegg Conservative-Liberal Democrat Coalition Government 115
Career Entry Professional Programme (CEPP) 158
Carr, J. 10, 11, 27, 46, 79, 116–117, 119, 128, 142; *Comhairle Múinteoireachta. A Teaching Council*, 1990 letter on 144–153, *148*; term as INTO teacher and trade union official 119–139, 168; *see also* global neoliberal policy regime, Ireland in
Carter, B. 192
Catholic Clerical Managers Association 111
Catholic Emancipation 51
Catholic Headmasters Association (CHA) 121
Central Executive Committee (CEC) 29
Chamney, R. 24, 53, 75; editorial, 1868 56–59
Chuinneagáin, S. 80, 81–82
Claidheamh Soluis, An (Gaelic League paper) 79
Clann na Poblachta 106
Clarke, K. 101
Clemans, A. 10
Cochran-Smith, M. 27
Colgan, B. 54, 76
Comhairle Múinteoireachta. A Teaching Council, Accessible, Accountable Autonomous (INTO policy document) 149
Committee on National Teachers' Salaries 121
Conway, P. F. 7
Coogan, T. P. 100
Coolahan, J. 51, 75, 125
Cosán, development of 161–162
Cosán at a Glance: Draft Framework for Teachers' Learning (Teaching Council) 162
Cosgrave, W. T. 86
Cosgrave-Corish Fine Gael-Labour Coalition Government 128
Coughlin, M. 158, 173
Cowen Fianna Fáil Government 11
Cumann Múinteoirí Éireann *see* Irish National Teachers Organisation (INTO)
Cumann Na mBan 106

de Buitléir, Seamus 129–133
Department of Education and Skills 2–3, 180; *Advancing School Autonomy in the Irish School System* 143; *Looking at Our School: A Quality Framework for Primary Schools* 28; *Minister's Brief Overview* 37–41; Quality Improvement Framework 28
Derrida, J. 191
Derrig, T. 87, 100
de Valera Fianna Fáil Government 96–97, 99–101, 103
Devine, D. 7
Dewey, J. 137
Doing My Bit for Ireland (Skinnider) 106
Doyle, M. 66
Droichead: An Integrated Induction Framework for Newly Qualified Teachers (Teaching Council) 159
Droichead policy, action 65 158–161
Droichead: Teaching Council Policy on a New Model of Induction and Probation for Newly Qualified Teachers (Teaching Council) 159
Droichead: The Integrated Professional Induction Framework (Teaching Council) 160
Dublin Central Association 51
Dublin in 1913: Lockout & Legacy (Granville) 76–77

Easter Uprising, 1916 77, 78, 96
Education Act, 1998 29, 46
Education Policy and Politics (Lingard and Ozga) 10
edu-politics, future of 172–176
80 Years of Progress (INTO) 111, 112, 116
Elliot, J. 157
Emergency Powers Act, 1939 96
European Union (EU) 3
Evers, J. 7
Experience and Education (Dewey) 137

Fennell, D. 8, 65–66, 89
Ferriter, D. 14–15, 54, 66, 72, 77, 79–80, 82, 86, 89, 96, 101, 105, 106–107, 109, 116, 167

Fianna Fáil Government 11, 89, 96–97, 100, 121
Fine Gael 2, 9, 38
Flanagan, F. 78–79
'flipping the system' 1–2, 28, 166
Follet, M. 131
Foster, Vere 6, 24, 27, 75; Chamney's editorial, 1868 56–59; letter from, in *The Irish Teachers' Journal*, 1868 53–56, 167; letter to *Northern Whig* on teachers' protests, 1878 62–65; overview of 50–53; teachers' evidence to primary education commission, 1869 59–62; teachers organising and 50–66
'Framework to Consider the Quality Assurance of Schools, A' (Hislop) 34
Free State of Ireland 89, 96, 105
Furlong, J. 11–12, 177
'Future Development of Education in Ireland, The' (Quinn) 27

Gaelic League 51, 65
Gallagher, C. 7
Garvin, T. 89
General System of Recognition of Higher Education Diplomas Awarded after a Minimum of Three Years Professional Training, A (INTO) 144
Gilliland, A. 4, 28
Gleeson, J. 176
global education reform movement (GERM) 6–7, 13–14, 50, 136
Global Financial Crash (GFC) 1, 32
global neoliberal policy regime, Ireland in 119–139; INTO position paper on curriculum prescription, 1988 133–138, *134*; introduction to 119–120; New Curriculum, 1971 128–133; teacher education, INTO commentary on HEA report, 1970 124–128; teachers' salaries, 1969 INTO submissions on 120–122; teachers' salaries, INTO first submission, January 17, 1968 122–123; teachers' salaries, INTO second submission, February 24, 1968 123–124
Glyde Court 11, *11*, 27
Gorton, J. 163
Granville, G. 76–77
Gray, A. 192
Griffin, M. 120
Grummell, B. 7

Hall, S. 27, 76
Hardiman, M. 14, 15, 43
Haughey Fianna Fáil minority government 135
Haughey Fianna Fáil Progressive Democrats Coalition Government 144, 145
Held, D. 73, 117
Henly, J. 51–52, 58–59
Heresy. The Battle of Ideas in Modern Ireland (Fennell) 8–9
Higgins, M. D. 180
Higher Education Authority (HEA) 126–127
Hillary, P. 125
Hislop, H. 3, 14, 24, 156–157; on quality assurance of Irish schools 31–37, 45–46, 182; reforms, as regulated professionalism 166
historical revisions 27–47; *Action Plan for Education* 41–44; Hislop on quality assurance 31–37; Inspectorate and 44–46; introduction to 27–29; *Minister's Brief Overview* 37–41; teacher union research 29–31
historical truths 168–172
Historikerstreit 6, 80, 81, 173
'history from below' 14, 23–24, 29, 36, 62, 66, 72, 80, 97, 104, 109
Hogan, P. 135–138
Hursh, D. 190
Hyde, D. 51, 65

ICTU *see* Irish Congress of Trade Unions (ICTU)
Inspectorate 44–46; Whole School Evaluation and 29–30
Inspectorate and Teaching Council 37
INTO *see* Irish National Teachers Organisation (INTO)
'INTO and the 1946 Teachers' Strike, The' (McCormick) 97, *98–99*, 99–101
InTouch (INTO magazine) 45
Investment in Education (OECD) 120
Irish Congress of Trade Unions (ICTU) 7–8
Irish Examiner 107
Irish language question, INTO inquiry into 86–89
Irish national schools 95–112; Hislop on quality assurance of 31–37; INTO plan for education, 1947 101–106; introduction to 1–4, 95–97;

100 Years of Progress 108–111; self-evaluation of 35; Skinnider INTO presidential address, 1957 106–108; Smart Regulation and 3; teachers' strike, 1946 97–101, *98–99*; teacher union research 4–6, 29–31; Teaching Council and 3–4
Irish National Teachers' Association (INTA) 5, 75
Irish National Teachers Organisation (INTO) 2, 4–5, 37; activist teachers and 75–90; anniversary book project 11–14; Central Executive Committee 29; commentary on HEA report, 1970 124–128; February 24, 1968 second submission on teachers' salaries 123–124; ICTU and 7–8; incidental inspections and 30; inquiry into Irish language question 86–89; January 17, 1968 first submission on teachers' salaries 122–123; Mahon and 80; national schools and 14–18; 1969 submissions on teachers' salaries 120–122; Nunan on 12–13; plan for education, 1947 101–106; position paper on curriculum prescription, 1988 133–138, *134*; professionalism and 33–34; research activities of 6–11; Skinnider presidential address, 1957 106–108; women's struggles and 80–82
Irish Primary Principals Network (IPPN) 37
Irish Proclamation of Independence, 1916 72
Irish Revolution, The (Ferriter) 80
Irish School Weekly 56, 103, 109
Irish Teachers' Journal, The 24, 75; Chamney's editorial, 1868 56–59, 167; Foster letter in, 1868 53–56, 167
Irish Times, The 76
Irish Trades Union Congress (ITUC) 81, 108–109

Jones, K. 108

Kelleher, D. 102, 103–105, 120
Kenny, E. 38, 180
Kenny-Gilmore Fine Gael-Labour Coalition Government 11, 13, 14, 27, 46, 178
Kenny-Varadkar Fine Gael-led Coalition Government 6–7, 14, 24, 37, 110, 115, 153

Kerr, G. 171
Kindling the Flame 150 Years of the INTO (Puirséil) 58
Kneyber, R. 7

Land War 51
Lee, J. J. 65, 112
Leitch, R. 176–177
Lemass Fianna Fáil Government 119
Lenihan, B. 124
Lennon, C. 136
Linehan, M. 87
Lingard, B. 7, 10, 11, 15, 173–174
Looking at Our School: A Quality Framework for Primary Schools (Department of Education and Skills) 28, 157
Lukacs, J. 96, 112
Lynch, K. 7, 11, 174, 174, 176, 180
Lytle, S. L. 27

Mahon, C. 72, 80–82, 106–107, 124–125, 167
Management Bodies and Patrons 37
Massey, D. 27, 76
McCormick, E. 97–102, 106, 110, 112, 116
McCulloch, G. 15, 24, 31, 77, 81, 99–100, 107, 111, 144
McCune Reid, H. F. 53
McGarry, M. 149–150
McKinsey and Company 3, 27, 72
McNamara, G. 7, 157
McNeill, E. 86, 125
McQuaid, J. C. 110
Meta-regulation 50; defined 37
Mills, D. 15
Mills, M. 7, 11, 174, 177
Minister's Brief Overview (Department of Education and Skills) 37–41, 167
Moroney, M. 65, 80
Mortimore, P. 13, 179
Morton, M. 15
Mulcahy, R. 121
Munn, P. 7, 11–12, 174, 177–178
Murder Machine, The (Pearse) 77–80, 104, 167
Murphy, D. 135
Murphy, R. 7

National Association for the Promotion of Social Science 54
National Certificate of Educational Achievement 37

National Council for Curriculum and Assessment (NCCA) 35–36, 37
National Economic and Social Council 3, 34, 36, 143
National Education Association 189
National Education Welfare Board (NEWB) 37
national programme of primary instruction, 1922 82–86
National Wages Standstill Policy 101
neoliberalism, negative effects of 2
Nevo, D. 156
New Curriculum, 1971 128–133
New South Wales Priority Action Schools Project 13
Nic Craith, D. 7, 46, 80, 143, 149, 150, 158, 171–172, 182
Ní Chinnéide, M. 72, 84, 85
Ní Scineadóra, M. 106; *see also* Skinnider, M.
Noonan, S. 8
Northern Whig, The 62, 64
Nunan, S. 12–13, 46, 169

O'Brien, J. 108
Ó Buachalla, S. 120–121
Ó Conaill, T. 84
O'Connell, D. 51
O'Connell, T. J. 72, 81, 84, 87–88, 89, 90, 95, 102, 108–111, 119
O'Connor, S. 25
Ó Donnabháin, D. 176
O'Donnell, M. 7, 178
O'Donnell, P. 96
O'Donohoe, P. 115
Ó Foghlú, S. 43, 154
O'Hara, J. 7, 157
O'Kelly, S. T. 95
O'Laighin, L. 146
O' Loingsigh, D. 97
O'Malley, D. 121
100 Years of Progress (Skinnider and O'Connell) 72–73, 108–111, 112, 167
Organisation for Economic Co-operation and Development (OECD) 3, 27; Education Directorate 72; *Investment in Education* 120; *Review of National Policy on Education* 147, 151
O'Rourke, M. 135, 144, 145–146
Ó Snodaigh, A. 106
O'Sullivan, D. 7
O'Toole, J. 9, 13, 30, 80, 82, 95, 97, 142, 149

Owens, R. C. 81–82, 84
Ozga, J. 10, 15

Passy, R. 192
Payment by Results System 65
Pearse, P. 72, 105; bilingual concept 79; *Murder Machine, The* (1916 pamphlet) 77–80, 104, 167
performance-related pay, teachers' protests on 62–65
Peters, R. 137
Plan for Education, A (INTO) 103–104
Plowden Report 137
Policy Futures 27
Political Writings and Speeches (Pearse) 77–78
'Politics of Social Partnerships, The' (Seddon, Billett and Clemans) 10
Powis Committee 59, 75
Powis Report 59
Primary Curriculum and Related Matters (INTO) 136
Professionalism in the 1990s (INTO) 30
Professor Seamas Ó Súilleabháin Memorial Lecture 31–32
Programme for the International Student Assessment (PISA) 7
Puirséil, N. 58
Punch, K. F. 15
Purvis, J. 81

Quality and Standards in Human Services in Ireland: The School System No. 129 (National Economic and Social Council) 3, 36
quality assurance, Irish schools, Hislop on 31–37
'Quality Assurance of Irish Schools and the Role of Evaluation, The: Current and Future Trends' (Hislop lecture) 3, 31–32
'Quality Education: Teacher Responsibility and Accountability' (O'Donnell) 7
Quigley, G. 9, 129, 133, 142, 144, 145–146
Quinn, R. 13, 14, 27, 32, 46, 156; Forum on Patronage and Pluralism in the Primary Sector 39–40

Radio & Television Ireland (RTÉ) Radio 1 78–79
rapprochement 192
Raworth, K. 116
rebuttal, described 165

regulated-regulation of teaching *see Action Plan for Education* (Bruton)
renewal 192
Renshaw, P. 15
Report of the International Review Panel on the Structure of Initial Teacher Education Provision in Ireland (Sahlberg, Furlong and Munn) 11–12, 177
resistance 192
Responsive Regulation 34, 50; defined 36–37
Review of National Policy on Education (OECD) 147, 151
Reynolds Coalition Government 147
Rise and Fall of Nations, The (Sharma) 3
Rooney, M. 106, 112
Royal Commissioners of Primary Education in Ireland 59
Rustin, M. 27, 76
Ryan, L. 121

Sachs, J. 71
Sahlberg, P. 11–12, 177
Saorstát Éireann 89, 96, 105
Saunders, L. 41
Schleicher, A. 174, 175
school autonomy, defined 178–179
school-based evaluation 155–158
Schools Must Speak for Themselves: The Case for School Self-Evaluation (MacBeath) 156
Secondary Teachers Registration Council 144–145
Seddon, T. 10, 37, 46, 72
Self-Evaluating Institution, The (Adelman and Alexander) 46
self-evaluation of schools 35
Sharma, R. 3
Sheridan, J. 103
Ship of Fools. How Stupidity and Corruption Sank the Celtic Tiger (O'Toole) 32
Skinnider, M. 72; INTO presidential address by 106–108, 167
Smart Regulation 3, 34, 35, 46, 50, 143; defined 37
Social Insurance and Allied Services (Beveridge) 57
Stanley, Lord 51
Stenhouse, L. 27, 174
Stevenson, H. 4, 7, 28, 192
Strabane Teachers' Association 75
Student Voice Forum about Wellbeing 36
Student Voice Forum on Assessment 36

Studies in Education (journal) 137
Sugrue, C. 7, 179, 181
Sweeney, P. 7–8

teacher professionalism 33–35, 50
Teachers as Learners (Swan) 10
teachers' 'case for the defence' 142–163; *Action Plan for Education* 153–155; *Comhairle Múinteoireachta. A Teaching Council*, 1990 letter on 144–153, *148*; Cosán, development of 161–162; Droichead policy 158–161; introduction to 142–144; school-based evaluation 155–158
teachers organising, histories of: essay concerning 23–25; Foster and 50–66; introduction to 16; revisions 27–47; *see also* historical revisions
teachers organising, politics of: essay concerning 115–117; global neoliberal policy regime and 119–139; introduction to 17–18; teachers' 'case for the defence' 142–163
teachers organising, theories of: essay concerning 71–73; INTO, activist teachers and 75–90; introduction to 16–17; Irish national schools and 95–112
Teacher's Perspective on Professionalism, A (Carr) 10
Teachers' Registration Movement 150
teachers' strike, 1946 97–101, *98–99*
teacher status 33–35
teacher union research, Ireland 4–6, 29–31
teacher union research, lessons learned about 165–183; edu-politics, future of 172–176; historical truths 168–172; ideas, battles of 167–168; introduction to 165–167; oppositional consensus 176–178; rebuttal 178–181
teacher unions and archives, politics of 186–194; archive 190–191; introduction to 186–187; politics 191–193; research 187–188; teachers 188–190
Teacher Unions and Public Education. Politics, History and the Future (Bascia) 171
Teaching Council 3–4, 9, 10, 144; Congress resolution of 147–149; duties, functions, composition

and structures of 152; historical background to 150; Nunan on 12–13; policy document on establishment of 149; rationale for 150–151; Teachers' Act parliamentary bill 152–153; *see also* teachers' 'case for the defence'
Teaching Council Act 3, 10, 152–153, 161, 181
Thompson, D. 23
Thompson, D'Arcy 54–55
three message systems of schooling 189
top-down policies 4, 14, 23, 29, 36–37, 115–116, 166
Tosh, J. 100, 107
Towards a General Theory of Curriculum and Evaluation (de Buitléir) 129
trait model 188–189

University Act, 1908 124

Varadkar, L. 38
Vere Foster Public Lecture Series 11
Verger, A. 187, 192–193
Voice for Teachers 171

Wall, E. 7
Wall, P. 135
Whitty, G. 4, 11, 13, 28
Whole School Evaluation 29–30
'Who Was Vere Foster' (Coolahan documentary) 75
Williams, M. 163
Women of the Irish Revolution (Gillis) 106
'Women Teachers and INTO Policy 1905–1916' (Chuinneagáin) 80
World Trade Organisation 3, 27, 72
Wrigley, T. 163

Young, T. 187
Young Irelanders 51